PAW PRINTS
AT
OWL COTTAGE

ALSO BY DENIS O'CONNOR

Paw Prints in the Moonlight

PAW PRINTS
AT
OWL COTTAGE

The Heartwarming True Story of
One Man and His Cats

Denis O'Connor

Illustrations by
Richard Morris

Thomas Dunne Books
St. Martin's Press ⋈ New York

THOMAS DUNNE BOOKS.
An imprint of St. Martin's Press.

PAW PRINTS AT OWL COTTAGE. Copyright © 2010 by Denis O'Connor.
All rights reserved. Printed in the United States of America. For information,
address St. Martin's Press, 175 Fifth Avenue, New York, N.Y. 10010.

www.thomasdunnebooks.com
www.stmartins.com

Library of Congress Cataloging-in-Publication Data

O'Connor, Denis, 1934–
  Paw prints at Owl Cottage : the heartwarming true story of one man and his
  cats / Denis O'Connor.—1st U.S. ed.
    p. cm.
  ISBN 978-0-312-57707-0 (hardcover)
  ISBN 978-1-250-03718-3 (e-book)
1. O'Connor, Denis, 1934– 2. Cat owners—England—Biography. 3. Maine
coon cat—England—Biography. I. Title.
  SF442.82.O26A3 2013
  636.80092'9—dc23
  [B]

2013024572

St. Martin's Press books may be purchased for educational, business,
or promotional use. For information on bulk purchases, please contact
Macmillan Corporate and Premium Sales Department at 1-800-221-7945,
extension 5442, or write specialmarkets@macmillan.com.

First published in Great Britain by Constable,
an imprint of Constable & Robinson Ltd

First U.S. Edition: October 2013

10 9 8 7 6 5 4 3 2 1

I wish to dedicate this book to the memory of my uncle, Captain John Watson of the Church Army, whose library of the classics was a reader's treasure chest for me.

This book is also for Catherine, my wife, without whose loving support it would not have been written.

The heart has its reasons which reason does not know.

Blaise Pascal, 1688

CONTENTS

BEGINNINGS

My extraordinary life with Toby Jug, the hybrid Maine Coon cat whose companionship and love gave me such happiness during my twenties and thirties, sadly came to an end in 1978 when he tragically died. We had enjoyed life together since I had rescued him as a tiny, sick kitten lying alongside his dying mother and brother. Owl Cottage, with its beautiful garden and rural setting, became our refuge and sanctuary over the eventful years we shared together. After his death the poignant memories of him were too sorrowful for me to carry on living there.

In 1980 I moved to Newcastle where I already had been appointed to a lectureship at the University of Newcastle upon Tyne. Later I worked at Durham University tutoring students in Educational Studies until I retired in 2000. In 1998 Catherine and I were married and since we were both contemplating early retirement we began to look for properties in rural areas because of our attachment to North Northumberland. Fate took us in hand and I was able once more, with Catherine at my side, to return to Owl Cottage and revisit the home where in my younger life I had spent such happy and memorable years with the cat called Toby Jug, whose adventures inspired *Paw Tracks in the Moonlight*.

Returning to live in Owl Cottage at West Thirston was for me the consummation of many years of longing to escape the city for life once more in the countryside. West Thirston is one of a group of hamlets, extending eastwards to the town of Amble and the North Sea, which lie astride a rocky ridge above the River Coquet. Owl Cottage is built on a site adjoining a minor road which leads westwards to Linden Hall, Rothbury and beyond. No doubt the area occupied by the cottage has witnessed many habitations throughout the ages but the present structure is built almost entirely of stone and dates from around the middle of the nineteenth century. The front of the cottage runs parallel to the road, leaving the back, which faces south, secluded and private.

The garden is extensive and comprises over fifty trees of various kinds including oak, beech, whitebeam and birch. There is also a small orchard of apple, pear, plum and nut trees, and a meandering swathe of grass bordered by flowering shrubs and flower beds, giving an overall effect of a woodland glade. Wildlife is welcome here and thrives in the pesticide-free environment. My wife Catherine and I refer to the garden as our 'Shangri-La' because of its beauteous tranquillity and natural appeal. There are stories from local folk who say that it is enchanted and inhabited by fairies, although we cannot confirm this from our own experience. Yet on summer nights, whilst songbirds are singing their songs and slanting sunbeams create green-grassed areas of golden meadow, there is an enraptured feeling about the garden at Owl Cottage.

It is certainly a wonderful place for cats and has been much loved by them, not least by our four Maine Coon cats respectively named, according to age, Pablo, Carlos, Luis and Max. These special and affectionate cats comprise our family and their unique and fascinating personalities and activities form the basis of this true to life account of our lives together with them at Owl Cottage. In many respects this book is the continuation of the story that began in *Paw Tracks in the Moonlight* because returning to the cottage and describing the adventures of our present cat family have revived the memory of some additional tales of the legendary hero of Owl Cottage. After all, Toby Jug's spirit endures in every tree and stone there.

PABLO

P ablo was the first kitten to live in Owl Cottage since the death of Toby Jug and we welcomed him, quite literally, with open arms. He was a pedigree Maine Coon. In appearance he was surprisingly large for such a young kitten, with a pointed face and extra large ears. His front paws were enormous and he had a long fluffy tail. His eyes were golden brown and his coat a cinnamon colour like oak leaves in autumn, with some darker markings which would become more distinctive and elaborate as he matured. Pablo had the build and markings of his ancestor, the Norwegian Forest cat.

On his birth cum pedigree certificate he was formally named Pablo Picatsso, son of Billyboyblue and Huffenpuff, and was officially designated a brown tabby. He was born in October 1999 and given to me as a present by Catherine, my wife, who had lived at Owl Cottage with me since we had bought it in 1998. Pablo proved to be a wonderful cat, affectionate and lovable, and he provided us with many fascinating insights into cat behaviour. But perhaps first I should relate how it happened that we acquired Pablo in the first place and how I and Catherine came to be living once more at Owl Cottage. Despite my earlier protestations – at the time deeply felt and firmly held

– at long last I had returned to the home where Toby Jug and I had been so happy in the past.

It all began in the spring of 1997 when Catherine and I decided to take a holiday in the north of Crete. One beautiful sun-filled morning, as we sat on the veranda of our apartment looking out over the azure blue Mediterranean, we heard a cat calling. It was not a distress call, just the kind of cat-talk that some felines make when they see something interesting or wish to express their feelings. I looked over the grey rocks and scrub that extended away from the holiday chalets. In the distance was the mountain known locally as Zorba's Rock, which reputedly was the location for the famous Greek dance sequence performed by Anthony Quinn in *Zorba the Greek*.

Suddenly, I spotted a small figure scurrying straight towards us. In a moment a neat and very petite charcoal-grey, short-haired she-cat introduced herself to us. She was obviously accustomed to people, since she immediately commenced purring and brushed herself against us in the most affectionate manner. I realized at once that she was focused on an agenda which was meant to manipulate us. No doubt she was in the habit of exploiting the charity of kind-hearted holiday-makers. This greeting display by the cat undoubtedly served her purpose which was to remind us of our obligations as hosts. And so it was that a late breakfast of corned beef and boiled ham was served up to her and very well received. I admired her social skills and wondered just how many other tourists had fallen under her spell and been cajoled into offering handouts.

My assumptions about her motives were soon confirmed because she came to visit us every day for the rest of our stay and we became quite fond of this dainty little beach cat. Each time we fed her we were, of course, rewarding her friendly behaviour and so, in terms of psychological theory, reinforcing her activities. Likewise she, this clever little cat, was reinforcing my act of feeding her by jumping on my knee and purring her thanks as a reward for me. Cats are great manipulators of humans and our guest cat proved no exception to this rule. She would arrive either mid-morning or teatime and, having been fed, she would linger next to us, sometimes gracing one of our laps as we relaxed and watched the sun go down. For the moment she had adopted us.

I really liked her, but then I always find it hard to resist a friendly cat. Catherine was not so sure. She is concerned about stray cats when we are abroad in case they carry disease. I tend to fuss the cats I meet on our travels and usually they respond well to me, and so I attributed nothing out of the ordinary to our visiting cat and simply enjoyed the contact for what it was worth until something extraordinary happened on the last day of our stay which gave me pause for thought.

Since our flight departure time was at some unearthly hour during the night we spent the early morning packing and then went for one last trip around the north of Crete in our hire car. We drove first to Maleme and the site of the German War Cemetery. We found it to be a peaceful and poignant place covered in an abundance of deep-red wild flowers which outlined the precisely placed granite-grey headstones stretching out of sight in regimented rows. All was kept in perfect order and obviously tended with great care and reverence for those who had given their lives in the Second World War. We then decided we would just about have time to go on to Agios Stefanos for a brief visit before returning to the apartment. We drove south through the countryside to this tiny tenth-century church which is reached by following a narrow track shaded by oak trees. En route Catherine, to her great pleasure, discovered on the bankside a rare white cyclamen for which this place is famous. *Cyclamen creticum* is found nowhere else in the world. The delicate white flower quivered slightly in the gentle breeze from the sea as we walked by. We were even more pleased we had made the decision to visit the church when we saw its thirteenth-century frescos of the Nativity and Pentecost which were still showing clearly after all this time.

Too soon we had to leave for Chania and make our final preparations for home. This last trip, however, had filled us with special memories of Crete to carry home with us and dwell on at our leisure. We were not back in our apartment until late afternoon and therefore I did not expect to see our feline friend again. But, just as evening was settling in, a frantic scratching at the balcony door roused me from a restful doze. I slid back the door and there she was, anxiously greeting me, tail up and mewing her request for a late supper. After feeding her I sat out on the balcony to keep her company. Together we watched the remains of the day, the last of the deep red sunset over the sea.

Soon she showed her gratitude by slipping on to my knee from where she treated me to a resonant purring session. I was at pains to explain to her that I was leaving and would not see her ever again but I would always think of her as a friend. Since I was talking to her in English and the language of her country was Greek I couldn't be sure if she understood me at all, but then I have heard tales of cats having the ability to read minds and I suspect it might be true. As the last glow of the setting sun changed to a darkening pink, she rose and, without a backward glance, disappeared amongst the rocks. I retired inside the apartment to snatch a couple of hours of sleep.

Some few hours later as we prepared to leave I realized that I had left my sunglasses on the balcony. As I opened the glass door and walked on to the balcony I almost trod on something. In the darkness I couldn't at first see what it was. Stooping to retrieve it I was amazed to find myself holding a short length of vine on the end of which was a single, ripe, red tomato. My wife's urgent call for me to hurry up or we'd miss our flight startled me out of a whole range of emotions that suddenly surged through my mind. Covertly I placed the find inside my jacket pocket. Thinking about the incident during our flight home I felt confused and uncertain. What was this about and why had it happened?

On our local walks I had spotted miniature tomato plants in cultivation on the outside walls of some of the houses in the surrounding residential area, but there were none near our holiday apartment. Part of me felt that I had been given a coded message. Had the cat put the tomato there as a goodbye gift? Why a tomato? In the subdued lighting of the aircraft, whilst most of the passengers, including my wife, were sleeping, I carefully retrieved the fruit from my pocket. The little glistening object lay in the palm of my hand, undamaged in any way. It reminded me so much of a tiny red ball. A cat I had known a long time ago had loved to play with red balls and had stolen some tomatoes from a neighbour's greenhouse to supplement his supply. His name, of course, was Toby Jug. I began to conjure up a scenario that this was a message of some kind, the significance of which was about to unfold. Weary with thinking about it I fell asleep with the thought that only time would tell.

One of the most irritating things about returning from holiday is to find the space behind the front door jammed with a bulk of mail, most of it of the junk variety. Searching through the accumulation, a postcard caught my attention. It was from Carol, one of our friends, and it simply said, 'Have you seen that Owl Cottage is up for sale?'

The feeling that raced through me at that moment was electric. Was this a coincidence? Or did it herald tidings of a change in the air? Was this related to the present of a tomato from a cat in Crete? I began to feel that somehow, in a way unclear to me, destiny was nudging me towards a reunion with the past. Such a return was not now out of the question since both Catherine and I were contemplating a move away from Newcastle upon Tyne. With this move in mind, since we both loved the countryside, we had been looking at properties for sale in Northumberland but had not searched the locality where I had previously lived. We discussed the news about my old cottage at length and then decided, on impulse, at least to have a look at the place and agreed to view Owl Cottage as soon as it could be arranged.

Then something else occurred which resonated with everything that was currently happening. One night I dreamed that I was living back at Owl Cottage as it had once been. Everything was extremely vivid and real. I was taking a walk along a path between the River Coquet and a line of oak trees where Toby Jug and I often went during a summer evening. Suddenly, he was there before me looking resplendent and radiant with glossy black-and-white fur and sparkling green eyes. 'There you are!' I exclaimed, almost as if our meeting had been arranged and I was expecting him. He ran to me and greeted me in his familiar fulsome manner by leaping on to my shoulder and rubbing his face and whiskers against my cheeks. After a short while he jumped down and ran a few yards ahead, turned and stopped to face me. Then a voice spoke clearly in my head: 'When can we be together again?' Startled, I realized the question was somehow coming from Toby Jug. Taken aback with surprise I stuttered helplessly to find an answer. 'I don't know.'

Then came the next question: 'Will it be soon?' Feeling the shock of disbelief at what was happening I groped again in my mind for an answer as best I could. 'I don't know when, Toby Jug, but whenever it is it will fill me with joy to be with you again.'

Finally, the voice said, 'I'll be there waiting for you.' And with a flick of his bushy tail he disappeared. I looked around searchingly but he was nowhere to be seen.

When I awoke the dream was fresh in my mind as if it had really happened. The memory of it was so surreal it bothered me all day. I couldn't dismiss the thought that perhaps the dream was somehow related to some of the other things which had recently happened, stirring up reminders of the past. A further consideration was that the dream happened to coincide with the initial launch of my book, *Paw Tracks in the Moonlight*, and overwhelming feelings of nostalgia at considering a return to Owl Cottage.

The estate agent made an appointment for us to view the cottage. As we drove back to the place that was filled with so many memories for me I could not stop wondering how the cottage had fared without me and Toby Jug. When we arrived and I gazed once more at Owl Cottage my heart missed a beat and floods of emotion and an overwhelming feeling of yearning for what had been swept through my mind.

As soon as Catherine and I stepped into the hallway I was saddened to see how neglected the place had become. Everything was in a pitiful state inside and also outside in the garden. But as we looked around my distress was suddenly lifted by a wave of good vibrations which, as we both recollected later, we felt at about the same time. Intuitively, I could feel the cottage crying out for us to take care of it and make it whole again. It was a cry from an old friend and it touched my heart.

That night in a pub in Newcastle upon Tyne we talked it over and I discovered that Catherine felt as I did and we decided to sleep on it before coming to a decision. The next morning after breakfast we were still both of the same mind and determined to go ahead and make an offer which hopefully would secure Owl Cottage for us.

When at last the sale was completed and I had the keys in my hand it was October and the countryside was bathed in vivid autumnal colours. As I turned the corner into the quiet village lane I stopped the car by the thick wooded copse on the side of the road. Ahead lay Owl Cottage, bathed in bright sunlight. My eyes were drawn to the gate pillar at the entrance to the driveway where a pink floribunda rose I had planted in the 1960s still bloomed robustly. Something had brought me back here – call it nostalgia or just a longing to recapture the sentiments of happy times past. I felt my mind whirling with a multitude of images. For a moment I was overcome with blissful remembrances: I was home again at last.

One of my first duties would be to pay homage to the old apple tree where Toby Jug had been buried. I stood near his grave for a long while to tune back into the ambience of the cottage garden and how everything used to be. When I previously lived at Owl Cottage I had often sensed good feelings in the surroundings, in the very walls as well as the garden. Possibly these were emotional resonances of the lives of people who had spent fulfilling times here in the past. Now I simply longed to renew my relationship with the cottage.

When we took possession it was like I had never been away and I rejoiced in my heart at the homecoming. Happily for both Catherine and for me the cottage seemed the right place for us to be, although there was much to do to make it comfortable. My thoughts turned to remembered times with Toby Jug. He was by now a distant memory yet his image was always with me, couched somewhere in the back of my mind. It was because Toby was so very dear to me that the shocking experience of his death led me to have to leave the cottage. At that time I felt that I could no longer bear to live there without him. He had been such an important part of my life. Although kind friends and neighbours had offered me kittens to replace Toby I could never bring myself to accept any of them. In the light of my feelings at that time it wouldn't have been fair to the kitten, however desirable, because I would have constantly compared him to Toby Jug who was, to my mind, irreplaceable.

By the time Catherine and I were more or less settled in, with all the essential repairs and improvements to Owl Cottage having been carried out and the interior painting and decorating finished as well, it was the beginning of July the following year.

Now July is the time when the Felton and Thirston Fair is held and I must confess that going to the fair to witness all that enthusiasm for the egg-and-spoon, three-legged and running-backwards races, amongst other events like crockery-breaking and chucking-the-welly, does nothing for me. I just want to slink away and hide. In this respect I am not at all the socially minded person that, by nature, my wife is. I therefore really did not want to attend the fair at all. Catherine had other ideas. She had entered one of the flower competitions in the spirit of joining in and also because that year she was particularly proud of her roses. She thought her Rosa Remember Me with its bronze, yellowish orange petals, stood a good chance of winning a prize. So despite my protestations I was prevailed upon to go and I am indebted to Catherine for evermore for dragging me there against my will.

As my wife was enjoying herself making the rounds of the local stall-holders, I managed to slip away to a remote corner of the field to examine a vintage bus. With its elongated bonnet and bulbous headlights perched on top of huge wide mudguards which protected the wheels, it was just the type of bus Catherine and I travelled to school in during the 1940s and early 1950s. Fully occupied in having an in-depth discussion with the enthusiast who owned the bus, I failed to notice the figure of my wife tearing across the field towards me with a look of 'I told you so' on her face. She wasted no time in breathlessly telling me that there was an exhibition tent with a range of pedigree cats on show. Then she triumphantly told me that one of the booths was reserved for Maine Coon cats.

With my mind in a whirl of expectation I duly arrived at the tent. It almost defies description to give an account of the exhilaration I felt as I entered and gazed upon the most beautiful cats I had ever seen. In a corner was a bench on which lay a creamy white and red she-cat that looked to have been fashioned by the Walt Disney Studios. She was the first pure-bred Maine Coon cat I had ever seen outside the pages of a book, apart from the severely injured mother cat I had rescued on the night that I found the half-dead kitten who survived to become Toby Jug. I was totally overwhelmed and entranced at the same time.

On meeting the breeders, a couple called Jane and Dave who subsequently became our friends, I immediately placed an order for a male kitten. We agreed that both Owl Cottage and ourselves had waited long enough without a cat with which to share our lives. Perhaps with a new cat in my life here at Owl Cottage I would be able to lay to rest the ghost of Toby Jug. Time has a way of healing sorrows and now I felt it was the right moment to allow another cat into my life. We decided to call our new kitten Pablo because, after an eventful short holiday in Madrid, we were imbued with an affection for things Spanish. I recall the first time we were invited to visit Jane's house and to choose a kitten from the litter of six.

Catherine was somewhat shocked as she preceded me along the hallway of Jane's house to be confronted by the largest domestic cat she had ever seen. His name was Hamish and he was the alpha male Maine Coon of the household. He was most definitely inspecting us in case we posed any threat. With his large head and intelligent eyes I thought he was marvellous. Catherine was rather more uncertain. When we knelt to peer into the cushion-lined box which housed the squirming kittens I could feel Hamish scrutinizing us and as I turned two fierce golden eyes met my gaze as if to warn us that that these kittens were under his protection. By now, much to my amusement, Hamish was circling the box housing the kittens and glaring at me for daring to handle one. 'It's alright, fellow,' I said to him affectionately. 'Your kitten will be safe and much loved by us.'

Over a cup of tea and a pleasant chat we discussed some details with Jane about caring for a pedigree Maine Coon cat. Then Catherine insisted that I do the choosing and so I hand-picked a burly kitten who appeared to be already asserting himself over the rest of the litter by standing in a biscuit tray and making unmistakeable kitten growls to prevent the others from eating until he had his fill. I picked him up and had a good look at him. I was impressed by the firmness of his chunky little body. After paying a deposit to secure the sale we were told to expect him in the regulation three months' time. And that is how we chose Pablo and subsequently took him into our home and into our hearts.

Now that we had chosen a new kitten I felt that the yawning gap in my life, brought about by the demise of my exceptional Toby Jug, had been satisfactorily bridged at last. With it I felt a sense of relief, as if I was making a new start. Once again, whatever I was doing day-by-day would be enhanced by the company of a cat, just as it had been for the greater part of my life. Even as a baby I remember the silky and furry presence of a cat called Fluffy, a kitten given to my parents as a wedding present. The company of cats has always been a source of comfort to me and throughout my childhood they served as playmates and as imaginary confidants who would listen to my problems and, by doing so, help me to sort out what I should do.

I have always talked to my cats and I always believed that they understood me. The Ancient Egyptians apparently ascribed divine powers to their cats in the conviction that they possessed supernatural powers and many people have noted their mysterious air of awareness of things that mere humans cannot perceive. A notable example of this was an article in the *New England Journal of Medicine* in 2005 which reported on a very special ability which a cat living in a care home for the elderly displayed. He could predict when an inmate was about to die and would visit that person and stay with them, presumably trying to comfort them, until they passed. How the cat named Oscar was able to identify in advance with remarkable accuracy the particular patient who was about to die mystified the medical and care staff at the unit.

The doctor in charge of the nursing home, David Dosa, who was not especially fond of cats, came to realize that Oscar, just an ordinary black-and-white tabby, had an almost psychic sensitivity to human beings. Dr Dosa wrote a book called *Making the Rounds with Oscar* about life at the nursing home and about how Oscar the cat helps staff and inmates there.

Most certainly, from my own experience, I have noted how sensitive my pet cats have been to my mood states, especially when I have been upset. On such occasions I have become aware that my cat has attempted to soothe and succour me by a friendly presence on my knee and the balm of a session of vibrant purring. I must admit, despite my lifelong exposure to cats, I remain at a loss to understand fully what a cat is all about.

A cat, Sigmund Freud might have said, is just a cat, but William Shakespeare might well have added: 'What a piece of work is a cat.' Coupling these two statements together highlights the ambiguities with which cats are perceived. To me, they are extra special animals, not least because, by tradition, they have the most prodigious capacity for survival against the odds. Hence the popular saying: 'Cats have nine lives.'

As the tales I tell in this book reveal, even if many cats look alike, they are not the same by any means. Just like people, each individual cat has a unique personality of its own. But this personality is only likely to reveal itself to humans where the relationship is a close one.

For instance, cats who spend most of the day resting and sleeping, and are put out at night, sometimes have only the most superficial contact with the people they live with. In this environment the cat's relationship with the people in the house might be very basic and consist merely of being fed, watered and given a place to sleep during the day. As a result the cats will tend not to show how interesting they can be because they need unconditional love and attention to bring that out. Put simply, it is necessary 'to make something of them' in the same way as one nurtures and encourages the development of a child. Given these conditions a whole new world of cat 'personality' is opened up as the cat feels secure enough to show its real self. The early days with our new Maine Coon cat reveal something of what I mean.

It was a bitterly cold day in March 2000 when the kitten called Pablo arrived at Owl Cottage. No kitten could have had better preparations for his coming than he did. There was a pedestal with a fur-lined tunnel, two platforms and several scratching posts. There was a large cushion-bed for him, a warm blanket, feeding and drinking bowls, and an elaborate enclosed litter box since we were advised not to let him roam freely until he had been neutered at the age of six months. We had been informed that there was a rule affecting pedigree cats involving the necessity for a special licence in order to breed from them.

When Pablo arrived at Owl Cottage we gently placed him on the top platform of the pedestal so that he could have a good look around and familiarize himself with his new home. He slowly looked about, stared hard at Catherine and then focused his huge amber eyes on me. And next, to my astonishment, he leapt up on to my left shoulder, the one always favoured by Toby Jug. I was naturally quite overwhelmed and somewhat nonplussed. I hoped that this would become a habit but regrettably it was not to be. That was the one and only time he jumped on my shoulder in all the nine years he was with us.

The rest of that first day was spent in lots of play activities of the getting-to-know-you kind. True to his cat nature, Pablo immediately set about establishing his own agenda irrespective of any arrangements that we made. This state of affairs became abundantly clear at bedtime. Our idea was that he should spend the night in the heated conservatory where he had a choice of sleeping areas and where his loo-box was conveniently situated.

Since cats are nocturnal creatures by nature we drew back the conservatory blinds so that, if he so wished, he could observe any wildlife going about outside.

On that first night we put Plan A into action. We placed him on a cosy bed-cushion, gave him lots of strokes, left him biscuits and water, bade him a loving goodnight and closed the door. Hardly had we reached the upstairs landing leading to our bedroom than the whining, punctuated by howls, began. Obviously, Pablo had other ideas and was not prepared to fit in with ours. He was clearly indicating that he was not prepared to spend the night alone. Steadfastly, we decided it best to ignore these protestations as we did not wish to encourage our kitten to think that he was boss. However, as cat lovers the world over have come to realize, dogs may have masters but cats make servants of the humans with whom they live. So it was to be with Pablo. The uncertainty about the outcome was soon resolved totally in Pablo's favour.

After an agonizing twenty minutes spent trying to close our ears to the noise coming from the conservatory, we capitulated. When we opened the door we were heartily greeted by a diminutive figure who commenced a welcome dance around our legs and joyously followed us upstairs to confirm his right to sleep where he liked, which in this case was on our bed. After treading his 'I'm getting ready to snuggle down' war dance on our best duvet, he eventually lay above our heads against the headboard with his face resting on Catherine's pillow near, and sometimes on, her long hair. During the night when either of us moved he began a loud husky purring sound which I referred to as the 'Donkey Serenade'.

We allowed him to sleep in our bedroom for a few weeks and then, as he grew accustomed to the house and became confident in our love, he decided that it would be more fun in the conservatory at bedtimes because he had posts to scratch and balls to chase, and sometimes there were exciting things to watch happening outside in the garden at night.

As he grew bigger and matured over the next few months we became aware of his complex and dynamic personality. Pablo's intelligence was remarkable and, short of speaking English, he had his own precise way of communicating with us through cat sounds and body language: he was, as many cat lovers will understand from their experiences, a 'Talking Cat'.

Sometimes when he was in full flow, conversing with us on some priority of his, jumping on our knees and rubbing his huge head against our legs and arms, we would wish he would shut up and give us a rest. But inevitably we would sooner or later realize what it was he wanted. Perhaps, as happened on several occasions, he had upset his water bowl and, fastidious cat as he was, wanted it put right. Or, as happened during his first encounter with springtime outside, there was a cock pheasant in HIS garden and it was bullying him. He wanted us to make it leave. In our life with Pablo we began to appreciate the wide range of sentient responses of which Maine Coon cats are capable, all of which reminded me constantly of how Toby Jug had been with me. Pablo loved our company but was suspicious

and often alarmed by strangers. He would respond most enthusiastically to us whenever we focused special attention on him. At
other times he liked to lie near us when we were talking
together, as if listening to what was being said. I often had the
impression that he was studying us as much as we were seeking
to understand him. His manifest affection for us was unlimited
and we grew to love him more and more as time went by.

There were many impressive characteristics about Pablo
which emerged during those early days, often related directly
to the special relationship developing between him and me. In
late evening, after dinner and before I joined Catherine in the
sitting room to read or watch television, I liked to sit alone in
the conservatory with all the lights out and stretch my eyes to
witness silently what was going on in the garden. I call this my
private thinking time. It was winter when Pablo came to us but
to my delight he made a habit of joining me, forsaking the warm
fireside in the sitting room. He and I would sit together peering
into the dark shadows cast by the bare branches of the mature
garden trees, many of which I had planted all those years ago.
Sometimes the darkness was so absolute that we spotted
nothing, but if there was a moon, even if it was merely a sliver,
parts of the world outside would open up to us. One night we
watched a tawny owl hunting through the trees, a sight which
filled me with excitement and sent Pablo into a frenzy, but then
he could see in the dark much better than I could.

Since no pesticides or other poisons are used in our garden,
it is a haven for wildlife and so Pablo and I shared the

enchantment of watching the nocturnal creatures which inhabit the nearby woods and gardens and which often chose to roam about near our trees and bushes to satisfy their needs and wants. Even better, when there is a full moon the garden assumes a fairytale silver mantle in which mysterious shapes move and are revealed as hedgehogs, rabbits and field mice going about their natural ways. They moved in a hushed, muffled manner, unaware of two rapt witnesses, a trembling young cat and a fascinated man, peering through the conservatory windows at the wildlife show outside. On some special nights our patient observation was rewarded and we were privileged to witness a variety of animals behaving naturally. Once we viewed a large mole emerging from the eruption of his tunnel exit to rummage in search of supper and to get some fresh air. One moonlit night in mid-March we saw a pair of hares boxing under the apple trees before racing off to continue their mating somewhere in the wide expanse of the farmer's fields beyond. Most wondrous of all, we once saw a huge white barn owl dismembering and eating what appeared to be a rabbit on the roof of our garage. Unfortunately, she quickly flew off as she caught a glimpse of Pablo's gyrations as he raced back and forwards on the window sill because the sight of such a large bird had sent him berserk.

Of course, on some nights we saw nothing because the sky clouded over or a neighbour's alert lights forced the creatures of the night to seek the shadows. Nevertheless, such times did not dissuade us from mounting a garden wildlife watch whenever the opportunity presented. Although I felt that it was I who was teaching my cat by sharing my interest in watching the nightlife in our garden, I eventually came to appreciate that cats come already programmed not only to know about nature but also intuitively to understand their place in it. Pablo had much that he could teach me and I had a great deal to learn from him. His natural-born skills were far superior to mine. His eyes could see much better in the darkness and his sense of smell and hearing were even more acute than his sight.

I was soon to be shown practical proof of this when I decided to train Pablo to wear a harness and accompany me on night-time walks beyond the confines of the cottage area, just as I had once done with Toby Jug. But first of all I had to persuade Pablo that wearing a harness would increase the opportunities for walks outside the vicinity of our garden and that this would contribute to his overall enjoyment of life.

This was not easy and the first few attempts were total failures. He simply lay down and refused to move. Then I decided on a plan to deny him an early breakfast. I then carried a pocketful of his favourite biscuits with which I enticed him, one at a time, to keep walking. In no time he got the message and began trotting alongside me with his harness on, as long as he received an occasional much-desired treat. Also, he began to delight in being outside in the fresh air. He was only in our garden but it did give him the chance to sniff around, startle little birds and partially climb some trees. Furthermore these garden trips helped Pablo and me to bond closer together and so it was that a stubborn cat turned into a willing cat for our walks. Eventually, Pablo was able to have his breakfast at the usual time, as soon as we got up, and I didn't need to dispense so many treat cat biscuits. We were now ready to travel beyond the confines of the cottage and to experience again the man and cat affinity that I had so enjoyed all those years ago with Toby Jug.

Since I am by nature a night owl, a habit formed in student days, I am rarely in bed before three in the morning, so I was able to choose to time our first nocturnal excursion as late as possible in order to reduce the possibility of encountering any dogs. We set out at midnight. Above us was a clear sky glittering with stars and a half-moon casting a silvery gleam though the trees. To be out at night in the countryside is an exhilarating experience; it is like being in another world.

We headed along a woodland path, well-defined and much used by anglers. Pablo walked ahead of me, lead taut, sniffing the fresh night air. Soon we heard the sound, of the weir and then saw that the river was in full flow due to recent rains. It was late April and it had rained a lot that spring, which was nothing uncommon in our part of the world. Pablo was buoyant with expectation, turning his head this way and that and raising his nostrils to savour fully the exquisite scents of the riverbank. Maine Coon cats are most highly sensitive to their environment and charged with quick responses to the possibilities of any situation. By the light of the pale moon I could see his body all aquiver with the excitement of exploring and savouring this new environment. I noticed that at almost four months of age Pablo had nearly trebled the size he was when he came to us, but he still had a long way to go in that respect because his breed do not reach full size or maturity until the age of four years.

At last we reached the side of the weir where the roar of the river tended to blanket all other sounds. It presented a picturesque sight as we gradually discerned through the shadowy trunks of the trees the translucent misty vapours rising above the waterfall like ghostly apparitions in the chill night air. Water has a charm of almost universal appeal to people and animals alike. It affects the tired mind like a balm and inspires the soul to contented contemplation. I pushed open the sprung wooden gate that gave access to the path alongside the weir and Pablo pulled me along by his lead in his enthusiasm to explore the way ahead. We stepped out onto the rocks that rose high above the tumbling waters and surveyed the vista before us. Moonlight rendered the gushing streams of white water into cascades of silver spray which splashed against the rock walls above where we stood. We moved along towards a great stony outcrop above the river and I sat down on a huge flat-topped boulder. Soon Pablo, tingling with excitement, jumped up to sit at my side. We shared a midnight feast of pork pie and I drank coffee from a flask. We sat together on the rock in comfortable repose, much as I had done previously with Toby Jug such a long time ago. Time had not visibly changed the river but now I was changed from an eager young man having a fun night-time ramble with his cat to an older, more mature person who was reliving the past in the company of a different cat. This experience was more mellow, but nonetheless memorable for all that.

As we made our way out of the woods I reflected that the trip had proved to be a success for both of us but especially for Pablo, who sniffed obsessively at mysterious animal tracks all the way along our path homeward. As we reached the open road I could see the snowy outline of the Cheviot Hills and in the far distance the Cheviot itself, which brought another raft of memories of a special cat, a horse called Fynn and days spent on lonely trails through the beautiful Northumberland wilderness. That night, before I turned in, Pablo treated me to an affectionate purring session with much rubbing of his body against me. His huge amber eyes conveyed a glowing appreciation for all that he had experienced during our walk. The big cat knew how to say thank you.

In the weeks that followed I took Pablo on many late night jaunts and used the time to train him to respond to my whistle by administering tasty treats. He was a fast learner and I always kept him on a short lead because I knew that there was always the unexpected to consider. How right I was to do so as subsequent events would prove. Our walks together served to give us both a welcome form of exercise since we were each housebound most of the time, Pablo because he wasn't allowed to roam freely yet and me because I was busy writing at my laptop. There was another benefit. The walks that brought us closer together as partners sharing in the raptures and the mysteries of nature also served to tune us in to each other's thoughts and feelings as we went along. But this halcyon state of affairs was not to last much longer and could well have caused the demise of one or both of us.

When Pablo was about five months old and growing larger by the day an incident occurred on one of our walks which could have resulted in serious injury for either one of us or, in the worst scenario, death. It happened during a warm spell of weather in May. We set off from the cottage around half-past-eleven and were soon deep in the woods approaching the weir. As Pablo and I wound our way along a narrow trail, flanked by banks of willow trees on one side and scattered broom on the other, we could hear the thunder of the weir coming closer. Suddenly Pablo stopped and refused to move despite my urgings. I always carried a small torch with me on these night-time excursions and I took it out now and shone it around, thinking that Pablo must have discovered something that I could not see. The torch slipped out of my hand and, just as I bent down to retrieve it, a shotgun blasted twice from very close by and I heard the whistle of the pellets as they ripped through the branches of the trees above and around us. Abruptly Pablo's lead was jerked out of my hand as the terrified cat ran for his life. If I had been standing then I surely would have been hit. Bent double for safety I threw the torch light to one side in an attempt to draw fire away from us.

Hearing men's voices approaching I raced crazily back along the path, tripped twice over tree roots and fell headlong on the rough ground. Eventually, bruised and bleeding from cuts to my hands, I made it out of the woods and stopped panting with the exertion of unaccustomed running. I strained my ears over the thumping of my heart to hear if I was being pursued.

Of Pablo there was no sign. I whistled and called softly and whistled and called again and again, but there was no response. Since it was now after midnight it was really dark, too dark even by the dim light of the stars to look for where a shocked and frightened cat might be hiding. Having regained my breath, if not my composure, I headed for home in an angry and bitter state of mind. What madman would be out at night in an English wood, blasting off a shotgun so wildly? I determined to investigate the matter thoroughly with the help of the authorities but for now I desperately needed to find and comfort my cat.

Soon I reached the garden drive and, as I fumbled in my pocket for keys, a dark form moved out of the shadows and meowed. It was Pablo, unhurt, safe and sound and still trailing his lead behind him. I cradled him in my arms and the stress drained out of both of us. I murmured words of relief with my mouth pressed against the thick fur of his neck and he made little whimpers of what I understood to be sheer joy. We were alive and well, and secure on our own home territory.

The next morning I gave Catherine a modified account of what had happened and she told me off for acting so rashly, confining her sympathy to Pablo who slept, as cats do when troubled, the entire day through. Later I telephoned the police and explained what had happened. The response was unsympathetic to say the least and amounted to a verbal reprimand for my alleged stupidity in wandering the woods at midnight when licensed hunters were out shooting rabbits and foxes. Suitably chastened, I didn't dare mention that I had a cat on a leash with me or retort that neither foxes nor rabbits carried torches on their nocturnal wanderings.

Well, after that I thought, I wonder what the locals will make of it; perhaps someone could cast some light on the matter. With this in mind I joined the throng of regulars at the Northumberland Arms which nestles at the foot of the bank down the road from our cottage. Glass of wine in hand, I recounted my tale to a group of habitual drinkers at the bar whom I knew had lived in the area for most of their lives. The end of my account was greeted by a stunned silence. Then the whole group, including the barmaid whom I had expected to be more sympathetic, broke into peals and guffaws of laughter. Shocked by their reaction I demanded to know what there was to laugh about. It was several minutes before the roars and chuckles of merriment subsided sufficiently for anyone to give me an answer. Then in broad Geordie accent I was told, 'Well, you know, you go out in the middle of the night for a walk in the woods and, worse still you take your pet cat with you; it is no wonder somebody took a shot at you. They probably thought you were a lunatic or a werewolf!'

More hilarity followed. Aware that my dignity had been severely compromised I managed a rueful grin and accepted several friendly slaps on the back as gracefully as I could manage. Joan the barmaid asked how big my cat was, a question that aroused another bout of hysterical laughter. Desperate not to appear a complete idiot I told them he was a Maine Coon and about as big as a Yorkshire terrier but anything I said simply made them erupt in giggles and sniggers. When I looked round at the group, some had laughed so much that their faces were tear-stained. I felt I couldn't win and made to leave but they prevailed upon me to stay. Somebody bought me a drink and gradually the mirth subsided and I was able to make my escape accompanied by jestful remarks such as 'Remember to keep your head down!'

Once outside I was joined by Derek, who had worked as a gamekeeper and water bailiff, and he explained to me that gangs from the city areas came up to the river at night using nets to poach fish, trout and salmon, which they then sold from the back of a van on the black market around the backstreets and to some restaurants in the Newcastle and Gateshead areas. It was big criminal business and in the past water bailiffs had been attacked and injured. The police had a file on it but nothing much seemed to have been done. It was probable that those people who shot at me mistook me for a game warden or bailiff and were determined to frighten me off to avoid arrest.

'Well they certainly succeeded,' I said.

'You'd best steer clear of the river at night,' Derek said. 'Sometimes they've been known to bring big dogs with them. If you want a walk at night go down to the coast; it's a lot safer!'

And with that he bade me goodnight and went on his way and I reflected with horror on what he had told me. I realized that Pablo, by abruptly stopping, had saved us from a fate too terrible to contemplate.

I returned home in sober mood and indulged Pablo with lots of strokes and endearments. I informed him that there would be no more midnight walks in the woods by the river. He stared at me gravely as if to say, 'I second that!'

The experience in the woods by the river that night had given me much cause to ponder the changing world in which we now lived, so different in essence from the beloved England into which Toby Jug had been born and raised over thirty years earlier.

When he reached the age of six months we took Pablo to the vet's to be neutered. I hated to do that to him but it was regulation for pedigree cats and it also meant that he wouldn't wander miles away to pair up with female cats in heat and have to fight off other tom cats for the opportunity to mate with a she-cat. Whenever any of my cats need to be taken for veterinary procedures I find it an anxious time, whatever the treatment might be. I know it is possibly an irrational response but accidents do happen and I am always worried until my cats are back with me safe and sound. So it was with Pablo. I took him at the arranged time and left him. He looked at me nervously on leaving and I knew that he would be fretting because he had not been fed that morning on vet's orders, as he was to be given a general anaesthetic. I was told to come back in two hours during which time I nervously drank coffee in a local cafe and attempted to read my newspaper.

When I went back to collect him there was a most awful din going on in the surgery, mainly caused by several dogs barking, especially one large and vicious-looking German Shepherd which appeared to be trying to escape his lead and attack some other dogs waiting there. No one appeared to be in control as I approached a harassed-looking young receptionist sitting in front of a computer. I asked her if she knew anything about my cat. She told me she didn't but she mentioned there had been several emergencies during the morning but hadn't heard whether a cat was involved. After hanging around for several more minutes I began to feel really concerned and this information from the receptionist had done nothing to mitigate my apprehensions. So without any further hesitation I charged into the inner sanctum of the surgery to be confronted by a tall gaunt woman dressed for the outdoors in muddy green wellies and smelling of cowsheds and farm animals.

'I am looking for my cat; he's in here to be neutered,' I ventured in the face of her inquisitorial stance.

'Please return to the waiting room and your cat will be returned to you!'

I was not to be so easily placated but tried to remain polite. 'My cat has been here for almost three hours; I am worried about him and want him back now!' I said forthrightly.

Just then, before the moment of confrontation could develop into a more serious exchange, the tousle-haired figure of a veterinary nurse appeared in the corridor and exclaimed: 'Oh, Dr O'Connor, your cat is now ready for collection. Please follow me and I'll show you the way.'

Avoiding the haughty and disapproving stare of the woman vet in the smelly wellies, I hurried to catch up to the nurse. 'Had a busy day?' I asked as we strode together down the passage.

'It's been like World War Two!' she said, grimacing, but later managed a smile.

We entered a cubicle where, safe in his carrying box, lay Pablo, smelling strongly of anaesthetic. He gave me a mournful look that said: 'Do you know what they've done to me?' Sighing with relief at the sight of him alive and well, I thanked the nurse and carried him out of the bedlam of the waiting room to the car. All the way home I praised him and promised to personally look after him for the rest of the day.

When we arrived at the cottage Catherine was waiting for us and gave Pablo some very gentle hugs and lots of words of welcome, but probably equally important from his point of view was that she had his dinner and bowl of biscuits ready for him. Although he appeared at first to be somewhat groggy, our growing cat, who seemed to be getting bigger every day, soon became his normal self. Sniffing and sneezing at the scents of the medication on his skin, he gave himself a thorough tongue-wash and then relaxed on a window sill in the sunlight.

During the days that followed his operation Pablo seemed to want to be closer to us than ever before, probably as a reaction to the trauma of being separated from us as well as the procedure itself. Cats are capable of storing memories and the emotions aroused cause them to feel vulnerable long after the actual event. This is why Pablo needed some extra loving from us to tide him over the experience.

He loved to play with us so when he pulled himself together we played together often. We had bought him a number of cat toys which he tended to play with during the night when he was alone in the conservatory. Often we could hear him racing around and jumping about. In the morning we would find his toys strewn around, well-bitten and torn. But he preferred to play with us.

Catherine had bought a brightly coloured cloth bird which was attached to the end of a stick by a piece of elastic. When we waved it about in front of Pablo the result would be the most extraordinary display of acrobatics, including outstanding leaps, bounds and twists of his body whilst airborne. But Pablo's preferred form of play was a rough and tumble with me. This usually involved me grabbing him and rolling him about on the floor whilst trying to avoid his big sharp claws. Another thing he enjoyed was when I ran along the hallway with him in hot pursuit, grabbing and biting at a trouser belt which I trailed behind me. These activities usually escalated to the point where he would wrench the belt from my hold, tear upstairs with it in his mouth and then lie on the top landing waiting for me to mount a counter move. Usually, I was the one who ended up exhausted and, much to Pablo's disappointment, would retire hurt with several scratches requiring medication and needing a rest.

Once Pablo was allowed to roam free, I would play this game

with him in a modified form out in the garden where I would run about trailing a length of rope behind me with him furiously chasing me. One day this playtime ended in a shock trauma for him when he sped off with the end of the rope in his mouth and me running after him; he made a detour over the compost heap where a cutting from a rose bush became entangled in his fluffy tail. Unable to free himself from it he panicked, dropped the rope and raced away into deep undergrowth to hide. I was convulsed with laughter at this turn of events but Catherine, who had been watching from the kitchen window, was more sympathetic and hurried to the aid of the terrified cat. Removing the offending branch from his tail she carried him into the cottage for treats and sympathy. Later, I received a deserved scolding. Following some soothing strokes from Catherine and after consuming a mouthful of tasty treats, Pablo was once again ready for action, cried to be let out and ran to join me. He didn't seem much bothered by his recent scare but for the sake of our continuing good relations I offered him my apology for laughing at him. Cats hate to be laughed at and go into a great huff when it happens, but in this case Pablo seemed more interested in resuming play. To please him we did a few more run-arounds before I called it a day and we retired indoors for tea and relaxation.

Generally, Pablo soon recovered his aplomb following situations like the one above and in a short while played as enthusiastically as ever. Because he liked both or at least one of us to join his games, he developed strategies to ensure that we did. When he became bored he resorted to a number of antics to attract our attention. These included knocking the telephone off the hook; thudding his body against the sitting room door; and clinging by his claws to the top of the opening door to hitch a ride. If these tactics didn't work then he would charge up to us with a ball or piece of ribbon in his mouth. He also loved to race upstairs via the wooden banister and then hurl himself back down in leaps and bounds. None of this does any good for the furnishings and decor, of course, but Pablo was so lovable and dependent on us that we could not resist just hugging him and even encouraging him so that we could laugh at his clowning around the cottage.

But Maine Coon cats, especially the males, tend to grow very large as they mature and once they become heavier the possibility for destructive rumbustious behaviour becomes alarmingly evident. The problems caused by a kitten running helter-skelter through the house can be bad enough but a burly Maine Coon with an abundance of energy can do considerable damage to the happy home. As Pablo grew bigger he needed to learn some discipline and, since his breed is noted for its intelligence and willingness to please, it was not difficult with patience to teach him acceptable behaviour in our cottage.

It is worth describing the first day that he was old enough to be let out by himself because it illustrates the true nature of his character. At first he just stood as if rooted to the spot. Then he turned and looked at me as if to say, 'Why aren't you coming?'

'Go on, enjoy yourself. You're a big lad now and you're free!' I said to him.

Eventually he moved off, if somewhat diffidently. I turned and went back inside the cottage for a cup of coffee and to hear the news on the radio. Suddenly, Catherine called me from the conservatory. 'Come and see Pablo; you must not miss this!' I hurried outside into the garden and abruptly became aware of a terrific clamour coming from a copse of tall trees at the edge of our garden. 'Can you spot him? Look, there he is!' she said pointing to the said trees.

And then I caught sight of him high in the topmost branches of an ash tree; he was swaying back and forth as he fought to maintain his balance. The clamour was being caused by a crowd of rooks who were noisily buzzing him. For his part Pablo was trying to retaliate by swiping out with his huge paws at the circling birds. 'Don't think I'm afraid of you lot!' he seemed to be saying, as far as I could make out. The sight of him swinging around in the spindly branches, his bronze and sable-coloured fur gleaming in the morning sunlight, was for me a foretaste of the way in which Pablo's personality would emerge as 'the wild cat within' and increasingly come to dominate his life. Regrettably, this would eventually result in his death but for the present we shared his joy at being free.

'Should we go and call him down?'

'No,' I said. 'He's only having fun. Let's leave him be.'

With that said we both went back into the cottage, although Catherine kept going to the window and anxiously looking into the garden to see what he was up to.

Later, Pablo gave us both a scare because he did not return

that night. Around midnight I took my large-beamed lantern and, at Catherine's urgent request, went to look of our missing big cat. I searched the garden, called, whistled and shone my light all around the trees and hedgerows adjacent to our property, but of Pablo there was no sign. I must admit that at this stage I wasn't worried unduly. As I explained to Catherine, it was a warm summer night and there were a lot more interesting things for a cat to investigate than thoughts of home. But we were both showing signs of parental concern at our missing child substitute.

In the morning all apprehension was relieved by the appearance at the conservatory door of a bedraggled Pablo whining loudly to be let in. As I moved to open the door, Catherine called from upstairs telling me not to do so as she could see from the window a row of rodent bodies lying on the patio. Obviously, Pablo had been hunting through the night and was the perpetrator. Catherine didn't want him carrying any of his kills inside the cottage.

'It's OK,' I called back. 'I'll grab him and lift him in.' Opening the door in one quick motion, I reached down and grasped Pablo around his middle, hauling him indoors whilst slamming the door shut. He stared up at me as if to say, 'Have you seen what I caught for you? Aren't I clever?' after which, head held high, he trotted proudly towards the kitchen for his breakfast to be followed, no doubt, by a well-deserved cat nap.

Meanwhile, there remained the problem of the line of rodent corpses outside. 'If we don't get rid of them he might start to eat them and be sick!' said Catherine, who was surveying the dead bodies.

'It's alright,' I said. 'I know what to do. I've been here before.'

And memories flooded back of all the times over the years I had needed to surreptitiously dispose of dead mice and voles before my cat became aware of what I was doing. As I set to clearing away the rodent corpses another more poignant memory came back to me which involved a different cat and an earlier but happy time in my life.

I recalled an incident that took place in Owl Cottage when Toby Jug was about two years old. I was busy in the kitchen when I heard some strange noises coming from another room. When I went in to investigate I was confronted by a strange sight. Toby Jug was standing, body arched, rigid on all fours, in a hunched crouch, staring at something by the fireplace. Worse still, he was making hissing and spitting sounds which I had never heard from him before. It was February and the room, having no lights switched on, was in semi-darkness. I strained to see what was arresting Toby's attention. Something moved in the shadows by the fireplace, eliciting a throaty growl from Toby Jug. At once I spotted it – the largest mouse I had ever seen. Surely it must be a hybrid, I thought. But what struck me as most bizarre of all was that the creature was baring its teeth and making muted snarls in the direction of Toby. I assumed that this was a developing situation which could only end one way and that was by Toby Jug killing this rather obnoxious-looking rodent. In order not to precipitate the matter I withdrew to allow what my medical friends term 'a therapeutic wait', wherein things can change for the better without further intervention. It was after five o'clock and, since I had been working hard in the kitchen, I poured myself a glass of claret, sat down in an easy chair and awaited the outcome.

When I checked, the stalemate was still ongoing: it was what you might call a 'Mexican Standoff'. From my vantage point beside the door I came to the conclusion that Toby was afraid to attack; he didn't know what to do. After all, he hadn't ever had an experience of killing anything since his mother had died before she had the opportunity to train her kitten in life skills for cats. Well, I thought, it is beyond my capabilities to emulate a female cat in respect of hunting and killing a mouse, however urgent it is for Toby to learn. He'll have to learn some other way. With that, I charged into the room and scared the big mouse away. I noticed, in the receding daylight, as it bounded and leapt away, that it had a patch of brown fur over its black back, like a cloak, unlike most house mice, which have grey fur. This gave it a most sinister look. Furthermore, it had very pronounced ears that were roundel-shaped like those of Walt Disney's Mickey Mouse. This thing was a monster, no doubt about that. I watched it exit through a hitherto unnoticed crevice in the stone wall of the room and told myself that I would need to give that some attention as soon as possible.

Next, I turned my focus on Toby Jug and picked him up. I got the feeling that he needed a cuddle because he'd suffered something of a shock. 'You and me both, pal,' I said, adding, 'You've a lot to learn yet, though; don't worry too much about it for the present.' Several times that evening Toby went to the gap in the stone wall where the mouse had gone through and gave it a thorough investigative sniff as well as several fierce hisses. 'Don't distress yourself!' I told him. 'Tomorrow we will go to a shop I know in Rothbury where I can buy just the thing to deal with Mr Mouse.'

After breakfast the next morning I set off in my white Mini for the rural market town of Rothbury, with Toby Jug catnapping on the front passenger seat. The town was bustling with early shoppers as I parked opposite the butcher's shop, famous throughout the area for game and special-recipe luxurious sausages. The shop I wanted was some distance up the sloping street and so, leaving Toby in the car, I crossed the road, trying to ignore the inviting smells of freshly made meat pies emanating from a home bakery, and headed for the store which had the local nickname 'The Old Curiosity Shop', after Dickens'. Inside the store it was gloomy and there was just one light bulb hanging above the counter for illumination.

The glum expression of the proprietor matched the dingy interior of the shop but it purported to stock every hardware item you might want.

'What are you after, then?' he grunted in a far from welcoming manner.

'I would like a "live" mousetrap. Even two if you have them, please,' I added politely. The vehemence of his response surprised even me although I was aware of his irascible reputation.

'It's only fools that would want to keep rodents alive. What you should have are killer traps or poison,' he said, glaring at me.

'Do you have any humane traps for sale?' I persisted.

He sighed, gave me another hard look, then muttered, 'There might be a few left of the ones bought in for the nuns at Lemmington Hall. What are you wanting to do, train them to sit up and beg?' With this last rejoinder he came as near as he could to smiling, only it wasn't a smile; it was more of a sneering smirk. Then he disappeared into the dim interior of the store. Several minutes later he reappeared carrying two lengthy wooden boxes with wire trap-doors at each end, all covered in dust and cobwebs. 'These will have to do for you,' he said ungraciously. 'That will be four shillings for the both of them.'

I paid him without further comment and with a cheerful 'cheerio' left the shop, stopped to buy two hot meat pies at the bakery and rejoined Toby Jug. He was sitting waiting inside the car on the shelf of the rear window and attracting curious stares, sometimes smiles, from passersby.

'We'll soon be home,' I told him as he leapt to my shoulder and purred all the way on the drive back. 'I've got us a pie each for lunch!' I said. At this, his purrs resonated even more loudly. Maybe he couldn't understand my words but he could obviously smell the pies and put two and two together. Smart cat.

When we arrived back at the cottage I examined the traps. They were rather scruffy but I thought that might be an advantage in luring the mouse into one since a clean trap with my scent all over it might make it wary and I really wanted to catch the creature. Toby, true to his nature, was full of curiosity and watched my every move. First, I rubbed the inside of the trap with a piece of cheese to awaken the mouse's interest and then I put two cubes of cheese inside the trap. I did the same with the second trap and set them ready. I placed them along the wall where the mouse had made his exit and awaited developments, although I realized that it would probably be sometime in the middle of the night before the trap would be sprung. That is, if our adversary deigned to appear.

Then, after giving my hands a good wash to clean them after handling the traps, I turned my attention to our lunch. Cutting Toby's pie in half, since a whole one would be far too much for him, I set his tray down for him. By the time I had served up a mixed salad with the pie for myself, Toby Jug had consumed his in double-quick time and was now busy licking gravy stains off his lips and preparing to give himself a tongue-wash.

In the afternoon I attended to some chores of the tidying-up variety around the garden. Toby Jug sat in his favourite old apple tree and I could tell from his expression as I glanced towards him occasionally that something was bothering him. It didn't take me long to guess that he was still worried about the mouse he should have caught yesterday. Later, while I relaxed with a book and a drink in front of the fire, Toby Jug couldn't settle and kept pacing back and forth around the traps, wondering what might be going to happen.

'Time for bed,' I said, and headed up to the bedroom followed by a cat who appeared to be in two minds as to whether to go to bed or stay on guard downstairs, ready to confront the mouse. After an uneventful night we rose in the morning and I set about preparing breakfast only to find that Toby Jug was nowhere in evidence. On hearing a scraping sound from the sitting room I hastened to investigate. The sight that greeted me took me by surprise even though it was half expected.

Toby was circling one of the traps, which had been sprung. Even more surprising than this quick result was the fact that the trap was being continually bounced over the floor by the creature inside. It was banging and crashing against the doors of the trap, trying to burst out. But the big mouse was well and truly captured. I picked up the trap to view the captive. The first impression I had was of a very large rodent unlike the small grey and brown creatures I was accustomed to seeing around the garden and driveways. It was a male and he looked ferocious. He glared back at me and recommenced thrusting against the trap door that had him imprisoned.

'Right,' I said. 'The sooner we get rid of you the better for all of us. Come on, Toby – we've a journey to make.'

Wasting no time I backed the car out of the garage and was quickly joined by a curious cat who was determined to see this through even though he had not yet had his breakfast, which normally would have been an immediate priority. We had a monster mouse to deal with. I placed the trap with the mouse into a shopping bag and put it on the floor of the car by the passenger seat, watched all the while by a bemused if somewhat apprehensive cat.

The informed rural advice regarding how far to take captive rodents before freeing them was about two miles; this was to ensure that they did not return to the place where they were caught. With this in mind I drove several miles down the A1 and turned off on the outskirts of Tarbrook Farm. Leaving Toby Jug in the car I took the trap to the border of a leafy lane overgrown with weeds and levered it open. After a moment's hesitation the mouse hurtled out into the coarse grass for a short distance then, amazingly, stopped, turned, raised itself upright and glared back at me, chittering like an angry squirrel before disappearing into a darkened ditch. To say the least, I was dumbfounded. I had never seen anything like it.

As I walked back to the car I smiled at the sight of Toby glued to the windscreen so he could witness proceedings. He seemed relieved to see the back of the little beast, but no more than I was. Later that day, I decided to address the problem of the hole in the wall, through which I'd seen the mouse leaving. From the greenhouse I brought a smoke bomb which was used to fumigate the place at the end of the season. Now, returning indoors, I lit the blue fuse end, pushed it into the wide crevice and then taped it into position. Next I went outside in the garden to view the other side of the wall. Sure enough a tell-tale trail of smoke was issuing forth from around a stone at the base. I chalked the spot and determined to fill the opening with cement as soon as possible. It would be a weekend job, which I thought I would probably do the next day. Whilst all this was going on I was followed about by a most interested cat who kept well away from the smoke but watched attentively from a safe distance.

Watching Toby, I was reminded of his behaviour the previous evening when he had, in a perplexed manner, kept returning to the entry crack in the wall, sniffing warily and then spitting a warning at the place where the mouse had disappeared. I suppressed a smile as I looked at him still trying to work out what he should have done when he first confronted the mouse. He couldn't quite sort it out in his mind but I knew that eventually he would when he grew and matured some more. 'Never mind Toby; I'm sure you'll have other chances to deal with mice,' I said to him lovingly.

Later that week, in a conversation with Richard Morris, my illustrator, he told me that mice of this kind were to be found in some country areas around the south of England. My intruder had obviously been a migrant. I hoped he would be the last. And so, with the thought that the past is always with us, I ended my ruminations about life with Toby Jug at least for that day and turned my attention back to the present and the disposal of Pablo's kills.

Pablo rejoiced in the opportunity he was given to wander at will and with the availability of lush woodland, open fields and river banks adjacent to the cottage he was spoilt for choice. Whilst the countryside around us mainly comprises traditional farmland there are hidden areas of wooded copse and overgrown bush-covered gullies in which wildlife thrives. In one covert domain rabbits and hares, foxes and badgers, weasels and stoats, colourful cock pheasants and partridges, redshank and woodpigeon, to mention only a few, live in secluded sanctuary. Here and there in this area you can still come across a green meadow, open to the sky but surrounded by dense foliage and tree growth which may harbour an abandoned gamekeeper's wooden shack. Not far away, there may be a tumbledown barn in which owls, swifts and swallows roosted and where poachers once took refuge. Now, such an area is the province of an itinerant population of wildlife refugees who are looking for a home to raise their young and to live peaceful lives.

Sometimes in the middle of a large field wild zones can be found which the farmer has not cultivated, possibly because it contains weighty rock mounds, or simply because he is a kind man who believes in conserving animal- and bird-life. These small plantations provide precious habitats for flora and fauna which would otherwise be denied living space. Happily, more farmers are now being encouraged to set aside land for such purposes.

I know of a stretch of land nearby which is littered with scattered boulders and rock outcrops, fringed with self-setting saplings and overgrown with broom and brambles. It provides an ideal environment for numerous small species of mice and shrew, as well as ground-nesting birds such as the skylark, to breed and flourish. In a dip in the land there is a drainage ditch which has been left undrained and, fed by the rains, it has grown into a pond providing suitable conditions for eels and exotic-coloured newts to thrive, as well as iridescent dragonflies and damselflies which flit and hover around the water's edge like vibrant humming birds. In time, coots and moorhens will most probably take up residence here and in a short while the area will be a thriving wildlife habitat. While wandering around such an environment, Pablo will be perfectly at home; it is, after all, his natural-born heritage as a cat.

In the early days of Pablo's life with us, like any pet owners we had to learn to accommodate him and he, us. For Pablo this involved accepting the need to treat the carpets, curtains and furniture with a certain amount of respect and to acknowledge the need for hygienic toilet practices. For our part, life with Pablo demanded a tolerant attitude to his preference for leaving animal and bird carcasses at the back door as offerings to us on a very regular basis. It also required forbearance towards a drenched presence plaintively wailing for entry after a stormy night spent hunting in the woods and fields. After his expeditions we would often have to spend time cleaning him up, drying him off and picking the burrs and thistle heads from his tangled fur. Pablo would look up at us and sigh as if to say, 'Well, you know all this is what cats have to do.' The process was a two-way track. We sought to teach him about our way of life and he encouraged us to understand and participate in the ways of the wild and the way of the cat.

As the evening developed into darkness Pablo would come to me and indicate that it was time for a prowl. He would signal this by raising himself on his back legs and padding his paws up and down on the glass door of the conservatory. When I opened the door, and just before he made his exit, he would usually turn and look up at me as if inviting me to accompany him like the times in his youth when I took him for walks on his harness.

Sometimes when I am free to follow my mood I will grab my coat and torch, and tag along with him. The first time I did this was a delightful experience during which I was initiated by my Pablo into the world of the cat. I left the conservatory and found him waiting for me by the beech tree in which the ring doves build a nest each year. As I joined him he paused to give his chest a quick lick and then padded off with a purpose in mind. Excited, I followed him. Once outside the garden I couldn't see a thing. More to the point, I couldn't see Pablo.

Then I heard a familiar throaty meow and felt him brush against my leg. I got the feeling that he was intent on guiding me on a tour of his making, like a child showing a parent around his playground. He stayed behind me for some reason and then approached me from the rear as cats are wont to do. I stroked and praised him and he led me forward only for me to lose sight of him once more. I took out my torch and shone it around to see where he was. Then I spotted a startled brown furry face slightly to the side of me and suddenly realized how stupid my action had been. Artificial light at night is anathema to wild creatures; it is an unnatural abomination associated only with human kind. For the nocturnal residents of the countryside improvised light is an unwelcome intrusion which deprives them of their visual acuities and frightens everything, both predators and game, away. The experience caused me to reflect. Here am I in the outdoors at night, an outsider divorced from the natural ways, by reason of being 'civilized'. My cat's senses of hearing and smell, as well as his vision, are infinitely superior to mine and without the trappings of my domesticated environ- ment I can no longer lay claim to belong to the natural environs which initially bred humanity. This was a sobering thought. In this setting, I was inferior to my cat and just about every animal that lived out there.

I found Pablo lying some distance in front of me in a crouched pose, intent on something out there in front of us. He acknowledged my presence as I joined him with the merest flick of his tail, which is a cat's way of responding to someone without breaking concentration.

We were situated at the edge of a mown hayfield which extended a vast distance over rolling landscape. Pablo lay motionless, nose and ears twitching now and then with the scents and sounds wafting over the soft autumn breeze. This was his method of reconnoitring the ground over which he would soon be moving. At last he turned and looked at me, and made an affectionate throaty sound. 'Can you understand what I see and hear and scent?' These were his unspoken queries. His bright eyes, shining like huge emeralds in the light from the moon, implored my comprehension. I struggled mentally to appreciate what he was experiencing and the quality of it. Suddenly, in a burst of intuition I became aware of what my Pablo was thinking and feeling. I strove to fine tune the meanings flowing between us.

'See how the grasses flow before the wind, hiding the creatures I would hunt. I can scent rabbit and partridge. There are field mice and shrews; I can hear them eating worms and scrunching beetles. Over by the fringes of the wood I hear bats fluttering and squeaking as they make ready to fly off to hunt. On a branch of the oak I can see the little owl waiting to pounce.'

Such a rush of perceptions stunned me and left me blank. I could see and hear nothing of it. To me it was just darkness and silence except for the sighing of the wind. Then the moon emerged from behind the clouds and blanched the landscape. Pablo glanced up at me in farewell and then, with innate stealth, he faded into the rippling grasses with no more than a hint of shadow. He had left to follow the call of the wild.

I felt a sense of loss at his going, a lonesome feeling that I took away with me as I retraced my steps homewards. He left me because he knew at that point of time that I was incapable of entering and sharing his world either physically or mentally. I just couldn't tune in and match his natural-born prowess.

Later in the cottage, in a thoughtful mood, I reflected that with increasing human dependency on scientific technology we are losing contact with our natural origins and preventing ourselves from accessing the vast reservoir of innate knowledge which is intuitively available to us, thus forfeiting the fund of wild wisdom which is freely available to cats and other animals. Thinking about this night's experience with Pablo I became aware, not for the first time, of the cost that civilization has imposed on us. Because of this I feel myself drawn progressively closer to the domain in which my cats live and through which they function. What happened that night triggered and re-awakened a vestige of what lay dormant within me. I retired to bed with these thoughts on my mind and with the hope that in the morning when I came downstairs and drew back the curtains the first thing I would see would be Pablo, safe and sound, waiting to be let in.

Pablo was affectionate and responsive to our overtures to tame and discipline him but yet he retained the right to fulfil his origins as a cat. He was usually quiet and withdrawn in his manner and temperament, and became more so as he matured and did his own thing. If he was a human being we would probably call him introverted. Whilst we adored Pablo and he obviously loved us, he could at times appear remote, totally engrossed in his own world.

In reading through a cat book I saw some photographs of silver-grey Maine Coon cats who were purported to be outgoing and dashing. Perhaps Pablo, I thought, was missing the company of his own kind and another cat, a playmate, would bring him out a little more satisfactorily for them both.

Pablo will return to our story later, but first I want to begin to tell the tale of our first silver-grey Maine Coon, an interesting and remarkable character, whose friendship did just what I wanted for Pablo and who initially brought chaos into our reasonably well-ordered lives.

CARLOS

'He's one in a million,' Jane said to me over the phone. 'I could have sold him many times over as soon as I put the pictures of his litter up for sale on my website. But he's all yours if you still want him. He's five weeks old now so you can come and see him. What would you like his pet name to be?'

'Carlos!' I said, the jubilation rising within me. I had been speaking to Jane, the Maine Coon breeder from whom we had bought Pablo. For the reasons I gave above I had contacted Jane and discovered that she had recently sent her silver she-cat Florence to be mated with a superb silver stud called Oscar. The litter had duly arrived and her phone call to me was about one of the kittens who was a striking silver-grey in colour.

Of course, all kittens look appealing but he was exceptional. The first time I saw him I was truly amazed. He was the most beautiful kitten I had ever seen and I loved him at first sight; a tiny fluffy ball of silver fur with a baby round head, minute pointed ears and piercing blue eyes that held a sparkle of intelligent depth about them. He was irresistible.

But there was something else about him that I could not at first identify; then it came back to me. It happened when I was on holiday in Zimbabwe. One day I had visited an animal sanctuary where injured animals and orphans of the bush were fostered until they could fend for themselves again. What I saw in the eyes of a leopard cub, which snarled at me, was also there in the eyes of my new kitten, Carlos. It was an almost indefinable wild glint of life from the jungle depths which Rudyard Kipling had ventured to describe in *The Jungle Book*. 'He's been here before!' exclaimed Jane knowingly, nodding towards the kitten nestling contentedly in my arms.

The next time I saw him he was ten weeks old. In another two weeks I would be able to bring him home but I just had to see him again. The regulations governing pedigree Maine Coons, as indeed with most other pedigrees, stated that kittens had to be three months old with all their health jabs before they could be allowed to join the new owners. Carlos didn't disappoint me. He was so full of life that he could hardly stay still even for a moment. He impressed me as being a little cat with a big mission. He seemed determined to investigate everything in his world that came even remotely into his line of vision. And these things, whatever they were, had to be explored robustly and at full gallop, which inevitably caused chaos in Jane's house.

One particular incident led to a medical emergency. Carlos had been playing chase games with some of the other kittens when it all got out of hand. He was on the top of the stairs when in a state of mega-excitement he took a flying leap through the banister rails, missed the kitten he was aiming at and crashed into the wall halfway down. He rolled to the bottom of the stairs and lay still.

Fortunately, Jane was on hand to witness this leap and its consequences. She was horrified. Suspecting that Carlos might be seriously injured she wrapped him in a towel, rushed to the car and drove as fast as she could to the vet's. Charging into the consulting room she pleaded for him to be examined immediately as a matter of emergency. As the duty veterinarian unwrapped the towel, Carlos, looking decidedly dizzy, was just beginning to regain consciousness. To Jane's relief he was unhurt or damaged in any way, just a trifle shocked and shaken. During the rest of the evening he was moderately calm and restful, which gave the rest of the cat family, as well as Jane and Dave, a peaceful respite. She was quick to inform me of this incident and the outcome but she was also anxious to mention that she was praying for the time when he would come to me.

'So am I,' I told her.

When I told Catherine of this latest episode in the riotous life of our new kitten she remarked: 'Well, you wanted a commando and now you've got one.'

Thinking back to that time, I can recall that look in the eyes of Carlos, how lucid and startling they were in a savage and primitive but most appealing way. Looking at his photographs as a kitten I am instantly reminded of the saying that the eyes are the mirror of the soul. The eyes of Carlos held more than a hint of the wilderness in him.

It was a warm sunny day in early July when Carlos at last came to us. To look at, he was a veritable picture, the iconic chocolate box image. But his behaviour quickly made a shambles of our careful preparations for his arrival and at times bedlam reigned. I soon began to realize that Carlos, beautiful as he might be, was suffering a hyperactive condition to an extreme degree; he was blatantly out of control and in grave need of remedial training. The evidence for this became only too apparent the first night after he had arrived. Catherine had retired early to bed and had taken Carlos up with her in an attempt to calm him down. Suddenly, she appeared in the sitting room where I was watching television. She exclaimed helplessly, 'I can't deal with this kitten. He is completely out of control.' This statement, coming from an experienced education professional in the field of disruptive and deviant behaviour, caused me no end of alarm and I swiftly realized that a state of emergency was developing in our normally tranquil household!

It appeared that on entering the bedroom, Carlos had proceeded to rip the plush velvet headboard and began to tear ferociously at Catherine's Egyptian cotton pillow cases. Then he had raced around the top of the walls via the expensive embossed wallpaper and finally he had flung himself headlong at the fragile curtains at one of the windows, ripping them to shreds. This was all in the space of a few minutes and from a tiny little chap no bigger than a bunny rabbit. Catherine had at last managed to grab him and, furious at the havoc he had caused, angrily thrust him into my arms. 'You'd better deal with him or back he goes,' she said determinedly.

After his rampage upstairs Carlos came to me all sweet and

loving, purring like mad as I held him up to face me to give him a stern ticking off. By chance a stray strand of hair fell down on my forehead just as I was giving him a really hard talking to. Unable to resist the temptation he took a playful swipe at it and scratched me across the bridge of my nose, all in fun, at least from his point of view.

'That's it,' I cried, and stalked outside with him and shut him in the garden woodshed. 'Let's see what a spell of solitary confinement will do to your attitude,' I shouted at him. Then I retired to the bathroom for medication.

'Did you manage to sort him out dear?' Catherine called down from the bedroom. I ignored her as male pride would not allow me to answer. It was plain to see that Carlos would require all my skills as a psychologist and cat lover if there was to be any effective sorting-out to be done.

I left him in the woodshed for twenty minutes before I went out to fetch him. All the neighbourhood dogs were barking their heads off, even the distant ones, and I soon saw why. A stream of banshee like wails was issuing from the shed holding Carlos captive. I did not know whether or not he was in pain. Had he cut or impaled himself on one of the tools in there? In my anxiety I rushed to open the door and peered worriedly into the dark interior. The wailing ceased immediately. Then I saw him, a stumpy little figure all covered in cobwebs and sawdust. He darted out and I clutched hold of him. He gave a tiny kitten meow and immediately began to purr loudly. In moments he fell fast asleep in my arms.

I resolved to go out the very next day to buy him a kitten harness in order to begin to restrain and discipline him. For now, lying blissfully asleep on my lap, he presented a picture of baby cat innocence but I decided that I would have to be firm and not let him fool me or I might lose this kitten, who I had already begun to love.

At bedtime it was decided to lodge Carlos in the conservatory, with Pablo for company. Pablo wasn't very happy about this since he preferred to go out at night, but we thought it would only be for a short while and Pablo might be a good influence on the kitten. We were delighted to find that this arrangement worked. Although Pablo snubbed and spat on first acquaintance with the new kitten, Carlos appeared to ignore such rebuffs and at bedtime was able to overcome the older cat's aloofness by simply cuddling up to him and refusing to budge. Eventually Pablo, who had a gentle heart, allowed the little cat's perseverance to prevail.

The following morning I was sitting happily at the breakfast table awaiting my bacon and eggs and Carlos was gleefully chasing a table tennis ball around the floor with feline abandon. As Catherine handed me my food, a silver streak of fur, claws and jaws erupted onto the table via my leg and made off at speed with a rasher of my bacon in his mouth. This spur-of-the-moment, opportunistic raid left me flabbergasted at the alacrity with which it had been accomplished.

'Right! That's enough. He is not getting away with that, kitten or no kitten.' And at that Catherine charged after Carlos.

Several moments later I became aware of a series of bumps and thuds from the bedroom upstairs. Feeling obliged to offer re-inforcement to what I expected to be a one-sided contest, I entered the bedroom. I was right. There I found Catherine lying full length on the floor with one hand under the wardrobe groping behind a line of her shoes. 'Got you!' she cried triumphantly as she dragged out a squirming kitten and handed him over to me.

'To the woodshed?' I ventured.

'At once,' she exclaimed. Of the stolen bacon there was no sign.

After the culprit had been locked away we resumed breakfast and held a council of war. The upshot of our deliberations was that Carlos should be restrained for at least part of the day by a harness and lead. And it was further decided that a consultation with the vet might help. Returning him to Jane for resale was, to my relief, not mooted at this stage.

As I drove up to Alnwick to purchase a suitable harness and lead for Carlos and to make an appointment at the vet's, I thought about what the best course of action was likely to be. What would be the best way to cope with our wilful kitten and curb his hyper energy? Eventually, an idea began to take shape in my mind, which I culled from my memories of my life with Toby Jug. It would be a solution requiring a lot of time and effort on my part but it might just work. In my heart I believed it had to, because I loved Carlos despite his aberrations and I could not bear to think of losing him.

It was a scruffy, dishevelled mini cat that greeted me when I opened the shed door on my return. Carlos hadn't been in the shed very long but he appeared to be contrite and immediately commenced rubbing himself against my sweater, with arched back and erect stub of a tail. Then he began an elaborate feline paw-padding rhythm that tore strands of wool from my jumper, but I must say I welcomed his attention and did not mind at all about the damage to my sweater. I guess he reminded me all too much of Toby Jug, who did the same thing.

I picked him up and held him close but not too close to my nose, just in case. I told him that from my point of view all was forgiven although I couldn't speak for Catherine. I reminded him that he was now part of our home and that we were his family, who loved and cherished him, but he must try to behave in a more controlled fashion. He stared at me as I spoke softly to him and I could identify the intelligence in that steady look of his and hoped the meaning of my message registered. His bright eyes looking up at me just melted my heart. 'Everything is going to work out fine,' I muttered, for the sake of both of us. Only time would tell.

'When is the vet's appointment?' Catherine asked.

'Tomorrow morning at 8.30,' I replied, trying to fit a harness on to the wriggling kitten, who regarded my efforts as something of a game. At last it was fastened securely and I attached the lead. 'I thought I'd take him for an introductory walk around the garden,' I said confidently.

'Good luck,' Catherine replied.

I picked up Carlos and carried him outside. Placing him on the edge of the grass to give him a chance to get his bearings, I waited for him to move, with the lead clutched firmly in my hand. Moving his head from side to side he surveyed the bushes and trees in front of him. Perhaps he's overawed, I naively thought. At that point he took off, literally. The best way I can describe his action is to compare it to a commercial aircraft roaring down the runway at a sufficient speed for the captain to issue the command 'Rotate', that is, to give it full power to enable the plane to blast off, straight up. If you can believe a cat could fly, Carlos did. He 'rotated'. The lead was jerked from my hand as he flew up from a standing start straight into the topmost branch of a young beech. From the height of his perch up in the tree he stared down at me as if to say, 'What would you like to see me do next?'

Luckily the lead from his harness was hanging down and by pulling it gently I was able to bring him within reach and catch him. As usual with this kitten, once I had hold of him he simply began to purr and rub himself affectionately against me. In such circumstances it proved difficult even to begin to reprimand him. One could only admire his quite exceptional physical prowess. The remainder of the so-called walk consisted of me dragging him along as he lay on his side, with part of the lead between his teeth, making robust attempts to break free. From the conservatory window Catherine witnessed it all and just had to laugh.

'Well, he's your cat,' she said despairingly, 'but he's going to wear you down before he tires.'

I decided that Carlos had that most enviable of dispositions: he was quintessentially happy-go-lucky. Life was his oyster and he was determined to live it with gusto.

After an early start I arrived at the vet's right on time with Carlos safely secured in an escape-proof carrying box as I ventured into the waiting room. There were already two other people there with dogs on leads. Carlos peered at the dogs through the bars of the door to his box and the dogs stared back with ears pricked and eyes set in curious mode.

Thankfully, we were called first. In the examination room a young vet introduced himself and took the box from me, opened the door and gently lifted out Carlos, who immediately started to purr loudly. At this point the surgery door opened and one of the clerks entered with some papers for signing, leaving the door slightly ajar. I was busy looking out of the window at the trees, which obviously needed a thorough pruning, and didn't see what happened next. Suddenly, I heard the vet cry out in alarm, 'He's gone!'

'Oh my God, no!' I cried, and we all set off down the corridor in hot pursuit.

Before we reached the waiting room, which was situated at the end of the corridor, the sounds of dogs barking furiously interspersed with cries of alarm and panic-stricken shouts filled me with fear and dismay.

I was fast coming to the conclusion that when Carlos cut loose those twin devils bedlam and mayhem followed in his wake. When I at last managed to push my way through a disturbed group of people blocking the doorway, I found chairs overturned, papers scattered over the floor and two dogs, a black-and-white sheepdog and a bull terrier, standing up on their hind legs baying like hound dogs at a diminutive figure perched on top of a large display cabinet. It was Carlos. I could not begin to fathom how he had got up there but what impressed me more was how in all the noise he was calmly staring down at the dogs, their frantic owners and the rest of us with sangfroid.

Due to the commotion other vets and assistants were pouring into the room and someone was only just stopped short of pressing the fire alarm. Finally, a tall gaunt vet, wearing a Barbour coat and long green Wellingtons smeared with something smelling strongly of horse, restored a degree of order by her very presence. She was the person with whom I'd had a contretemps on the occasion of my last visit with Pablo. When she spotted me her gaze moved from authoritative to downright unfriendly. Then she caught sight of Carlos, who was watching curiously from his high vantage point. She seemed to grasp immediately that he was the cause of all this upset.

'To whom does that creature belong?' she demanded.

Wishing that the ground would open and swallow me, I gulped nervously with embarrassment and said, 'He's mine. But he's only a kitten,' I added defensively.

The answer was as condemning as it was imperious: 'Remove him at once!' she barked.

There now followed a stressful interval, whilst someone went to fetch the caretaker's stepladder, during which the atmosphere could have been cut with a knife. With the help of the young vet with whom we had the appointment, I dragged Carlos from his resting place and locked him away in his box. This I carried out under the baleful glare of the alpha female vet. I made a hasty exit but just as we were leaving I heard one of the dog owners say: 'It scratched my dog's nose and she's bleeding.'

I didn't wait to hear more but rushed to the car, put the box containing Carlos on the back seat and drove away as fast as I could. What now? I thought. There would have to be a plan B; Carlos would have to be somehow transmogrified into a more peaceable cat. But in my mind I accepted that it would fall to me, not the vets, to think up some modus operandi to domesticate Young Master Carlos. Now to tell Catherine.

After another council of war, with the culprit nestling fast asleep on my knee, and my having consumed two coffees and a large brandy, a new behaviour management plan for Carlos was agreed. The main features of the plan were that Carlos would wear his harness, if not his lead, at all times until further notice so that he could be more easily restrained as necessity required.

I also decided that I would take him on trips in the car to wild places in order to make him feel vulnerable, perhaps even overwhelmed, and therefore more malleable to training. I expected, too, that our travels together would serve to bond him closely to me and hopefully that would afford a further degree of control over him.

As I looked down at him snoozing on my knees he reminded me of one of my grandmother's expressions: 'He looked as if butter wouldn't melt in his mouth.' I had to chuckle at his antics of the morning but I needed to rid myself of the feeling that Carlos and I were performing in one of those slapstick Harold Lloyd movies. It wasn't funny anymore. Tomorrow I would take him up the coast to Bamburgh and along the rocky seashore.

Strangely enough, for the rest of the day and evening he was remarkably quiet and well behaved. I wondered whether he had been mollified by the happenings at the vet's or whether he was just saving his strength for another day.

The next day I packed some sandwiches for me and biscuits for Carlos, because he preferred biscuits to meat or other cat food. I also filled myself a flask of coffee and took water for him. To carry Carlos, I had in mind to use a newly acquired papoose, a sort of carrying pouch for little dogs, with a small blanket in the bottom, because he would not yet walk on the lead.

When I was walking he would be in the bag, lying on the blanket, with only his head peeping out. He would be secured by his harness to the bag by a keyring. When I reached somewhere that I considered safe I intended to let him out and start training him to walk on the lead. I wanted him by our association and experience together to become dependent on me. The more dependent he became the more influence I would have over him. That was the plan but Carlos, I guessed, might well have other ideas.

As we set off, Carlos had his harness on without the lead,

which I was carrying in my pocket. He seemed to enjoy exploring the inside of the car in his usual intensive manner; nothing escaped his scrutiny. As we drove along the narrow winding roads of rural Northumberland, with their many bends and twists, a route I preferred to the traffic-busy A1, boredom set in and Carlos began to whine. The whine developed into a kittenish howl. I ignored it. Unable to attract my attention he resorted to physical measures. Jumping on my knees he clambered up my sweater and swaying with the movement of the car he proceeded to complain loudly in my ear. His tiny claws were like needles sticking into my arm and shoulder but I gritted my teeth and told him things were going to be different now and he shouldn't expect to have his own way all the time. I talk to my cats just as I would to a person in the belief that they somehow pick up my meaning.

He kept up his aggravations until at last we passed through Seahouses and the majestic outline of Bamburgh Castle appeared on the horizon. 'Now the fun really begins,' I muttered for the benefit of both of us. Carlos momentarily desisted from his whining as a low-flying flock of seagulls flew across the bonnet of the car. 'Come on, let's get started,' I cried as I lifted him out of the car and carried him over the dunes and down to the beach, where I sat him on the sand.

His first response was to sniff the area all around him in some trepidation. Then he just stood and sneezed several times. Suddenly a gust of cool sea breeze that is almost always present on the north-east coast ruffled his fur and caused him to shiver.

The end result was that he climbed up to sit on my shoe, looked up at me and whined.

'None of that,' I said, trying hard to be firm. 'You are the worst-behaved kitten I have ever met, probably the worst in the whole world, and it has to stop; so it begins anew here with some training in discipline for you.' He whined again, looking up at me with big, sad eyes. 'No complaints will be tolerated. Sorry,' I said harshly, tugging at his lead and heading across the beach to some nearby rock pools filled with sea water and minute marine life that I thought might arouse his curiosity.

The stroll on the beach involved me dragging Carlos on the lead across the sand. He just lay on his side and refused to walk despite being offered inducements of biscuit treats in the same way that I had trained Pablo. However, arriving in the proximity of the first pool changed this stubborn attitude. A small bird, which had been foraging for insects amongst the seaweed strewn around the sand, flew in alarm almost into the face of Carlos.

From then on my silver boy was on constant alert as we progressed towards the rock pools and he even stood up and walked to the point of pulling me along. All at once Carlos stopped and stared, with his whole body rigid, towards some rocks. He had spied something moving below the surface of the water. Flattening his body against the smooth surface of a boulder he slid forward until he could just see over the edge directly into the pool of seawater below. I guessed that it was a small fish or crab that had caught his attention. Sure enough there were several tiny crabs scuttling around the perimeter of the pool. Then I was taken completely by surprise again, although by now I should have expected it: Carlos, in ultra stealth mode, inched further towards his quarry, shook his rump once and then leapt into the pool.

I sighed. Carlos was never one to stop and stare when he could throw caution to the wind and leap into action. Indeed, if human, he would have been a natural recruit for the SAS. Soaking wet, bedraggled but defiant, I fished him out only to find he had a small crab in his mouth. Fortunately, Carlos had grabbed it from behind and the crab's nippers were facing out in front.

'Whatever am I going to do with you?' I grumbled as I levered the crab from his mouth and dropped it back in the water, where it raced off to hide, much to the dismay of a drenched kitten who was dripping seawater all over me. Afraid that he might become ill from his dunking, I hurried back to the car, holding him inside my coat and pressed against my warm sweater. I had an idea that I thought might work. Rather than driving all the way home with him in this state I drove along the beach road to Seahouses and parked outside the Bamburgh Castle Hotel because I knew there would probably be a warm log fire in the sitting room.

I explained the situation to the perplexed receptionist who thankfully recognized me from previous visits with Catherine, when we had enjoyed the special fish and chip lunch, so she did not treat me as a crank. But it was not until Carlos poked his little wet head out from my jacket that her manner melted and, chortling with sympathetic laughter, she led me into the empty lounge where there was indeed a huge log fire in the wood-burning stove, radiating warmth.

As I was settling the wet cat down in front of the life-reviving blaze the receptionist reappeared, accompanied by the housekeeper carrying a saucer of warm creamy milk for 'the dear little kitten' and a steaming mug of coffee for me. Tired out with my exertions (Carlos did tend to wear one down with his antics), I ordered a glass of ginger beer and a hot bacon sandwich and relaxed back into one of their most comfortable antique leather armchairs. Carlos, meanwhile, having consumed the milk, was indulging in a thorough tongue-wash in front of the fire, though he had to keep spitting out the seawater taste he was licking off his fur.

Just then a group of the hotel's guests crowded in from the bar, having been informed that there was a man by the fire who had rescued a kitten from the sea. I allowed this story to grow of its own accord, as rumours tend to do, and merely nodded my acceptance of their acclamation of my heroism. I need not have bothered because the focus of their attention was on Carlos, who was being enthusiastically admired by several of the ladies, each of whom was vociferous in their offers to adopt him.

'You'd get the shock of your lives,' I muttered to myself as I witnessed the fawning adulation being heaped on Carlos. True to his cat nature, Carlos was revelling in it.

It was late afternoon when at last we left and I removed a

dry and fluffy Carlos from his adoring audience, who meant well but were beginning to irritate me. Many heartfelt thanks were extended to the kind hotel staff and eventually we drove away, leaving behind our celebrity status as well as the lovely fire. Catherine was relieved to welcome us back. We noticed however that Pablo had the air of someone who was worried about the trouble that the new kitten was causing the family. He had never caused trouble like that and we began to think he was slightly miffed that he was being largely ignored of late. Or that was what we read into his non-verbal behaviour, and I made up my mind to play with him and fuss him much more than we had done of late.

That evening as I considered the events of the day I realized that I was becoming accustomed to the aberrations of Carlos, almost as if I had come to expect him to do something outrageous. But the day had not been without value for me as I remembered the lasting pleasure of experiencing the sight of an autumnal haze shrouding the misty outline of Bamburgh Castle against the big Northumbrian sky, always a sight worth seeing. Thinking about the castle set off memories of the many times I had taken Toby Jug there and picnicked amongst the sand dunes with steak pies from the famous butcher in the village. But I could never shrug off the thought that there was a strange air of loneliness about the castle, as if it did not welcome human habitation, although many people lived there in flats despite the many tales of hauntings. For many months of the year the castle and coast is subjected to cruel north-east gales which stir up fearsome storms and yet the castle and its surrounding beach area possess an ambience which exerts a positive, therapeutic uplift to the soul of the discerning visitor. Whenever I have visited the castle and the golden sands below I feel somehow spiritually refreshed and charged anew.

That evening, I recalled the long sands of the beach below the castle in the golden light of morning as we arrived and parked the car. I hoped the day I had shared with Carlos had led to as positive an effect on him as it had on me. As for me, I was now feeling emotionally and physically drained with the effort of coping with this unusual and highly volatile kitten. As if he wished to make it up to me, he jumped on to my knee and crawled right up my sweater until he faced me. He then proceeded with accompanying purrs to lick my forehead and cheek with a tongue that felt like sandpaper. I closed my eyes and endured it, and felt cheered that at least my efforts at bonding with this crazy little chap appeared to be working. Finally, he fell asleep, snoring softly, with his head tucked under my chin. I wondered as I dozed if he'd ever grow to love me as my other cats had but then I needn't have worried because cats know how to win the hearts of humankind – they'd been doing so for thousands of years. In this state we both slept until Catherine woke us just after midnight and ushered both of us off to bed.

During the next few weeks I took Carlos with me to many of the idyllic small country villages and hamlets that are delightfully characteristic of Northumberland. We travelled to Lindisfarne, which is also known as Holy Island, where Carlos chased and hunted sandflies to his heart's contentment whilst I lazed on the beach in the late autumn sun. Another day we drove to Craster and walked (although Carlos had to be carried all the way back) by the rough, rugged coastline that leads to the ruins of Dunstanburgh Castle, its stark outline dark and forbidding against the bleak sky.

That day we found a sea bass, beached by the rough seas, which was being ravaged by gulls. I could tell Carlos was desperate to chase the birds and so I let go of his lead. This afforded a unique opportunity for Carlos to indulge a machismo charge into the fray. Unfortunately, the gulls were not impressed and simply screeched fiercely and flapped their massive wings at him. I watched his face expressing fearful uncertainty, probably for the first time in his life, and concluded it would do him the world of good. Anyway, he came running back to me with many backward glances in case he was being pursued. He's learning that the world can be a dangerous place for little cats, I thought with a smile and a certain amount of satisfaction.

Another time we explored the village of Chatton, with its charming ancient church and cemetery, and we sat outside the Percy Arms where I had a large glass of merlot and Carlos demolished a meaty sausage roll. For me the experience was made all the more exquisite because the air tasted so refreshingly healthy and clean.

One day we toured the Cheviot Valleys, always a joy to me.

Carlos caught a snake while we tramped up Langleeford Valley. It was a non-poisonous grass snake but he was exuberant with his find. He wasn't so pleased when I took the snake from him and set it free it in a damp ditch. For the remainder of our walk that afternoon Carlos trotted along without having to be urged, strong in the belief, I'm sure, that at any moment he would encounter even more fascinating creatures. He was most intimidated by a fat toad he cornered when it spat in his face before it took an enormous leap into the stream that ran close by, but Carlos was having an adventure. As I watched him protectively I saw that he was thrilled by it all, which gave me no small measure of gratification.

As we travelled around I became increasingly enamoured of Carlos with his effervescent high spirits and his joyous attitude to life. Nothing seemed to daunt his gung-ho disposition. After a while he adjusted to travelling by car and was prepared to accept the restraining harness and lead. Sometimes, if anything interesting ahead caught his attention he would almost pull me off my feet with his enthusiastic urge to investigate. Small though he was, he had abundant strength. I began to feel that my plan to train him to my way of living was beginning to work without subduing his engaging spirit and his unique individuality.

I became convinced that if I had not been retired I could never have kept this kitten, with his mercurial moods, simply because I would not have had the time to spend with him.

Whilst on our excursions I was very apprehensive about

encountering people walking dogs or even, as sometimes happened, dogs wandering alone. To protect Carlos against any attack that might occur, I always carried a stout walking stick with me. I also practised swinging Carlos by his lead and harness up into my arms where I could hide him under my coat at the first sight of any problem. It did not surprise me at all that the few times I did this, Carlos seemed to enjoy it inordinately and when put down again kept looking up at me, expecting another swing – yet another example of his sporting character.

There was, however, an occasion when both Carlos and I could have been in serious danger, not from dogs, but from the elements and my own foolhardiness. I had motored away from the A1 and driven high into the moors above Chillingham within sight of the Cheviot and the foothills. The land there is exposed, wild and craggy but it provides spectacular views over open country to the distant north-east coastline.

I left the car parked just off a narrow road and headed over the moors towards a rocky outcrop where I let Carlos, attached to me by his lead, prowl among the stony crevices and boulders. It had been sunny and warm when we set off and in such conditions it is easy to travel further than intended and to forget how quickly the weather can change for the worst in high and wide open places.

Long before the storm hit us I should have noticed the signs. As I relaxed in the warm sunlight I had been unaware of what was ominously imminent. I had with interest watched a covey of small birds, probably grouse, as they erupted from the heather near to us and headed northwards. Instead of merely admiring the way in which the flock kept tight formation and moved in smooth coordination with each other until I lost sight of them, I should have heeded the warning. Wildlife, especially birds, do not move without urgent reason. If that sign did not alarm me then the sight of a low-flying squadron of wild geese fleeing towards the safety of the reed beds bordering Lindisfarne ought to have alerted me to expect a serious change in the weather. The signs are there for those who can read them. Ignore them at your peril, as I was soon to find out. The problem arose initially from the fact that I had my back to the crags and was gazing eastwards, admiring the scenic views over the moors to the sea. The storm was over us before I turned and saw, too late, the thunderous black clouds rushing at us from the west.

Within seconds, it seemed, the sky grew ominously dark, with thick cloud formations scurrying from behind us. Suddenly, it seemed a raging storm descended on us from out of nowhere. With wind and rain tearing at us we quickly became wet and cold. The weather struck at us in such a fearsome way that I completely lost my bearings and could see neither the car nor the road. We were lost in a storm and the air was becoming icy cold. The rain turned to sleet and the wind blasted us mercilessly and so with a very subdued little cat tucked inside my coat I looked for refuge.

Cold and miserable as we both were, all that I could think of doing was to wedge myself between two outcrops and wait for the storm to pass. Then I started thinking in alarm that should the storm set in for the night, and should we be obliged to spend the night here, I hadn't told Catherine exactly where we were going and she would be worried sick.

It was now so gloomy that it was quite impossible to see where we were in relation to the rest of the moor and, more importantly, the road where I had parked the car. Just as I was verging on the edge of panic I spied a welcome sight. Headlights were approaching fast. Taking Carlos out of my coat I set him down and we both made off in the direction of the approaching car. Stumbling and slipping on the wet ground I was pulled along at speed by Carlos who could obviously see better and run faster than I could. It seemed to take an eternity to reach the road but at least I could now discern the shape of my car which had been silhouetted by the lights from the passing vehicle which soon roared past us.

Whilst busying myself starting the car and turning the heater on full blast I hadn't time to think what the occupant of the car that passed us must have thought at the sight of two bedraggled figures, a man and a cat on a lead, running across the moorland in the darkness. I had parked within a mile or two of the medieval castle at Chillingham, about which there are enough tales of ghosts and ghouls to fill a large book. No doubt the driver of the car would be able to dine out on the story which, fuelled by local imagination, would enter the annals of weird hauntings.

As the warmth from the car heater began to circulate I experienced a brief spell of shivering, which soon passed. Carlos was meanwhile wrapped snugly in the car rug and seemed to be recovering well. When I turned the car round and drove down the moor to rejoin the A1 it was an easy journey back to the cottage.

Along the way Carlos poked his head out from the comfort of the blanket, stared at the road ahead and, with a little cry, gave me a long hard look. He was no doubt wondering what all that had been about. I had to chuckle because the bemused expression on the cat's face said it all. I had embarked on our excursion with only the best intentions but I realized it had been a daft and dangerous enterprise to risk our lives on a wild and desolate moor in the vicinity of the weather systems generated by the Cheviot Hills.

Soon I felt warmer and drier and was able to give Carlos my full, caring attention. He had no doubt been frightened at the turn of events but now, snug in the blanket, he looked positively his old happy self and my strokes elicited a stream of throaty purrs.

When we arrived home and I recounted our adventure, Catherine once again gave me a stern telling-off. Quite reasonably, in this instance. And we agreed I would limit such trips now that Carlos appeared to be more disciplined in his ways. From now on training for Carlos would be home-based. What a relief! Although I must say we had enjoyed some exciting outings together which I wouldn't have missed for anything.

As we relaxed together in the sitting room that evening, with

Carlos contentedly asleep with his body stretched out over my lap, I started to think about earlier times when I had ventured into the Cheviot foothills, also with a cat. Thinking along these lines I recalled a time when, at about the same period of the year, I had been asked by the principal at the college where I taught to take over the supervision of a group of mature men and women students who were going on a weekend residential course in environmental studies at the Howtel Field Studies Centre, north of Wooler. The students already had their projects planned but their college tutor had been taken ill and someone else was needed simply to take charge and to see that all went smoothly. I agreed to go as long as I could take my cat with me. The warden in charge at Howtel gave his consent and so I was able to break the news to Toby Jug, who gathered from my demeanour that something exciting was in the offing. I could tell from his bright-eyed, attentive look that he expected that we were about to embark on another adventure.

Once at the hostel, when it was time for lights out, Toby Jug could not at first be found until I discovered him in the women students' hut where he was being petted and given treats from cheese sandwiches. The students were reluctant to let me take him but I insisted for everyone's sake. He soon bedded down at the end of my bunk and so ended our first night at Howtel. I was looking forward to the weekend because my duties were limited to overseeing student welfare, leaving me free to further explore the valleys and the riverbanks with which I was already acquainted.

After breakfast on the Saturday morning, when the students had all been deployed to their various tasks, I set off in the car with Toby Jug towards the village of Etal. The narrow twisting lanes of North Northumberland wind along green corridors bordered by tall hedgerows where, in places, overhanging trees sublimely enclose the route into a verdant tunnel, above which sunbeams filter through the canopy of foliage and gleam between the leaves.

I parked the car in front of the Black Bull Inn, which is the only remaining public house in Northumberland to have a thatched roof. It is also reputed to be haunted by the ghost of a witch who lived in the seventeenth century. Regrettably the traditional hospitality of the inn did not extend to a man with a cat. We therefore repaired to the garden of the Lavender Tea Rooms opposite the Black Bull for rest and a snack. I ordered a glass of elderflower water and a slice of the cafe speciality, lavender cake. Meanwhile Toby Jug helped himself to a drink from the dog bowl near our table and watched in bewilderment the flocks of sparrows flitting between the legs of the tables, picking up scraps. I kept a firm hold on his lead but he seemed intimidated rather than aroused at their presence. He was five years old now but he had still managed to retain an ingenuous air in relation to anything which overawed him. As for the sparrows, they hardly seemed to notice him.

After a while we left the cafe and strolled along the road between the neat rows of cottages towards the ruins of Etal Castle, at the entrance to which stood a sixteenth-century cannon painted black, a grim reminder of turbulent times past in this border area between England and Scotland. We skirted the castle because I had something special in mind that entailed a journey by the little tourist railway which ran a short distance along the river to Heatherslaw and back. On our way to the railway we followed a path that wound through woodland which, at this time of year, was thickly carpeted with bluebells, and in some patches the flowers were an appealing mauve colour. Toby appeared to be so impressed by the sight of so many flowers that I guessed he wanted to run amongst them and so, there being no dogs around, I slipped off his lead and let him go. He ran off with the kind of wild abandon that only young children and animals can generate. In a short while I whistled and called his name and he came gambolling back to me like a spring lamb. This reminded me that earlier I had noticed, opposite the village cricket ground in Etal, a field full of black curly haired sheep and lambs which were considered to be very rare and hardy; it was believed by the villagers that they had been imported from the Hebrides over a hundred years ago.

Clipping Toby Jug's lead back on, I headed down a cutting to the old-fashioned railway station with the single platform. We didn't have long to wait before the train pulled in, but the noise of the little steam engine temporarily alarmed Toby, who sought refuge behind me, which he always regarded as the safest place to be. Soon we were able to board an open-sided carriage which we had all to ourselves as there were not many other passengers. The conductor appeared and I bought my ticket, though my offer to pay for Toby Jug was declined. A kindly man, he was much taken with mirthful amazement at the sight of my cat sitting upright and perky. Once the train began to rumble along the track Toby shot me an anxious look but when I simply smiled at him and gave him a reassuring wink he settled down to enjoy the ride. He adjusted, as always, very well to this new experience and before long he was jumping from one side of the carriage to the other whilst still secured, of course, by his lead. At the gentle speed we were travelling it was possible to view the scenery all around and Toby Jug was trying to do just that so that he wouldn't miss a thing.

Arriving at Heatherslaw we left the station and followed the footpath down to the working mill beside the stream. Here organic flour was produced and was available for sale in small bags, chiefly for the interest of tourists.

The return journey was pleasantly uneventful and Toby slept, no doubt soothed by the swaying motion of the carriage. He'd had a busy day but had taken it all in his stride. We were back at Howtel just before the students returned and, while they wrote up their reports, dinner was being prepared. Toby was meanwhile making friends with anyone prepared to give him some attention and kept going from one person to another. Watching him from my seat near the window I was suddenly shocked to see him confronted by a hairy miniature Yorkshire terrier. The two animals sniffed and inspected each other with cautionary care. Then the little dog gave a half-hearted bark, which sounded like a cross between a yelp and a snort, and ran off. To my amazement Toby Jug made off after him and I relaxed as the two of them had a real good play-game of chase-me. Apparently the dog was the pet of one of the women students and her husband had come to visit with her dog. As we sat down to dinner I was delighted to see the dog, called Dooley, and my Toby Jug stretched out side by side at the foot of the large oven. They looked as if they had worn each other out and were now resting. I wasn't surprised that Toby had made friends with the dog, who was slightly smaller than himself, because he had such an affectionate nature; obviously Dooley was like-minded and until the dog left the two of them got along fine. As usual, Toby joined me at bedtime but since the night had turned unseasonably cold he later worked his way under the blankets and slept cuddled into my back.

On the Sunday morning the students were again soon away, determined to complete their studies before departure that evening. I decided to take Toby Jug for a trip across the moors that lay surrounded by the Cheviot Hills. Driving to the far end of the moor I parked the car in a viewpoint lay-by and from our high elevation looked over the unspoiled clean landscape towards the sea glistening in the sunlight many miles away.

'Let's get walking,' I said to Toby, who was outside before me and already sniffing around the peaty ground with a scattering of heather covering. But the moor was windswept that day and although it looked scenically wonderful the wind tore at us in such a hostile fashion that we soon turned back for the shelter and comfort of the car. Toby's fur had been flattened to his body by the gale and both of us had been almost swept off our feet. Once inside the car the two of us began shivering.

'And so we say farewell to the Cheviot moorland and head for warmer climes,' I quipped as I put the car into gear and drove down to the village of Chatton. The Percy Arms was open and afforded a friendly welcome after the experience of being blasted off the moor. I ordered a bowl of hot vegetable broth to warm me up and the waiter cobbled together some meat scraps from the kitchen for Toby Jug.

Chatton Village is low-lying and receives a measure of protection from the bordering hills. It is one of my favourite places partly because the air is so sweet but also because the village embodies old English rural simplicity. As Toby Jug and I strolled down the lane towards the cul-de-sac that ended at the church we passed well-tended gardens and cottages, evidence that the people here really cared about their village.

The Church of the Holy Cross, which dates originally from the late seventeenth to early eighteenth centuries, is a formidable building of rough stone with a magnificent old wooden door reinforced with iron studs. The church yard has an ancient feel to it with its huge upright gravestones, rounded and weathered, the inscriptions now largely indecipherable. There is an air of melancholy yet peaceful repose about the lichen-clad stones and tree trunks with plots of wild flowers ornamenting some of the graves. Especially prominent were some fragile wild yellow field poppies and also the red variety of the same flower. Toby Jug was eager to investigate and so I let him wander at will, secure in the knowledge that this cat was tied to me by an emotional umbilical cord that had never been, nor would ever be, severed. In one corner of the church yard a flourishing yellow broom had spilled over the wall and it seemed most fitting that pretty little yellowhammer songbirds appeared to be nesting within its dense foliage. Everywhere I looked it seemed that nature had enfolded this manmade place and made it her own.

I lingered a while longer in the warm afternoon sunlight, reluctant to abandon the tranquillity I found there but a sudden summer shower cooled the air and hastened me away. I had no sooner unlocked the car door than I became aware of a frantic scrambling as Toby Jug negotiated the church yard wall and made a mad dash for the car in case I left him behind. I had to laugh because he was already sitting waiting for me on the passenger seat before I had the door fully open.

On our return journey I drove by the imposing castle at Ford, where I was often involved in specialist courses for teachers, and recalled, with a shiver, how cold the bedrooms were in winter. When I drove into the yard at Howtel I noticed that the students had already returned and then I spotted Dooley eating from a bowl. From his vantage point on my left shoulder, Toby Jug also caught sight of him and whined to be let out of the car, no doubt to join him for another bout of hectic play. Which is precisely what happened. After a cup of tea and some sandwiches everyone was anxious to be on their way. Last to leave, I thanked the warden on behalf of the college and, collecting my weekend bag and Toby Jug, who was looking rather forlorn since Dooley had already left, we set off for home. On arriving back at the cottage Toby Jug did his usual circuit of the garden, after an absence however brief, to check that all his familiar places were intact and he assumed his customary position high in the old apple tree from where he could survey the road, examine passersby and keep an eye on me in the conservatory. Watching him now, I felt so proud of this wonderful cat who behaved in such a familiar way with me, as if he truly believed that we were of the same family of beings and that I belonged to him as a relative. He thought that between us there were no species divisions but that we were one and the same.

Finally, I closed down my mind to these blissful yet traumatic memories and focused again on the here and the now.

Looking back at my expeditions with Carlos, my mind is tinged with happy nostalgic feelings of remembered days when he and I shared very special experiences that few cat owners would even contemplate launching into. These thoughts are mingled with much sorrow that Carlos, exceptional cat that he was, is no longer with us.

But I take comfort from those times because the strategy certainly worked. Carlos and I became so closely bonded that whenever we were in the house or garden together Catherine remarked on the fact that he stuck to me like glue. Wherever I went, he followed. He loved to join me as I pottered in the greenhouse during the spring and summer months, tending my plants. He would lie for hours in a discarded cardboard box or on a disused hessian sack (a particularly favourite spot of his) and watch my every move with his natural intensity. In response to his avid attention I would talk to him. I began to treat him like a gifted child and I remember explaining how the incredibly tiny seeds I was planting could grow into tall plants bearing luscious fruits such as exotic tomatoes and cucumbers.

Eventually, I admit it, I got somewhat carried away; I was flattered by his concentration and gave him parts of my introductory student lectures on astrophysics and psychology. Captivated by the sentience in his eyes I explained in primary-school terms the meaning of Albert Einstein's formula $E=MC^2$. Catherine overheard me one afternoon and thought that this might be going a bit far, but she was impressed by the total attention Carlos gave me. He did appear to soak it all up.

Sharing his company so intimately I concluded that Carlos had such an abundance of energy that he craved outlets for it in every situation he encountered; sometimes, as I knew only too well, it simply catapulted him into action and he couldn't help himself. I had grown to love him as one adores a brilliant and precocious child and in return he demonstrated unreserved love and affection for me.

This, to my mind, is the way it is with cats when a human being makes the effort to breach the defensive wall of reserve and independence with which cats are endowed as a birthright. Once the natural aloofness and introverted characteristics of cat personality are cracked through persistent and unconditional love and attention then the cat is yours for life. Given these conditions the cat in question will lavish you with affection and that rarest of emotional attributes: dedicated attachment. This is what I was now receiving from Carlos and from Pablo. But let the would-be cat enthusiast be aware that this feline love and loyalty is only won with continuous effort and is not to be achieved lightly or just because you give a cat a home.

I have described the process of ultimate bonding with Carlos as an example. I find it a matter of no wonder that the Ancient Egyptians worshipped cats: for them cats had a divine right and it was only what the cats richly deserved. I must admit that I am smitten and cannot contemplate life without the love and companionship of our cats.

As one pedigree cat breeder once remarked to me when I pointed out that there are many people who actively dislike and even hate cats she said: 'Those people can never have known a Maine Coon.'

Soon Carlos would have been with us for three months. That meant that he was approaching six months old and it was time for him to be neutered. Since it was approaching Christmas I thought it best to get it over with before the holidays. I felt it advisable with our past record not to go to the vets we previously used, where Carlos and I had most certainly upset the management. There was another vet's surgery and I took Carlos there to be neutered and have an identity chip inserted under his skin in case he was ever lost or stolen.

I was told to collect him after three hours and as usual I spent the waiting time in a state of nervous tension. This state of mind was in no way diminished when I arrived at the surgery to be told that a vet wished to speak to me. Once I was ushered into her office I was relieved to be told that Carlos was fine but that in order to anaesthetize him it had required more of the chemical than usual. Therefore, he was still rather groggy and would need to be kept warm and offered plenty of water until he recovered.

I thanked her and was shown to a room where a dozy-eyed Carlos seemed as much relieved to see me as I was to see him. He slept flat-out all the way home and when laid comfortably by the fire with a bowl of water nearby he perked up momentarily, though sleep swiftly overcame him again.

Later, when Pablo came in for dinner, the noise awoke Carlos and he tried in vain to get up and go to the kitchen to see Pablo and possibly eat a few biscuits, but his back legs wouldn't work. The sight of him in this state made Catherine most distressed and she lay beside him on the floor stroking and talking to him all the while. I sought to reassure her by saying that 'wound up for action' was Carlos' normal state, which is why he behaves in such a hyperactive way, but tonight, because he was so heavily drugged, he was completely relaxed. It seemed odd to us because we had never seen him like this before.

'I thought you had managed to change all that,' Catherine said.

'I cannot change what God put there,' I commented. 'But

now that Carlos is so attached to me I can control him more easily and that is all I can do because he will always be highly strung, which is why the vet must have had to give him a real "Mickey Finn" to knock him out. He'll be his old self in no time.'

When we were satisfied that he was resting peacefully we left him stretched out in front of the fire and retired to bed. I was exhausted; we all were: it had been quite a day.

Sure enough, in the morning all was well and after a good night's sleep Carlos had made a full recovery. After a hearty breakfast of biscuits (he refused to eat cat meat), he appeared ever ready to resume living life to the full. A domestic incident then occurred that just showed how fully recovered he was from the anaesthetic and back to his hyperactive self.

It took place in the conservatory when Catherine and I were having a mid-morning coffee break. Carlos was staring out of the glass door leading into the garden when, because some of his fine hairs had got up my nose, I sneezed violently. Carlos, taken aback by the sudden explosive noise, leapt or, I should say, levitated on all fours to a height of at least six inches: he looked like a Harrier Jump Jet doing an aerial take-off. That was how highly strung our silver cat was all the time. Needless to say, the sight of his reaction made us both roar with laughter, especially since Carlos, now grounded again on all fours, turned to look at me in amazement. He couldn't work out why I had made such a loud noise.

Now that he had been neutered it was time to liberate him

from, as it were, domestic house arrest and give him his freedom to wander at will. I can't say how many times I have regretted this decision which effectively sealed his fate but at the time it seemed the right thing to do and it was evident that Carlos was enthused with joy the moment I opened the door and let him go. He bounded out into the garden and then whimsically turned and waited for me to join him. 'Go on, you're free now!' I called to him.

Suddenly from further up the garden Pablo appeared with a small rabbit in his mouth. As soon as Carlos spotted him he raced up the grass to greet him and share in the spoils. Pablo, much startled at the sight of Carlos, dropped the rabbit in surprise. Instantly, Carlos rushed to pick it up but not being big enough as yet he couldn't lift it clear of the ground and, in a pathetically funny attempt to cope, began to drag the dead creature down the path towards me. The rabbit became entangled in his legs and Carlos tripped and proceeded to fall over. Pablo meanwhile stared at this performance in disbelief.

This farcical situation was ended when I retrieved the rabbit carcass from a confused Carlos and disposed of it out of sight of the two cats. Pablo, deprived of his kill, disappeared over the garden fence post haste, followed by Carlos, who considered this to be a wise move in the circumstances.

Meanwhile I was left in a state of hiatus wondering if I would ever see him again. But true to form they both reappeared some hours later for dinner, rest and recreation. Soon Pablo and Carlos were to be found lying side by side in front of the sitting room fire in a seemingly comatose state, as only cats can achieve at a moment's notice. Catherine and I looked at each other and sighed with contentment that peace at last reigned in Owl Cottage. But for how long?

It was a few days before Christmas Eve and the business of decorating the tree and hanging tinsel, coloured lights and red-berried holly from the garden was in full swing at Owl Cottage. Once the cottage was seasonally decorated the cooking preparations commenced with turkey, vegetables and various sweatmeats and desserts being assembled and made ready. To me there is an excitement about Yuletide which no other time of the year quite manages to achieve. Most probably that is to do with feelings of vintage childhood nostalgia.

On the Monday of Christmas week there had been flurries of snow all day and hopes were running high for a White Christmas. When evening came the air temperature dropped sharply and snow began to fall in earnest. Before long the topmost branches of the fir trees in the garden developed a frosty mantel, followed by rooftops covered in thick blankets of white and then the garden at ground level disappeared under thick, powdery snow.

It was on this night as I watched the snow falling that Carlos set off on a new escapade, although I must say it progressively developed into something of a nightmare, rather than an adventure, for the two of us.

Pablo came into the cottage at the appointed time, consumed

his dinner and then hurried off, no doubt on a hunting spree, since the rabbit population was at the climax of its breeding cycle and there would be some tiny newborn bunnies to be dug out from burrows to provide tasty after-dinner morsels. Of Carlos there was no sign. This was unusual because the one thing that the silver cat craved more than excitement was his supper of special cat biscuits containing high energy and vitamin nutrition.

Several visits to the garden failed to elicit a response from Carlos despite loud whistling and calling. In common with other caring cat owners, whenever a beloved pet fails to appear as expected it rapidly develops into a cause for worry. And so it was with me. I could not rest until I knew what had happened to delay him and, naturally, I began to fear the worst.

An hour later and still there was no sign of him. Really alarmed at this point I set out with torch and stick in hand to look for him. I searched first the roads in the near vicinity, which were the most dangerous areas for any animal but especially cats. Thankfully I found no squashed corpses on the tarmac.

Returning home cold, wet and covered in snow after a fruitless search of hedgerows and ditches, not to mention a foray into the eerie darkness of adjacent woodland, I was tired. But after a reviving cup of tea laced with brandy and moral support from Catherine, I was ready to resume searching since I couldn't relax until I knew what had happened to Silver Boy.

Outside Owl Cottage the wind had whipped the lying snow

into icy flurries that stung my face and hands. By midnight I was tired of trudging around snowy pathways and neighbours' driveways and returned to the cosiness of the cottage when just on the edge of the wind I thought I caught the sound of a high-pitched wail coming from overhead. There it was again. A piercing note of sheer desperation. I knew it had to be Carlos.

At first I could not locate the sound. Thinking it might have come from the top of one of the tall trees that line the roadside, I flashed my torch to sweep across the bare upper branches but nothing registered in the light beams. Then a slight distance away a movement caught the periphery of my eye. Walking nearer and shining my torch upwards in the direction of the movement I saw the bright green reflection of a cat's eyes. And there he was, marooned on the ledge of my next-door neighbour's tall chimney stack. It was Carlos sure enough. He sounded petrified. Shining my light directly on him I could see that he was dodging around the base of the chimneys pots in agitated movements, slipping slightly on the snow as he lost his grip. It was as if he wanted to climb down but each time he approached the edge he lost his nerve and retreated, howling. He needed help. He cut a forlorn, increasingly snow-covered figure, tiny against the dark sky.

I got as close as I could to him from my position at ground level. Moving my torch around I shone it directly on to the roof tiles below Carlos and called his name again and again in the hope of giving him reassurance by my presence so that he could feel sufficiently confident to clamber down and come to me. No matter how I urged him by calling out endearments and induce-ments he remained confined to the ledge. The only reply to my summons was another series of louder whines and wails.

At first I was at a loss to understand his reluctance simply to jump down and come to me. Then I recalled Catherine, who I had noticed that Carlos, unusually for a cat, did not appear to be adept at balancing on narrow ledges, and while sitting in the garden we had been amused at his clumsy manoeuvres when climbing in the trees. He could climb up well enough: it was getting down that posed a problem. In comparison to Pablo he had a lot to learn because the older cat was gifted with superb agility.

Looking up at Carlos now, shuffling anxiously in the snow around the chimney pots, it was clear that having jumped up on to the chimney stack he was too scared to come down. So began a number of ploys to rescue him. First I got the stepladder from the garage and heaved my by no means agile body on to the lower roof of my neighbour's house. Having gained a foothold on the now freezing snow I crawled my way up into a lead-covered gutter that led straight to the base of the chimney where Carlos was now reduced to sitting and uttering plaintive whimpers of distress. Unfortunately, the gutter was so slippery that my attempts to advance higher resulted in an unceremonious slide off the roof and, failing to grab the stepladder, I was dumped down into the snow. By this time Catherine had come out of Owl Cottage, just in time to see me fall. She rushed over to help me up, frightened that I had hurt myself badly. I hadn't but I was sure that I would feel bruised and sore the next morning. She advised me that it was now well after midnight and if the neighbours heard me thumping about they could well send for the police and I would be arrested.

Carlos obviously wanted me to come and get him but attempts to lure him off the chimney had failed completely and now my slide down the lower roof sealed his fate. I was beginning to feel very cold as the temperature continued to fall.

Just then Pablo, alerted no doubt by the goings-on, appeared on the roof from which I had fallen. My hopes of Pablo helping Carlos to find a way down grew. But that did not work either. Whether it was because of the cold or fear or maybe a combination of both, Carlos seemed almost unable to move. Completely exhausted by the whole escapade I could not think of what to do next. Catherine suggested we should go indoors before we caught pneumonia. She was right. Carlos would have to find his own way down.

I decided that if he wasn't down by the morning I would have to marshal help to rescue him but now bed and hopefully sleep beckoned, even though I hated the thought of abandoning him to the freezing cold weather outside.

Neither of us slept well that night. I tossed and turned in between short snoozes all night long. At last, when the illuminated dial of the bedside clock showed 6 a.m., I could no longer stay in bed and worry drove me to get up. Easing myself gently out of bed in the darkness so as not to disturb Catherine, whom I suspected was also half-awake because she was equally concerned for Carlos, I made my way quietly downstairs and had a reviving mug of tea. Not yet prepared to look outside I did not draw back the curtains covering the patio door adjacent to the kitchen, which is normally where both boys wait for us each morning after they have been out on their overnight prowls. But as I sat struggling with the dilemma of how to rescue Carlos there came a thumping and padding of paws against the door. That would be Pablo, I reckoned, back from his nightly excursions and no doubt with his superior feline senses he had detected that somebody was already up at this early hour.

'So why isn't the door open and breakfast served?' I guessed he'd be thinking. 'Well never let it be said that I am anything but a willing slave to the needs and wants of my cats,' I said to myself as I drew back the curtains. It was still dark outside and just as I opened the door, to my astonishment, a small grey and silver body shot inside, almost bowling me over in the process. It was Carlos, cold and hungry but otherwise unharmed. Following him at a leisurely saunter was a rather smug-looking Pablo, whose facial expression and body language suggested that he might well have had something to do with Carlos making a safe descent from the chimney. I hugged them both, Carlos especially. My feelings went into freefall and I could rejoice at all the good things in life once more. Just then Catherine appeared and together we were able to celebrate Carlos' safe return over breakfast.

Such are the problems to be expected when living with cats. Despite this episode and the snow, and in some respects perhaps because of it, we all had an especially happy Christmas at Owl Cottage. As ever, the cottage looked a picture with our Christmas cards, decorations and the Christmas tree itself, as well as the lights and candles, all enhanced by our newly acquired wood-burning stove.

The broader issue of training Carlos to become better disciplined was of necessity addressed by me every day and it soon reached the stage where I was able to say that it was working. I recalled a remark made to me by a horse wrangler I met when I was on a working holiday on a ranch in British Columbia in Western Canada: 'If you really want to tame a horse and teach it to like and respect you then don't set out to break its spirit. Talk softly to it. Spend time brushing it down whilst praising it for the horse you want it to be. Never use the whip. Then you'll have a friend and a helpmate for the rest of its life.'

It became clear in my mind that the same tactics could be applied equally to cats and indeed any animal to which you wished to relate. And by and large these were the tactics I had successfully used with my cats, not least Carlos who was now eight months old and growing fast, although he would never be as big a cat as Pablo.

By this time Carlos accompanied me in the car without demur and walked on the lead without complaint. But I feel I cannot overstate enough that the kind of interaction evident between Carlos and me, which resulted in these behavioural changes, was a two-way process. As the bonding grew firmer between us I became as closely attached to him as he was to me. A sort of emotional fine-tuning into what the other is feeling and experiencing occurs. I became aware that such an affinity was certainly beginning to grow between myself and Carlos just as it had happened in the past, only more so, with Toby Jug. In his case I only needed to look at him and I could weigh up his mood state. And it became obvious that when we were together Toby could respond to whatever I was feeling. If I was in a thoughtful mood he would join me on my knee and we would peruse the world together. If I happened to be low in spirit or upset he would do his best to console me by rubbing himself against me and licking my hand or neck and purring his song of love.

With Carlos the same sort of attachment was beginning to develop. One instance I can recall vividly. At the time it occurred it both thrilled and surprised me. I had noticed that Carlos, like kittens everywhere, liked to play with small objects, a rolled up piece of paper, a ball of some sort or just his own tail. But the difference with Carlos was that he would carry the object around in his mouth until he found a place to hide it. The next time I saw him do this I called him to me, rolled up a piece of paper and scrunched it into a ball. I showed it to him and he tried to take it from my hand but instead of giving it to him I threw it across the room. He stared at me in puzzlement and then charged after it, grabbed it in his mouth and disappeared into the hallway, obviously to hide it away. Later he came back into the room and sat by me.

'Why didn't you bring the paper ball back to me and then we could play a game?' He looked up at me with those large intelligent eyes and wandered off to sit near the fire. I returned to reading my book and thought no more of it.

Sometime later when Catherine came into the room, ever the tidy maid, she asked, 'What's that piece of paper doing down by your chair?' I glanced at the floor and there was the paper ball I had thrown for Carlos. He must have gone for it while I was reading and placed it near my shoe. But why? Surely he could not have understood my words. Had he read my mind? I told Catherine what had happened and she said, 'Why not try him again?' So I did. Picking up the paper I scrunched it in my hand until I attracted his attention and then I threw it to a far corner of the room. Without hesitation he galloped after it, took it in his mouth and raced back to me, dropped the paper ball at my feet and then stared up at me in anticipation of yet more fun. I stroked and patted him and told him how marvellous he was.

'Could be a coincidence, I suppose,' said my wife, mindful of me jumping to hasty conclusions. But after several repeat performances we became convinced that Carlos, incredulous as it seems, had understood what I wanted him to do. Highly elated that my cat was something of a genius I telephoned Jane, the breeder, to tell her about the incident, only to be somewhat deflated by her response. 'Oh there's nothing unusual about that with a Maine Coon cat. Many of my cats have retrieved and I've been constantly surprised at how quickly they pick up my thoughts,' she said in a matter-of-fact manner. Then she gave me a boost by adding: 'You need to remember that I am with my mother cats and their litters at the moments of their birth and for three months after that so they relate to me intimately, but you must have worked very hard with your kitten to achieve that quality of rapport.' I thanked her and rang off. Going back into the sitting room I picked up Carlos, hugged him and told him what a wonderful cat he was and how I loved him to bits. It had been hard work with him but now we were reaping the rewards.

After the several crises we had faced with Carlos, life at Owl Cottage at last began to resume its normal pattern. Together with our cats we were looking forward to the coming of spring. Each of the seasons has a distinctive charm but for me it is only springtime that has an appeal which is totally alluring. Here in Northumberland the snowdrops and crocuses usually come later than in the rest of the country but they are no less welcome. When I see the first daffodils flowering in the garden my spirit soars. The sight of those huge golden heads is uplifting, as is the appearance everywhere that I look of life renewing itself before my very eyes.

There is no green as vibrant and brilliant as the first leaves on our trees and remarkably each genus of tree seems to have its own unique shade of green. I so look forward to that time. When in tranquil moments, usually with a cat or two by my side, my mind becomes awash with the sheer beauty and inspiration of spring. I know that I am not the only one to be so stimulated because all around me the music of songbirds is heralding a time of rebirth. Above all, I am always relieved at the going of winter but I know that we will have to endure the snow and ice of wintry landscapes yet again because the exuberance of spring and summer needs some respite before we can be entranced by it once more.

And so I waited and prepared for the full onset of spring which was still some months away; it was time to turn my attention to the plants I grow each year in the greenhouse. My specialities are tomatoes and cucumbers, which I grow from seed obtained from far-flung countries of the world. This year I had an apprentice who would undoubtedly scrutinize my every move: his name was Carlos. Meanwhile, he liked to lie alongside my seed catalogues which were spread about on the table. Ever watchful, his attention followed whatever I did. Occasionally he would extend a paw and flick one of my pens towards him which he would then start to chew. If I got up to fetch something from the garage, for instance, Carlos would simultaneously rise, often from a state of apparent deep sleep, to follow me. It is what psychologists call 'pairing' or as my American friends put it, simply 'being buddies and pals'. I find it most endearing. You are never alone with a cat.

Since we got our boys I have found out that Maine Coons owe their existence to the actions of Marie Antoinette, the fateful Queen of France in the late eighteenth century. A virtual prisoner of royal protocol since her birth, she found solace and comfort in her pets and was especially fond of cats. She interbred some newly acquired Norwegian Forest cats, who were popular as rat-catchers aboard ships, with her long-haired pedigree lap-cats. Over several generations of breeding, a different type of cat emerged. These large and extremely handsome cats were considered to be exceptional because of their intelligence and affability. When the revolutionaries began to attack the French aristocracy, the Queen dispatched her beloved cats en masse by ship to the Americas, fully intending to follow herself. However, on her journey to the port, travelling in a coach bearing the royal insignia, she was stopped, taken captive, put on trial and ultimately guillotined. Her cats, meanwhile, survived and became most popular in that part of America called Maine on the east coast.

Since these cats shared a likeness both in appearance and habits with raccoons, the local populace mistakenly believed that they were hybrids produced by interbreeding the cats with raccoons, which is biologically impossible; hence they became known as Maine Coons even though they are most specifically of the cat species. Maine Coon cats are registered as a separate pure-bred pedigree cat nowadays and are extremely popular throughout the world.

In this period of relative calm at Owl Cottage I began to think that life with our two Maine Coons might endure in tranquil and uneventful mode for the foreseeable future. Then the unexpected happened. Pablo did not return from his Friday night out 'on the tiles'. Catherine and I had composed for our own amusement a fantasy storyline to describe what our magnificent cat did when he took off on his all-night prowls. My favourite idea was that he was on 'The Trail of the Lonesome Pine', culled from a song in one of the Laurel and Hardy films, because I knew that he ranged far and wide on his hunting excursions.

We had never been really worried about Pablo because he was so careful and cautious by nature, not at all excitable and impulsive like Carlos. He could be depended upon to have his jaunt every night and turn up tired and hungry each morning as regular as clockwork. That is, until one morning, which we never believed would come, when he wasn't there and did not appear all day. Later that morning I set out on that most feared duty of pet owners: the search for the body, dead or alive. Several hours later, I had no news for Catherine, who had been keeping watch for him at Owl Cottage. Of Pablo I had found no sign.

The next morning brought renewed hopes but there was no welcome furry presence at the patio door when we drew back the curtains. There was no sign of him for the rest of the day either or for the following two days. No sign or sight of him anywhere.

If you let cats roam free there is always the chance that you will lose them, victim to one or another of the myriad dangers out in the world. You take a real risk. Such were the thoughts going through my mind as it moved into hyperdrive and I began to imagine all kinds of disaster scenarios. Perhaps he was caught in a snare or trap like Toby Jug's mother had been the night I rescued her. There were still farmers and poachers in the area who laid traps. Perhaps he had been shot by a feckless poacher who hunted at night with lantern and shotgun and who would shoot any small animal that moved within range. Was he lying somewhere, wounded or dead? Reasoning it through, I determined to employ an age-old country remedy of using an animal to find an animal. I did not have a dog which I could use to track Pablo but I could hire the next best thing, a horse. Horses have extraordinary senses, as I had learned during my time on the trail in Western Canada. A horse is fundamentally a creature attuned to everything in the natural environment. My human perceptions could miss detecting an animal in distress but a horse would not. A horse would alert me to a suffering creature in the vicinity. And so I headed to a nearby farm where there was a riding school.

Green Meadows Riding School was managed by a pleasant lady named Molly who had that robust outdoor look, brimming with health. She listened sympathetically to my request to hire one of her horses for an unaccompanied ride around the local fields and woods. I didn't mention Pablo but simply explained that I had once kept a horse and now that I was retired I wished to take up riding again. I said I didn't need instruction and preferred to ride alone. She looked rather dubious at this and after some moments of deliberation she declared that I would need to demonstrate that I could ride safely in the indoor training ring. I had to agree. After all, it was only fair since I was a stranger to her.

I accompanied her to the stable area where she introduced me to a young mare called Starlight, suggesting that she might be suitable as a possible mount. However, the vibes coming from the horse were negative as far as I was concerned. For one thing she jerked her head about a lot, rolled her eyes and stamped a hoof as if she was anxious to be out and off. I imagined that Starlight would be something of a handful, more suitable to strong, older teenage girls than me. So I asked if there were any other mounts available. She pondered a moment and then she said she had a gelding called Rio who was a quiet, biddable ride and liked an easy life. 'I couldn't have put it better myself,' I said. Rio occupied a corner stall and looked out at me with mild liquid eyes and a steady gaze. I fondled his head and stroked his side and he stood without moving, enjoying the attention. I turned to Molly and indicated that I would try him.

Ten minutes later I was sitting astride Rio, wearing an infernal contraption called a safety helmet. I really did feel ridiculous but Molly insisted that it was regulation headwear, whilst staring disapprovingly at my past-their-best trainers and worn jeans. She also stressed the necessity of me donning a padded vest to protect my torso. If these safety measures had been in force when I first learned to ride then I doubt whether I would have ever started. I felt as if I were a jockey preparing to ride in the Grand National horse race. Struggling to hide my irritation I gave Rio a gentle heel and he lumbered into a jerky trot which I smoothed out by rising to the trot, although I much prefer the American western style of lengthening the stirrups and sitting solidly in the saddle. I feared Milady would not approve.

I circled the track a couple of times in this way and then pressed my knees slightly to spur Rio into a comfortable rocking horse canter. I reined him back and stroked and patted him a lot, all the while talking softly to him. Then I turned him this way and that, backing him up as if I were manoeuvring to open a gate, after which I rode him around again at a fast trot. I pulled up, looked over at Molly and asked if I'd passed.

'Well it's hardly "Horse of the Year Show" standard but I can see that you know how to handle a horse.' We then agreed terms and I paid her £80 for three hours. The price included the hire of the helmet, vest and also insurance. I considered it reasonable, especially if Rio helped me to find Pablo.

I mounted in the yard and urged Rio out on to the road, which I quickly crossed, and made my way along a farm track until I was well out of sight of the stables. Then I halted and, taking a green bin-bag from my pocket (I'd brought several with me in case I found Pablo's body), I placed the helmet and vest inside and hid the bag behind a hedge whilst holding firmly on to Rio in case he decided to head back home. Then, to Rio's growing interest, I took an apple from my pocket and cutting it in half I gave a section to him. He began to pay full attention to me now. I needed an alert horse under me and to achieve this I needed to have a degree of rapport with the animal.

Mounted again, with the breeze blowing in my face and ruffling my hair, I felt at home once more on horseback. I was now able to focus on the purpose of the ride as Rio trotted along the margins of the dormant fields. There was no sign of Pablo anywhere. No sounds of distress registered with either man or horse in response to my urgent whistles and calls. I rode by endless ditches and hedgerows, through scrub and deep copses, and picked my way through scattered and variegated patches of woodland.

I stopped and greeted two farmhands driving tractors over newly ploughed fields but they had seen nothing of a large brown cat. However, they did mention, just to make me feel worse, that they had seen a fox with cubs near the river. I dismounted and let my horse drink from a brook near the Coquet and considered my options.

I had been riding for two hours and was beginning to tire. I also felt that Rio had just about had enough. Besides that, my knees were in severe torment at the unaccustomed riding exercise and I felt it was time to call it a day. I fed Rio the rest of the apple and he looked at me with such big sorrowful eyes that I had to smile as I stroked him, although I felt far from happy.

As a last resort I led Rio up to the crest of a hill overlooking the river and using my small powerful binoculars I scanned the fields and the sky for any sight of buzzards, ravens or carrion crows which might be circling around a trapped or dying animal. There was nothing to be seen, the sky was empty of life and despite my thick sweater I was beginning to feel chilled now that the late February sun had clouded over. Remounting, I turned Rio for home and for the first time felt some exuberance in his fast trot and short canters. This horse liked an easy life and he had probably covered more ground that afternoon than he normally did in a week but he had done well for me. Also riding-school horses ordinarily ride out in a bunch and he had most likely missed the company of the others. Retrieving the bag in which I'd hidden the safety gear I led Rio on foot to ease my back and knees and handed him over to a waiting stable girl.

Returning home I could only wearily shake my head at Catherine's questioning looks as I headed for the bathroom and a welcome hot bath.

Lying awake in bed that night I tried to think of what else I could do to find Pablo. If he was dead then the least I could do was find his body and bring him home. But where could he be? It had been four days since we had last seen him. I was acting on the good old British Army strategy that there is always something more that you can do. After a while a memory from the past crept into my head of a friend called Duncan with whom I had, over a glass or two of wine, shared many discussions on such topics as folklore and psychology. As I recall, Duncan had either been related to gypsies, now called travellers, at a settlement near Yetholm in Northumberland, or had even spent some of his formative years in their company. He related to me many tales of gypsy power spells and magic practices which could be used to help with problems of everyday living, although we tended to agree that so-called 'magic' was an unconscious function of the human mind set on achieving something or other. Gypsy 'spells' involved ways of focusing mental powers in order to create good outcomes. I suppose this could be described as a means of praying or, as research in areas of phenomenological psychology states: if you can visualize something strongly enough then you can actualize it for real. That is, you can make things happen through the power of the mind.

As my thoughts meandered along these lines I suddenly realized that my brain was trying to figure out a solution to Pablo's disappearance. I recalled Duncan telling me that when someone went missing the gypsy method of guiding them home was to inscribe the person's name on a white candle and light it in a window to call the lost one back. It was a way of focusing the feelings to summon the lost one back home. Then my thoughts made another connection to a story by Charles Dickens in which a candle was left burning each night to lead 'Little Dorrit' home.

Excited now that I had something else to try I hurried downstairs. In our candle box I found a medium-sized white candle on which I wrote the name Pablo in red ink. This I placed in an antique candle holder that had once belonged to my grandmother and which we always used at Christmas. Lighting the candle with a hand that shook with all the nervous energy of worrying about him, I whispered a prayer that the light from this candle would bring Pablo home safe and sound. I carried the candle upstairs and placed it on the uncurtained hall window facing out over the garden and fields beyond.

I replaced the candle at regular intervals and kept it burning day and night. The next night as I mounted a vigil by the open window, a curious silver cat joined me and kept watch with me each night afterwards. I realized that it gave me something to do which gave me hope, but gradually my hopes for the return of our lovely big brown boy were fading as the amount of time that had elapsed since his disappearance increased.

On Friday it would be a week since he had last been with us. If he were alive but trapped somewhere without food and water then his chances of survival were minimal. Catherine and I both became convinced that we would never see him again and with that realization melancholia set in. We did not talk much. We each moved quietly about our business of the day with heavy hearts, as if we had only just grasped how much the presence of Pablo meant to us. Without closure of some sort we could not begin to put our memories to rest.

Late on Friday evening Catherine and I sat talking in the conservatory. I could tell that she had shed a few tears over Pablo but I did not remark on it because I also felt devastated. She and I agreed that it was not realistic for either of us to go on hoping for his return. We knew that everything that we could do to find him had been done. We commented that since he had an identity chip he could easily have been identified if he had been found then. But a large cat like Pablo could range over great distances and we had to accept he might never be found. Anything might have happened to him. We had given him his freedom which he seemed to enjoy and this was the price we had to be prepared to pay for that.

Many people in our little hamlet and the extended village of Felton called to sympathize with us once they heard about our loss. Catherine had told the girls at the hairdressers and I had put a notice in the post office window. In our small rural community, where most people know each other, there prevails a sense of communal concern for neighbours when any kind of problem or tragedy happens. The Village Coffee Shop is more than just a cafe as it tends to be a meeting place for local folk where news is dispensed via the grapevine and it was my hope that eventually someone would find out what had happened to Pablo.

As Catherine and I sat talking we began to share some of our personal memories of Pablo. She recalled how on some mornings after he had eaten his breakfast he would insist on coming to lie in her lap and refuse to budge until he had his expected half-an-hour stroke and cuddle.

For my part, and I had not told her this before, I remembered how if he was in the mood he would greet me by jumping on the table or windowsill and, rising up, he would place his massive paws on my shoulders and rub his face against mine, especially the sides of my head. Of course, I loved this display of affection. And cringing somewhat to disclose such a private moment to another person, I recalled my use of a silly affectionate pet name for him: I called him my 'Big Teddy Bear'. Also I sometimes would pick him up two-handed, with his front paws in my left hand and his back legs in my right hand, swing him over my head and wrap him around my neck like a scarf; he loved it and would purr away loudly to let me know how pleased he was.

And so we talked away our sorrows as the evening progressed until at last we felt a little better and decided to call it a day. As I headed up to bed I took a last look out the window where the candle was still burning as a testimony to our love for our missing Maine Coon. At midnight it would be three days since I had lit the first candle. With a jolt I remembered Duncan's words: 'In gypsy lore the candle will work within three days or not at all.' Oh well, I thought, at least I tried everything.

Just then Carlos joined me noisily on the window sill. He put his face close to the glass window and cried excitedly. 'I don't think so, Carlos,' I said and opened the window so that we could both look out. 'See,' I said to him, 'there's nothing there. Pablo will not be coming home but he'll always be with us won't he?' Just as I uttered the words a whiff of air blew out the candle. 'There you are! That's an end to it.' And I closed the window. Then I opened the back door for him to saunter forth.

We slept later than usual and so it was nearly 9 a.m. before I ushered Carlos in from the garden to feed him. After his breakfast he liked to retire to the conservatory to watch the birds and the garden, and to indulge in a morning nap after the exertions of prowling throughout the night. I was feeling desperately low.

Later that morning I took my third cup of coffee into the study to do some reading as I didn't feel up to writing. Catherine was meanwhile working on the computer to prepare some items for the forthcoming Parish Council Meeting for which she was Clerk. She looked unhappy. However, outwardly it appeared that all was calm within Owl Cottage. The bright early morning sun was melting last night's harsh white frost which covered the entire garden.

Suddenly, there came a tremendous crash and sound of breaking glass. Catherine beat me to the scene of the disaster and I heard her exclamations of dismay. I bet it's Carlos, I thought. Surprisingly, my wife's cries changed to ones of jubilation. 'Denis,' she shouted. 'Come quickly and see. Your "Big Teddy Bear" is back! He's here now.' I literally could not believe my ears. With my heart thumping as if it would jump out of my chest I walked disbelievingly into the conservatory to see my wife on her knees, hugging a ragged looking Pablo.

'Well I never, how on earth . . .' I began. 'Pablo!' I shouted and then the feelings aroused were beyond words. The two of us simply petted and stroked him until we had the sense to appreciate that he must need water desperately and some food. But Pablo did not seem to mind and obviously enjoyed the attention he was getting more than anything else.

He did drink thirstily when we offered him water but ate only sparingly. What he seemed to need most of all was to be with us. After the initial petting session we examined him thoroughly and concluded that he had not been living outside. His fur was too smooth and dry and the pads of his paws, especially the claws, showed no sign of wear and tear. I was mystified as to where he could have been.

We wondered if someone had kept him prisoner, but then quickly dismissed that explanation since Pablo did not take to strangers easily and would become fierce if coerced in any way. Eventually, we assumed that he must have wandered into an open garage or outhouse and became captive when the owners locked up and went off for a week; this was probably the most likely explanation. It was highly unlikely that we would ever know for sure where he had been. He must have had access to water, possibly condensation on a window or steel door. It was all a puzzle to us.

We spent most of that day stroking and talking to him. For his part he simply lay there, enjoying the loving care and attention we lavished upon him. Relief was palpable in us all. We were both absolutely delighted and Carlos too seemed pleased. It was a momentous occasion, one to be recorded in the annals of Owl Cottage. Catherine opened a bottle of champagne she had been saving and I indulged a glass of single malt whiskey from a bottle I'd specially put aside. Pablo had come home and all was well with the world once more. Incidentally, the loud crash we had heard was caused by Carlos, (who else?), who must have spotted Pablo and became so excited that he ran amok and knocked over a vase of flowers. As we too had experienced a range of emotions over Pablo, we felt we could hardly blame our impulsive silver cat who still exhibited hyperactive tendencies from time to time. So what if the vase was broken and water spilled all over the hall carpet? (No cat is perfect.) Carlos welcomed Pablo back enthusiastically but insisted on having his fair share of the strokes being given out.

Later in the day I noticed that Catherine had already tidied away the antique candle holder and wiped up some spilt candle grease from the window sill. The sight of this started me thinking about what Duncan had told me regarding old-fashioned gypsy spells. Pablo had returned after the candle had burned for three days. Duncan had said everything works in threes, for example, three wishes, three coins in the well, cross your fingers and count to three, etc. I began to think that perhaps there was something in those old mystic lores that could not be easily explained away. I shook my head in disbelief as I reflected that there is much about this world that is beyond my understanding. But I was glad that Pablo was back, however it had happened.

Soon our minds were attuned to happier thoughts and feelings as spring finally arrived and all at once the garden and the trees began to show new life. It is at this time of the year that I most enjoy walking around the garden, usually in the early evening when the sunlight dims to a hazy glow and the earth shines in a golden half-light which the Scottish call the 'gloaming'. Then the colours of the flowers and the fruit blossom seem to radiate a lustre of their very own, as if they are giving back sunshine to illuminate the air. It is a special time for insects, too, among which only the bumble bees work with feverish haste in contrast to the fluttering butterflies, with wings softly hued, and flimsy damselflies iridescently shimmering as they hover above the waters of the bird bath. Such sights inspire the human heart and mind with poetic images and nourish the soul. In this vein of sheer delight, who would dare call my all-time favourite wild flower, the cowslip, a weed?

Reflections like this awaken nostalgic reminiscences of earlier times in my life when I'm afraid I became an inveterate truant from school. If on my journey to school a passing gleam of sunshine touched me then my longing for the dense greenery of fields and inviting riverbanks, the path through the woods and the excitement of the lake seen distant through the trees would turn me away to cavort as a free spirit among nature's bountiful offerings! To watch the nesting songbirds and to listen to their sweet whistling, to glimpse hares running wild across fields of waving grasses, to lie at ground level at the side of a pond and gaze in curious wonder at a stickleback in full mating regalia of black and red, weaving his nest of slime-green moss to attract a mate – this was the education for which I craved even though I knew that that a heavy punishment would be meted out both at home and at school when I was found out. I didn't care: it was worth it. That inevitable outcome never deterred me from my wild gambols with mother nature.

One morning as Catherine and I ate breakfast the boys, as we nearly always referred to Pablo and Carlos now, started making a real fuss at the conservatory window. When we looked out we saw what had bothered them: two frisky red squirrels were feeding from the peanuts we put out for the birds. I addressed

Toby Jug appeared to me in a dream.

The rooks buzzed Pablo for climbing high in the tree.

Toby Jug is confronted by a hostile, big mouse.

Carlos coolly looks down on the chaos he has caused at the vet's.

I took Carlos to the beach at Bamburgh Castle.

I raced for the car with Carlos to escape the storm.

We lit a candle in the window to call Pablo home.

Max, the red kitten, is comforted by his little twin brother.

the cats in human terms but they understood the tone of my voice alright: 'You've had your breakfast. Don't begrudge other animals a bite or two!'

While my cats show remarkable empathy towards us I'm afraid that does not extend to other species. And so, in spite of their insistent demands to be let out, I refused and watched in fascination the acrobatic antics of the squirrels who were hanging upside down, taking nuts and seeds from the bird-feeders. Both cats continued to make throaty growls, turning their backs to me in a huffed posture and declining to make eye contact for the rest of the morning.

But this was unusual; normally we are easy with each other, born out of the reciprocity I described earlier. The cats and I spend blissful hours together just watching the garden, the trees, the birds and the wildlife and I assume that they, like me, enjoy it. We stare out of the large windows of the conservatory, sometimes at a sky laced with orange and yellow woven against a backcloth of azure and indigo as the evening sun softens into lingering twilight. A faint breeze might stir the grass and bushes around the trunks of the trees, disturbing a male blackbird who screeches and tweaks his tail in a spasm of agitation before flying on to the top of the garage roof to deliver his evening serenade. Much later, the creeping darkness hides everything until a three-quarter moon lightens up the sky and intensifies the watching as the creatures of the night begin to emerge. Along the fringes of the far line of trees at the end of the garden and, in the patches of meadow, moonbeams call out hedgehogs, moles and field mice to move afoot in their everlastingly urgent search for food. A whole array of moths takes to the air with the inevitable consequence that the bats, lying in wait, indulge in a feeding frenzy.

For my two cats this heralds a call to action; it is a time for stalking and the thrill of the chase, though I am confident that they won't overdo a killing spree because they are too well fed. The chase will be solely for fun. As they disappear into the night I move to relax my cramped limbs and go in search of a cup of tea and possibly a sandwich.

As the months passed, Catherine and I decided that we were in need of a holiday and on impulse we decided to go to the Isle of Wight. We organized a stay at the Blue Lodge, a local cattery, for the boys and although we knew they would have only the very best of care and attention, it was nevertheless a traumatic experience for all of us to be separated.

When we were ready to depart, we put Pablo and Carlos into a large carrying box together and placed it on the back seat of the car. The cats became aware that they were being taken either to the vet's or to the cattery and, although Carlos is used to the car, he joined in the whining distress calls of Pablo, which sounded dreadful. We became upset but we gritted our teeth, turned up the radio and reasoned that since we rarely go away, the cats would just have to make the best of it.

We returned home to finish packing. The cottage felt so empty and strange without our felines that we were glad to leave. We drove south on the M1 on a bright sunny morning in

June. We reached our night stopover just outside Oxford in the early evening. After a brief rest and freshen-up we went to a well-known watering hole called the Trout. The lovely day turned into a delightful warm evening full of sunshine and bird song. The Trout was situated in a charming old-world setting. From the car park we crossed a quaint wooden bridge over the river to enter, via a rustic gate, the Trout's open-air dining space which was shaded by an ancient oak tree growing in the centre. We chose a table lodged against the trunk of the oak, where we had a clear view of the river and a variety of water fowl which seem uncommonly tame. The young waitress who served us was a student in her second year studying languages at one of the colleges of Oxford University and we had a pleasant con-versation with her about her home in South America.

The meal was excellent and the wine superb but just as we were lingering over a final glass, enjoying the balmy late night air, we were jolted out of our reverie by a hideous scream from some animal or other. We looked around and saw that many of our fellow diners, who were obviously regulars, were simply nodding and smiling at each other as if there was nothing untoward about the noise.

I followed the direction of their glances and spied a whopping great bird on the roof which was instantly accompanied by another. They flapped and strutted around, and then we heard strident screams repeated several times. I realized that we were being treated to an encounter with peacocks. These majestic birds with their fabulous fantail plumage must be a speciality of the inn but not for the menu! I expect that they are a customized extra to attract visitors because they certainly add something unusual to the already impressive ambience of the Trout Public House.

All at once one of the peacocks began to clamber in an ungainly but effective fashion down the tree under which we were sitting and, by a series of wing flaps and teetering grabs at the lower branches, the creature arrived at the base of the tree adjacent to our table. Subjecting us both to a goggle-eyed stare, it felt safe enough to thrust its long neck forwards and, dipping a coloured beak into a bowl on our table, began to consume mouthfuls of brown sugar. To our amazement this continued for some time until a passing waiter intervened and chased the bird away, whereupon it flew to roost on the roof and commenced more screaming. Turning to us the waiter remarked by way of explanation that this peacock was addicted to sugar and chocolates and the staff were under instructions to prevent the bird indulging.

As we left the restaurant we were passed on the bridge by a cream-and-auburn-coloured cat who did not acknowledge my greeting and hurried on inside, no doubt for a feast of meaty leftovers. Later, as I went to bed, my thoughts as ever switched to a place in Northumberland where I believed two Maine Coon cats would be thinking of us and I hoped they would know that we were missing them, too.

The next day we drove through the New Forest and savoured the experience of watching a group of wild ponies grazing in picturesque settings of the time-honoured variety, which served to remind us what we had read about the culture and history of this unique place. I would have liked to linger and absorb the vibes of the forest but Catherine, who is much better than I am at keeping to a timetable, urged us to press on for the car ferry. My lasting image of the area is a view of hazy sunshine outlining the silhouettes of horses and trees in woodlands looking much as they must have done for hundreds of years. It was almost like a watercolour painting.

A couple of hours later we began to feel that we were really on holiday when in warm sunshine we boarded the car ferry for Yarmouth, Isle of Wight. Driving around the island during our week's stay gave us a lot of pleasure. A special favourite route was the scenic road along the east coast up to Osborne House and Cowes. But we also enjoyed walking along the coast towards the Needles and the famous Alum Bay, with its multi-coloured cliffs and sand. Our seven days passed quickly and after taking a final coffee at a fine old hotel in Yarmouth we were on our way north. I was glad to be going home; I was seriously missing our cats.

This time our stopover for the night afforded us the opportunity to visit a hostelry dating back to Tudor times called the Coach and Horses Inn which had oak beams and white plaster walls, and was full of old-world charm. As we sat in antique chairs at a table which must have been early Victorian I felt fully relaxed in spite of the muted noise from a World Cup football match on the television in the bar next door.

After a very good dinner we sat relishing the last of our wine and the cosy comfort of the lounge when I noticed the entrance of an exceptional dog. He was long in body with the rangy look of a hound, possibly a wolfhound with some of the lurcher about his slender, smooth-haired frame. I frequently find that now I am retired as a psychologist, which involved a heavy clinical commitment to people, I take immense pleasure in applying my psychology to the study of animals, whether they are birds, horses, dogs or, more especially, cats. This dog looked a promising subject. It glided into the room as unobtrusively as a breath of air and his demeanour oozed breeding and class. His master sauntered into the bar as easily and nonchalantly as his dog and casually took a seat, which appeared to be reserved for him. His dog was already lying beneath the appointed table as if he and his master belonged there by right.

Although there were no other dogs around, no one seemed to object to this dog's presence, which surprised me. This dog was really far too big to be in this low-ceilinged, modest-sized room with what we decided must be the regular Saturday night crowd. The dog's owner, a man in his late fifties, evidenced an air of nobility and privilege in common with his dog. He appeared to be perfectly at ease with the world and himself. In keeping with his aristocratic airs he had an aura of eccentricity about him, too, as witnessed by the trousers he was wearing which appeared garish in their design of black stars and spots on a white background. The fact that he had the confidence to wear them in a public place and to bring with him a huge hound indicated that he probably belonged to the local gentry and this assumption was born out by the deference the staff showed towards him.

But more than the man, it was his magnificent dog which arrested my attention. He lay on the floor half underneath his master's table and only his eyes moved to convey that he was alert to everything going on in the room. In a while he sensed that I was studying him and gave me a long scrutinizing stare and then, concluding that I was without menace, he resumed his watchful gaze over the room. To give a dog like him the exercise he needed to keep fit would, I believed, require someone with a horse prepared to ride several miles a day. He seemed to be in magnificent condition judging from his well-groomed, fine-haired coat of muted brown. I sensed that his owner, who never once had to speak to him but did occasionally caress his ears, thought the world of him. I enjoyed the evening for many reasons but the sight of that superb animal in such harmony with his master, who obviously treated him very well, made the experience complete.

We made our way back to our hotel by taxi through the grandeur of richly endowed countryside which was a pleasure to see and was rendered all the more pastoral by the silver moonlight. I reflected on the sharp contrast between this lush landscape through which we were travelling and the harsh wilderness of the moors and hills of Northumberland where we lived. It made me think of how fortunate we are to have large tracts of land consisting of such diverse features of rural terrain covered by multiple flora and inhabited by a wide variety of wildlife which inspires the spiritual as well as aesthetic appreciation that has been lyrically described as 'Forever England'.

As I lay awake in our hotel, which nestled in woodland near a lake and was a fair distance from the M1 motorway, I could hear through the partially open bedroom windows the soft hooting of owls and once or twice I thought I caught the sounds of foxes barking a communication to each other as they hunted rabbits in moonlit meadows. Such sounds are a source of solace to me whenever I hear them and I believe them to be healing for anyone with a stressed or troubled mind. Humans cannot afford to separate themselves from the natural life of our planet. It set me thinking of how our domesticated creatures can provide us with friendship, solace and succour and how helpful and supportive these relationships can be especially when we are troubled.

For example, I was told about a woman who lived not many miles from us in a fishing village who could often be seen walking around with an exotically coloured parrot on her shoulder. This large bird was, it would seem, so attached to her that he demanded to be taken along wherever she walked in the locality. One summer evening I was extremely surprised to see this same lady as she entered a fish and chip shop where I was waiting my turn. On her left shoulder was perched the parrot, which proceeded at intervals to address the queue and the assistants with remarks such as 'Turned out nice again' and

'Two fish suppers please with batter'. These utterances were accompanied by much bowing and bobbing. The fact that no one else seemed to find this unusual convinced me that this was a regular performance. It was clear that the lady herself was extremely proud of her pet and his prowess with language as she stroked and cosseted him in a most loving manner. That woman and her parrot clearly gave each other a great deal.

Perhaps the English, as the saying goes, are truly a nation of animal lovers, although some events would appear to contradict that opinion, including an incident that happened in the neighbouring village of Felton. It was so extraordinary that it made local, national and then international headlines. It began first as a rumour spread by a few avid gardeners who circulated their anecdotes at the bar of the Northumberland Arms, which stands just over from the old bridge at Felton.

The story was that a giant rabbit was raiding crops of vegetables from the village gardens and allotments. Jokes galore made the rounds about the Giant Beast of Felton which could strip a garden of all its produce in a single night. At first the jokers had their way and every one believed the stories to be an elaborate hoax until a local housewife of mature years, and not one given to practical jokes, reported seeing a huge rabbit thundering across her lawn in the early morning rain. Other sightings followed and the continuance of the raids on vegetable plots by the strange creature outstripped the jokers and moved one besieged allotment holder, sixty-three-year-old Jeff Smith, to attempt to mobilize support from the local community, including the Parish Council, to eradicate this nuisance. With this in mind two local gamekeepers were instructed to stalk and shoot the animal. Immediately, there arose a concerted outcry from many within the village, including myself, and when the news got out people from outside the village voiced their protests at this draconian measure.

One misty morning I spotted this great rabbit moving around the far end of our garden. He was indeed massive, far outweighing the local population of wild rabbits, and I guessed he was a pet rabbit that had either been abandoned or had made a break for freedom. I watched him serenely cropping some long grass growing near a pear tree and as I moved from my seating position in the conservatory he saw me and did not take fright, thus confirming my original view that he was a tame pet rabbit. In contrast to my response, my cats were really spooked and were literally climbing up the walls in shock horror. I watched him as he loped off and bade him good luck: he would need it.

Heated arguments both for and against killing the monster sustained the public attention until it was suddenly realized that the rabbit had simply disappeared. Then further rumours began to disseminate regarding the fate of the creature and soon conspiracy theories, most of which were fuelled by alcohol, started to orbit around the town.

About a month after the gossip about the rabbit subsided I met up with a young lad I had known previously as a waiter in the Northumberland Arms but who was now working in a supermarket in Alnwick. We got talking and I mentioned the mystery of the 'Felton Rabbit'. He drew me aside in a secretive manner and confided that his uncle told him that a group of allotment holders had lain in ambush for it one night, shot it dead, skinned and barbequed it, and fed the meat to their dogs. I never found out if this was true but if it was then the poor rabbit had failed to understand that human domination of the animal kingdom is absolute and, although his life was as important to him as anybody else's is to them, once he came into conflict with man's interests he had to die.

This tragic affair called to mind how scientific institutions abuse animals for their own research purposes and I remember learning that one highly esteemed director of an animal research unit had published a paper describing an experiment in which twenty cats had been deliberately blinded to advance knowledge about eyesight. During my own university studies for a bachelor of science degree, in which I had to attend laboratory sessions in the department of zoology, I was made aware that compassion for our mammalian brethren was non-existent in the cause of science. It happened that one day my assignment in the physiology laboratory was to create a diagram of the organs and innards of a rat. I began carefully to copy the relevant details from the physiology chart manuals I had to hand when a lab assistant handed me a typed note which instructed me to kill one of the pure-bred white lab rats, then dissect it and note down the spatial distribution of its organs. Just as I finished reading the instructions I was handed a box full of cotton-wool pads, a bottle of chloroform and a live white rat. I need to point out that the white rats bred for experiments bear little resemblance to the wild brown breed that inhabit our countryside or the disease-carrying black rats of the sewers. The creature that sat on my table had pure white fluffy fur and pink eyes. In appearance it looked as harmless as a kitten and I truly felt that I was in the presence of a healthy, sentient animal. As I stared at it in consternation it ambled across towards me and licked the back of my hand.

I said, 'Don't worry, I won't kill you,' and I stroked its head. Then I became aware of a figure standing off to my right. It was the professor in charge of the session.

'This is not Pet's Corner, O'Connor. Complete your assignment.'

'Sir,' I called out, because he was already moving away. 'Please, sir, I don't need to kill this creature because I already have a detailed anatomy chart of the rat right here, which I'm in the process of copying. Also, I'm a psychology student not a medic!'

If you have ever been in the presence of a human being who looked as if he would explode then you will recognize my experience that afternoon. In short I was told that if I refused to carry out this assignment then I could say goodbye to any chance of graduating. In a frame of mind akin to being encased in a block of ice I did what I was expected and vowed that I would never ever again wittingly cause the death of an innocent animal. When I left the session I fled to the lavatory area and vomited. That evening I could not face dinner and sat in the student bar sipping a pint of lager and reflecting on Wordsworth's words about what man has done to man. And no, I didn't sleep well that night; I kept seeing a little white rat staring at me accusingly for taking his life as if it meant nothing. The note which passed my assignment as satisfactory added a cryptic footnote which said: 'There is no place in science for sentiment!'

As these memories of bygone days and experiences ranged hurtfully through my mind on the final night of our holiday, I suddenly felt very sleepy and the next I knew it was morning. As we ate breakfast the central thought in both our minds was that today we were going home to our cats and we would be happily with them by nightfall.

After an arduous journey by motorway we were reunited with Pablo and Carlos. The reunion was not without strain for us since we were treated, despite our enthusiastic petting and stroking, with the bland indifference that only cats can muster when they feel huffed by the absence of their loved ones. On arriving home friendly relations were only resumed after we had fed them and made an excessively big fuss of them both. Eventually Carlos, who could no longer maintain his aloofness, jumped on my knee and began to tread my sweater whilst emitting melancholy cries intermingled with purrs, just to let me know that he had missed me terribly but he was desperate to know why it was that I had left him anyway. Meanwhile, Pablo deigned to stretch his massive form across Catherine's lap and, in between a series of baritone purrs, commenced to lick her hand and arm. After a while feelings of domestic harmony pervaded the room and all was once more well at Owl Cottage. But this slightly tense reception by our cats due to our absence reminded me how much they were emotionally dependent on our presence and our love. The problem for animals is that when we leave them they cannot be sure that we will come back until we actually do return, which causes them extreme emotional distress. Being aware of this affects me so intensely that I have often considered whether I should ever leave them again for whatever reason.

The next day after we returned from holiday I resumed my focus of attention on training Carlos but I was beginning to believe that he had changed over the past few months and was fast becoming a more agreeable cat, although I understood that his personality would always retain a wild streak. He increasingly liked to spend time at my side, whatever I was doing. If I was still in bed in the morning he would seek me out and join me on the bed, where I was treated to a fulsome show of affection. If he caught me still asleep I would receive licks on the forehead and cheeks until I surfaced, blinking to find his handsome little face peering at me, exuding love and affection. Then he would work his way under the duvet and poke his head a little way out, which was a signal that he wished to be stroked. He would lie there next to me emitting throbbing purrs of sheer happiness which, in turn, made me happy, too. Since further sleep was impossible I would give him a few more moments of attention and then get up, escorted by this attentive cat who would weave between my legs as I descended the stairs, often in danger of tripping over because of him. Once I had my morning cup of tea he would jump on my knee, snuggle cosily into my dressing gown and look at me as if to say: 'Where are we going today, then?'

The intense look in his bright green eyes made to chuckle at the gung-ho, lively attitude of this cat. He truly was a rare phenomenon among his kind and I couldn't quite believe that in the short time we had been together he was beginning to mean everything to me. Each day I looked forward to his antics, which at one time had worried me. We were really getting to know each other. Lately, I had been concerned because of his preference for dried food over the meat varieties. I finally resorted to cooking chicken for the cats, especially Carlos, and even went to the extent of cutting fine slivers of chicken breast to tempt him. Whilst he would chew a couple of pieces just to please me he preferred to eat dry biscuits, which meant of course that he needed to drink lots of water. It distressed me to see how desperately he needed water: even though there was always a clean bowl of water for the cats in the conservatory, Carlos felt the necessity to stand on the edge of the kitchen sink, imploring me to turn on the cold water tap, and then eagerly lean forward to drink directly from the streaming water. This behaviour resulted in him becoming soaked to the skin on the upper parts of his body, though he didn't seem to care.

In the literature about Maine Coon cats there is particular mention made of their fancy to take to the water and all my cats, including Toby, loved washing a morsel of meat in their drinking bowl. Each summer we wash our cats in a bucket of warm water and they seem to really enjoy this for the soothing affect on their skin. We always choose a hot day so that they can dry off quickly. An exceptional incident of this kind took place with Toby Jug when he was about three years old.

One morning I was taking a shower and to my surprise he walked under the shower curtain and settled himself at my feet. Anxious that soap wouldn't get into eyes and hurt him, I switched off the shower head, lifted him out and commenced to dry him immediately. However, he appeared to be totally un-concerned and I do believe that the wily cat had kept his eyes closed. He repeated this deed on several other occasions when the weather was hot and more especially if I was having a cool shower after a day's gardening. Whilst Carlos never took a shower with me, he did enjoy taking a run through the automatic revolving garden hose spray when I fixed it to the lawn on especially hot sunny days.

Just as I became resigned the fact that Carlos would only eat dry biscuits I discovered that he liked milk pudding. One evening after dinner I opened a tin of creamed tapioca as a dessert for myself, since Catherine was enduring a self-imposed dieting regime. Once Carlos spied me eating the pudding he began to pester me for a taste. Assuming that Catherine's attention was elsewhere I poured a small spoonful on to a paper napkin for him to sample. Then two things happened at the same time. First, Catherine spotted what I had done in defiance of her right and proper ruling that cats were not to be fed at the table and I was subjected to a harsh reprimand. Second, Carlos consumed, in rapid time, not only the spoonful but also the part of the napkin on which it had lain. This feat reminded me again of Toby Jug, who also loved puddings, only in his case it was baby-food tins of chocolate pudding.

From that time on tapioca became a preferred culinary delight for Carlos, though he refused rice pudding and wouldn't touch semolina. For him it was obviously a matter of taste. In case he would felt left out and became jealous through sibling rivalry, a portion of tapioca was offered to Pablo. He sniffed it derisively then walked away with an expression which in plain cat language said: 'You can't expect me to eat that muck. Don't you know I'm a meat-eating cat exclusively?'

From then on the dry biscuit meals for Carlos were supplemented at intervals with a small portion of tapioca milk pudding, which caused me to reflect on the lengths to which I would go to please and care for our cats. Indeed, in so many ways life makes us hostage to the ones we love no matter who and what they are.

The emergence of other traits of personality which distinguished Carlos from other cats was epitomized by little incidents that occurred daily. When taking together all the facets and quirks of his behaviour, including his hyperactive approach to life, there was little doubt that he was a remarkable cat and that we had in our home a champion of the feline variety.

Carlos loved to play. He needed no prompting to race around the garden after me as I towed a length of plastic wrapping cord across the grass, though he found it too easy to catch me and so would attempt to rouse Pablo in a game of chase. One calm and sunny evening in May, Catherine and I were relaxing in the garden when we witnessed Carlos approaching Pablo, who was lying in the grass thinking cat things and doing nothing in particular. Carlos assumed an exaggerated side-on pose and pranced towards Pablo, who simply stared at him as if he considered this behaviour idiotic. Frustrated beyond bearing with the big cat, Carlos resorted to aggression and swiped Pablo across the face before racing off. When Pablo, looking dumbfounded, still didn't respond, Carlos charged him and a rousing chase and fight ensued with both cats running to and fro, accompanied by some squealing from Carlos as the larger, heavier cat sought to teach him a lesson. Eventually, the two cats lay down in the grass exhausted. But this incident made me realize that the over-the-top enthusiasm of Carlos did not gel with Pablo's more matter-of-fact, sober approach to living. We discussed the situation as we saw it and the upshot was that I determined to phone Jane, the Maine Coon breeder, the following day to order a new kitten to give Carlos a playmate. If I could acquire another cat of similar temperament to Carlos, but not excessively so, then it might satisfy his need to play and lift the onus from Pablo.

'I hope you know what you're doing,' my wife said.

'Well, he needs a companion something like himself so I'll see if Jane has any more silver boys on the way.'

'I just hope another silver kitten won't be as crazy as Carlos,' Catherine said.

'Don't worry. There couldn't be another the same as he is!' said I hopefully.

The next day Jane told me over the phone that her silver female called Florence had been mated again with Oscar, the six-times champion cat who had a formidable reputation as a stud and, incidentally, was the father of Carlos. I confirmed an order at once for a male, silver Maine Coon kitten. I had hopes that the new kitten would prove to be an appropriate playmate for Carlos, who, I could often see, became easily bored and frustrated with life.

This decision was to prove more propitious than we could ever have imagined at the time, but for the present life proceeded at the steady uneventful pace of ordinary living except for an extraordinary feat of heroism by Carlos which served to endorse our already developing love for him. The incident happened on one fine summer evening when Catherine and I were relaxing in the garden, enjoying the warm sunlight. We were sitting in the gazebo at the top end of the garden. The weather over the period of the previous two weeks had been extremely hot with little or no wind, a rare condition for the far north-east.

It had become noticeable how insect activity had intensified to the point where we were becoming increasingly wary of wasps, though we had not anticipated large hornets, which inflict a lethal sting for anyone allergic to their poison. Suddenly, a monster black-and-yellow banded hornet appeared and mounted a determined assault on Catherine. It might have been attracted to the scent of soap or perfume on her skin but whatever the cause it had her trapped in the corner of the shelter from which she could not easily escape. Our flapping hands did nothing to dissuade its attack and it began to buzz ominously. All at once, when the offending hornet was barely inches away from her face, a silver streak erupted on to the scene and knocked it to the ground. It was Carlos to the rescue and he now proceeded to whack the disabled insect until it was dead. We were at once relieved and amazed. We had not been aware of Carlos in the proximity – it was just as if he came from nowhere.

Catherine picked him up and gave him a loving hug in gratitude and carried him into the house to give him a treat. Later that evening, as we reflected on his heroism, we elected to award a special medal for him and determined that it should be nothing less than the Owl Cottage Victoria Cross for Cats.

'Do you think he'll understand?' Catherine asked.

'If he could understand that you were in danger and chose to intervene to save you from a very nasty sting then I think he will understand only too well. After all, Maine Coon cats are noted for their intelligence and loyalty to their adopted family. Anyhow, you said he was a commando and that's what commandos do!' I said, praising him.

The next morning Catherine removed his neck collar and sewed a silver star button to it which she had taken from her jewellery box. We arranged to have a special ceremony in the garden in the afternoon, when we would award the medal to Carlos, together with some special teatime treats. Although I know some people would view our actions as being the height of daftness I was aware from my reading that there had been many recorded deeds of heroism by animals, some by cats, which had contributed to saving the lives of humans and we were not going to deny Carlos a well-deserved meritorious award for his bravery.

Catherine concocted an award meal consisting of cold pheasant and turkey. It fell to me to articulate the award ceremony and it amused me to see the look of bemusement on the face of Carlos as I called him to me and the citation was read out to him. I hung his collar with the medal attached around his neck and kissed him on both cheeks as the ritual demanded. Meanwhile, the leonine face of Pablo peeped out from underneath a nearby bush, curious as to what all the fuss was about. Both cats showed no hesitation when presented with the meal, although Carlos only ate half of his and whined for biscuits, which I hurriedly acquired for him. Pablo, ravenous as usual, cleaned off both dishes. The evening ended on a most propitious note and we all retired happily to the cottage.

Good news arrived the next day with a call from Jane to say that her she-cat Florence had given birth overnight to a litter of six healthy kittens, which included a stunningly marked silver grey, the diminutive picture of his dad Oscar, who was mine for the asking. I rang her immediately to claim the kitten and to convey my congratulations to Florence.

Meanwhile, Carlos was showing a much more controlled and disciplined attitude to life and was less inclined to 'rush in where Angels fear to tread', as the saying goes. I was often pleased to see him, whenever we were off on one of our field excursions, wanting to rush away in a particular direction because of something that had aroused his attention. Previously, on occasions such as this, when the mood took him he would tug forwards with such force that I would almost fall over and he would suffer a fit of coughing because the harness had constricted his chest. But now, after all his training, I was glad to see that when he became excited he would turn and look back at me and whine as if he was asking permission. Usually I would say OK and he would lead me to towards whatever interesting scent or sight had attracted his attention.

He showed many other characteristics which were unique to his personality, two of which always made me laugh. Sometimes at the weekend when Catherine drove away on an early shopping expedition, I would allow Carlos to sit on the table near me while I ate a late breakfast. This was a special treat for both of us because I loved his company and it was a secret to be shared between us, a sort of buddy male pact. During this breakfast ritual I would enjoy offering him tasty bits of bacon and sausage. Then Carlos would interact with me in a playful and humorous way. He would lie full length with his face pointing towards me and pretend to be sleeping, only I could detect that he was peeping through his eye slits. Then when he believed I wasn't watching he would slowly extend a paw surreptitiously towards my plate. I would join in this game by permitting him to grab a morsel of bacon, which he would draw back towards him and eat still with his eyes closed. When he tried it again I would give the intrusive paw a rejecting tap. And at this his eyes would jerk open and if a cat could smile he smiled with me. It was fun for both of us.

Then there were times when I would be sequestered in the bathroom of a morning. While carrying out my ablutions, my attention would be drawn to a slight noise by the door. The first time it happened I watched in amazement as a paw covered in silver fur sneaked slyly through the gap under the door and groped around as if it could somehow gain entry. This was Carlos playing another game with me; he was letting me know that he knew I was in there and whatever was going on he wanted to be part of it. Also I believed he was trying to amuse me.

Another fun game we played was when I would suddenly make a dash at him while he was strolling along the hall. Instantly, he would respond in kind and make a mad dash upstairs then turn at the top, staring down at me with ears pricked. If I then ran away in mock fear to the conservatory he would hurtle down and chase me; then I would turn and charge at him again and the game would be repeated. I know it sounds juvenile but we both enjoyed such playtime romps.

He loved playing games with Pablo, usually of the chasing

kind, if the big cat was in the mood. If no one was available to have a play with him he would set about amusing himself and so would give an entertaining display of jumping and pouncing on stray leaves blowing in the wind or a fragment of twig dropped from a tree. I was often drawn away from my writing to watch him from a window, in awe at his capacity for exceptional light-hearted play and gamesmanship. These were memorable moments that I would store forever of a splendid cat called Carlos, of whom I dared ever to say was mine – as if anyone could possess such a free spirit. Unfortunately, our halcyon days were numbered, though neither of us, at that happy time, was to know how it would all tragically end.

The summer had proved to be exceptional and bird life in the garden had flourished, as had the crows nesting in the nearby rookery. I have ambivalent views about the crow family, which includes rooks, ravens, hooded crows and magpies. I know that they serve a useful purpose by disposing of carrion and lots of bugs that inhabit the rural landscape. I also know that they function as an intelligent community from the stories I've heard from farmers and gamekeepers who have told me of crows gathering to punish one of their group who has committed an offence in their colony. Recently, I read in the newspapers of magpies assembling to mourn one of their flock, but I did not credit the crows I see every day with profound emotional attributes until one summer when I witnessed the following incident.

I had observed a man in our community who waged a war

with his shotgun against wildlife in our area. He shot rabbits and hares, and he especially liked to shoot at crows. His killing sprees made me fear for our cats and indeed all cats in the vicinity. I had confronted him once in a field not far from our garden and I warned him about shooting indiscriminately. The more I witnessed this man's activities, the more I grew to dislike him.

One day I heard shotgun bursts coming from the rookery area and I observed the rooks detaching a squadron to circle above the shooter and vent their fury at his intrusions. I spotted him skulking away after failing to kill any of them. Crows are very clever and it is extremely difficult to surprise and kill any of them. But some people fire at their prominent nests built in the tops of the tallest trees in order to destroy the eggs.

It is often my pleasure to watch from our garden what is happening in the district. On a summer morning in June I caught sight of a female crow making an unearthly din from the copse of trees near the front of our cottage. When I investigated I found a huge male crow lying dead on the roadside. It was her mate and he had been shot. I guessed what had happened because in the competition for nesting sites this couple had built their nest in a medium-sized tree overlooking the road, affording the shooter an easy target. I was so angry that I printed notices from my computer declaring this area off bounds to shooting and then telephoned the police about the dangers of shooting near occupied areas, warning them about the man in the village who was the perpetrator.

Sometime later I saw that the lone female crow had reared a chick. She had probably only laid one fertile egg because her mate had been shot before they had got fully going with their mating. It intrigued me as I watched to see how she fussed and fostered the chick. It delighted me each day to observe how mother and son were always close together and often roosted on trees in our garden. She seemed so proud of him and he prospered under the lavish care he was receiving. In the evenings, because the nest was so close to our garden, I could hear their comfort calls as they settled down for the night. One morning I again found the mother crow in great distress and I didn't have to look far to find why. I found her son's body in the back garden. He had probably been shot as he left the nest to follow his mother, who often traversed our garden on her flight path to the farmer's field. I was in a rage and the next time I encountered the man whom I knew was responsible, I berated him angrily and told him that I would report him by name and address to the police.

Meanwhile, as I gathered up the body of the young crow I was impressed by his sleek black feathers, testament to his mother's loving care. She watched me from a nearby branch as I placed his body in the cleft of one of our trees and left her to privately mourn her son. She never left his body for five days and she stroked him with her beak and head, and cried piteously over him as I watched from an upstairs window. Then I decided enough was enough and buried his body in our garden because I could bear her sadness no longer. She watched me as I buried him and, job finished, I called out to her, telling her to make a new life. The next day she'd gone and I never saw her alive again.

It rained heavily in early July and after a few days of torrential downpours our conservatory began to leak. Later that week, during a dry spell, I summoned a builder to do repairs. He only needed a short time to find the cause of our leak. He called me outside to show me the dead body of a crow which had blocked the gutter on the roof, causing a flooding down the wall at the side of the conservatory. I recognized the body at once: it was the bereaved mother crow. Her body was emaciated, as if she'd starved to death. Catherine came out to see what was happening and I showed her the crow's remains.

'What's that?' she said.

'It's the mother crow that I told you about. Look at how emaciated her body is. She must have starved to death because she was pining over the death of her son. Somebody shot him and I watched her as she mourned him. This bird died of a broken heart. Amazing, isn't it? A bird feeling emotional sentiments comparable to humans. What will the cynics say now?'

All my life I have struggled to make people aware of the complexity of nature and how human beings drastically underestimate the abilities and skills of the wild creatures living around us. Since I was a boy, freely wandering the riverbanks and woods, I have become ever more impressed and enchanted by watching animals going about the business of their daily lives.

Far from being inferior, their capacity to cope with the exigencies of life far outweighs those of some of their human counterparts. In this respect I am constantly overcome with admiration for the qualities shown by cats in their relationships with people as well as the environment.

As June gave way to the promise of a hot July there was much excitement in the cottage because an important birthday was looming. On the 6th of July Carlos would be one year old and what a year it had been. We always celebrate the birthdays of our cats to show how much we love and care for them. I did it for Toby Jug and with our new Maine Coon cats, Pablo and Carlos. We intended to continue the tradition and establish birthday celebrations as an Owl Cottage custom. The day turned out to be fine and sunny with not a cloud in the sky and only a soft breeze slightly stirring the leaves of our trees. Carlos was enthralled to be the centre of attention and rejoiced with mad dashes across the lawns and the feverish scratching of tree trunks. To climax his display he showed how competent he had become in catching and returning small rubber balls we threw for him. Whilst all this activity was proceeding Pablo kept a watchful if sleepy-eyed view of the ceremonies from a thick branch of the old ash tree next to the barbeque area so that he could check what was cooking.

As we all gradually grew tired of playing in the hot sunshine it was, thankfully, time for the birthday tea. We had carefully prepared small pieces from our own barbequed food to entice

Carlos to eat meat. We didn't need to encourage Pablo as he was always up and ready for any meat dish. Catherine was having chicken breast and my preference was a thick sirloin steak. Carlos sniffed at the meat morsels and made a stab at eating some steak, but quickly abandoned the food on offer and stared expectantly at me.

'He's after biscuits,' Catherine said with a sigh because of the worries about his diet.

'I'll get him some,' I said resignedly.

'You spoil him,' she said. Then she burst out laughing because Pablo had jumped down to eat the morsels refused by Carlos. Meanwhile, Carlos was provided with a bowl of the best dry food biscuits we could buy and, as a special treat, a saucerful of tapioca pudding. Later, whilst we washed down our meal with a mug of coffee followed by a glass of wine, the cats retired to a garden bench and engaged in assiduous ablutions by means of prolonged tongue-washes. The day had given us a rare taste of hot summer without a cloud in the sky and now that it was drawing to a close a faintly cooling breeze was most welcome.

The fading sunlight cast golden rays across the freshly mown lawn, irradiating the grass with myriad shades of green and yellow, and as the daylight succumbed to the orange and red glow of sunset we all trooped wearily indoors to relax. It had been a grand day.

It proved to be an excellent week for weather, with sunshine and blue skies. We took advantage of it to carry out some essential gardening tasks. The two cats did their own thing except that Carlos seemed to know whenever I went into the greenhouse because he felt obliged to join me and scrutinize my efforts at pruning the tomato plants. He also liked me to talk to him and he would listen from a reclining position on the potting bench with eyes wide open as if not to miss a single word of my many tales of cats and wild country places.

Outside in the garden the swallows were busy in a frenzy of nest-repairing and mating and, no doubt, we would soon be greeted each morning with the excited calls of nestlings hungry for the next feed. When this time came we needed to warn callers at our front door that there was a swallow family living just above their heads high in the canopy and they could be very aggressive with visitors intruding into their space. Our postman was most at risk because his bald head had to run the gauntlet of their offensive swoops each morning as he delivered the mail. On days when we were at home we felt compelled to offer him the protection of an umbrella and I did promise him a sample of my tomatoes when they ripened as a palliative for his suffering.

Meanwhile, at the back of the cottage the house martins had almost completed their rugby-ball shaped nest of mud and spittle under the overhanging roof outside the window of the spare bedroom. Furthermore, blackbirds had invaded and occupied the ivy-covered wall adjacent to the conservatory, though it was the impudence of a pair of ring doves who had woven their nest into the Sky satellite dish that gave the most cause for amazement. The cats viewed this encroachment of the feathered brethren into our garden territory with steely eyed hostility but had long given up trying to catch the swallows as they swooped and dived in their aerial acrobatics as they took insects on the wing. In the long summer evenings, when we sat in the garden and we witnessed their tireless flights over our heads, I could not avoid thinking, while I listened to their muted calls as they winged their way around, that their vocal outbursts must partly be cries of sheer rapture at the joy of flying.

Saturday morning was golden with the sunshine which had graced every day that week. I had stayed up late to finish some writing so Catherine, who loves to walk through the garden on summer mornings, was first up. Carlos decided to search for me. Suddenly, I was awakened with a start from a deep sleep by a thud on the bed followed by a rasping wet tongue licking my arm and then my face, and finally the sound of loud purring in my ears. Carlos had found me. When he realized I was awake he started pawing the duvet, which was the signal for me to lift it so that he could crawl inside and lie on the sheet against me. As soon as he was between the bedclothes he nestled closer to me and eventually settled on my chest. I was half asleep but felt comforted by his presence so near to me. I decided to doze a while longer. Having completed all his positional manoeuvres he laid his head just below my chin, a mandatory invitation to me to stroke his head, which I duly did even though I was not quite fully awake yet.

I was surprised but pleased that he had remembered this bedroom ploy of his which he had done regularly as a kitten.

He had seemingly abandoned the practice of late when I was working on ways to bond with him. I savoured this intimately private time with him and was proud that he was maturing into such a wonderful cat, bright as a button with a gleaming coat of silver fur set off by the handsome dark leg rings of the true-bred Maine Coon cat. Had I known in advance what this day would bring I would have locked him away until the time passed but, as it is, I have sealed the memory of that morning's togetherness deep in my heart where it lives anew each time I think of him. Not a day passes but for a stray thought that takes me back to my time with Carlos.

We came downstairs and he sat by my chair as I ate a quick breakfast of tea and toast, since we were due to go shopping later that morning. As I showered, shaved and dressed, he sat on the laundry basket to keep me company. Then, as Catherine drove the car out from the garage, I opened the patio door to let Carlos out. It was the last time I saw him alive.

After we had done the shopping we broke for a light lunch at a small restaurant just by the back of the Alnwick Castle walls. It was early afternoon when we arrived home and, after unpacking the shopping, I strolled into the hallway to collect the post. Picking up the letters I noticed a handwritten note lying off to one side. 'Please call round when you get back. I need to show you something.' The note was signed by Julie, our neighbour.

I hastened round to her house to find out what the mystery could be. She spotted my approach and met me by her garage door, which was open. I looked at her and saw that she wore a markedly serious expression so different from her usual smiling greetings and I immediately became worried.

She said, 'I hope I'm wrong but I was walking up the bank with Jane and Clare when we discovered the body of a cat lying in the road. I do hope it isn't yours. It's in the garage.' She spoke quietly as if afraid of what I might find. In a quick movement she opened the garage door wider.

At her words my stomach constricted and my heart began beating wildly as I had an immediate premonition of tragedy. Sure enough, in the bright light from the open door, I saw the body of Carlos, curled unnaturally in the terrible pain of his death throes, lying on Julie's shovel. Feeling an icy dread beyond description, I somehow found the words to thank Julie for recovering his body from the road before the traffic squashed him into something unrecognizable. I picked him up and, cradling his body in my arms, I fled back home and went immediately to the greenhouse where I sat holding his dead body to my chest. I wept and in the weeping I could hear someone making anguished moans until I realized they were coming from me. Eventually, I became aware of Catherine standing in the doorway of the greenhouse. Her face was covered in tears but she tried to help me, knowing how close I had been to Carlos.

'Julie told me about Carlos. Your sweater is covered in blood. Shouldn't we bury him? Come on, Denis. We can't do anything more for him now.'

I heard her as if from a long distance away. I had retreated into a dimension of denial from which I was not prepared to resurface for some time. In my mind I was with Carlos, alive. At last I gave way to Catherine's gentle prodding and reluctantly carried his body to the place where he used to lie in the upper garden and Catherine followed me, carrying my garden spade. I told her to go and get my dark, nearly new fleece from the cupboard upstairs. This was what I had worn when Carlos and I did some of our later excursions together and I remember how he loved to cuddle into its warmth when I held him after our walks back to the car. I wrapped his still beautiful body in my fleece and began to dig his grave. It was as if I was sleepwalking. I can hardly remember the burial except that Pablo was there making hollow-sounding cries that became yowls, and I believe we cried over Carlos together. Before I filled in the grave, from my right wrist I unfastened the silver bracelet which Carlos had loved to grapple with and chew. I dropped it in his grave as a goodbye token of affection from me.

Pablo joined me and together we mourned Carlos at the side of his grave. Pablo whimpered and pawed the grass above the grave and looked up at me in incomprehension.

'I know,' I said to him. 'My heart is broken too; yet again.'

Later I brought a garden chair over to his grave site and mounted a vigil, despite Catherine's protestations. I was still suffering the shock of disbelief and although I had buried him and knew that he was in the grave in front of me, I kept glancing round expecting him to appear. The time passed very quickly and soon the daylight was gone and a pale half-moon appeared.

In the clear night sky, Catherine came out to where I was sitting and tried again to persuade me to come back inside the cottage. I explained that I could not abandon him to the cold ground and the darkness. His spirit would be confused and worried as he'd obviously been killed instantly. If his spirit knew that I was near it would comfort him until he was taken care of.

'I know he loved me and I cannot desert him,' I said with a sob in my voice. I realized that she was also upset at his death but she could handle it better than I could. After all, he had been very much my cat and we had been through a lot together. I missed him and always would. As a testament to this sentiment I carry to this day a photograph of him in my wallet. Sometime later, Catherine brought me a large glass of brandy and a thick blanket and then Pablo, with a soulful look at me, followed her back to the cottage.

Meanwhile, as I sipped the brandy and hugged the blanket for warmth, I viewed in my mind's eye the many memories of my times with Carlos and I softly spoke a message for him to the night sky, trusting that in some way the night would communicate it, telling him that I prayed his spirit would soon find peace and that nothing would ever stop me loving him.

As the first red streaks of the new day dawned Catherine came out in her nightwear and slippers and led me inside. I could not bear to go to bed and simply dozed in an armchair by the fireside. With the death of Carlos something had died within me also. A host of precious feelings had vanished and it reminded me how I had suffered at the death of Toby Jug.

For solace I turned inevitably to music as a balm for my feelings and selected a piece by Maurice Ravel, 'Pavane pour une infante défunte' ('Lament for a deceased princess'), as being the most appropriate, despite being for the wrong gender. After which Mahler and Wagner served to ease my heart somewhat during that first morning without Carlos' company. I found that I couldn't eat and just drank one cup of tea after another while staring out into the garden.

The days that followed the death of Carlos were unbearable for both of us and it was Catherine who suggested that we should plan to get away from the cottage, where everything reminded us of him, and fill our minds with new experiences such as visiting National Trust properties and the like. This strategy worked to a large extent but it would take a long time before I could think of Carlos without feeling pangs of anguish and hurt. Curiously, in the days that followed, both Catherine and I had dreams in which Carlos appeared to us as we had known him in happier times. After the dreams we each remarked how we had felt comforted. A week after I had buried Carlos I visited a builder's yard and selected a large grey stone scored with streaks of silver, which I placed on his grave. On the topside of the stone I scratched his name and dates. He had lived just one year and six days, but in that time he had made his mark and it was for me an unforgettable legacy of high spirits and humorous affection. Catherine and I visited a local garden centre and chose a hybrid tea rose to plant on his grave. It was purple with white and pink flecks of colour. It blooms with abundance each summer and serves as an annual reminder of his beautiful spirit.

LUIS

Now I had to address the problem of whether to accept the silver male kitten which I had ordered to be a playmate for Carlos. I could never ever replace Carlos and it would be folly to try but I now desperately needed a kitten to replace the emotional gap left by his death. Pablo was a fine, loving animal but he had his own, wild-wandering agenda. Perhaps a new little Maine Coon from the same sire and she-cat would have some of the spark and appearance which would remind me favourably of Carlos and console me for his loss.

'I'll know whether I want him when I see him,' I told Catherine as we drove down to Jane's house to meet the new kitten. It turned out to be a much better experience than I had expected. When we arrived Jane was outside, tending her garden. She immediately commiserated with us about the loss of Carlos but then made some interesting comments. She remarked that Carlos had inherited too much of the 'wild side' of cat nature not to act recklessly and to gamble once too often with his life. We met old cat friends like Hamish and Rory, who had matured but did not seem to have aged at all, a testament to Jane's love and care for them.

Becoming impatient I blurted out, 'Well, where is he, then?'

Jane gave me a hard look that was nearly an admonishment.

'You must understand he's no Carlos, but he's one of the handsomest kittens I've ever seen and he's a real little gentleman,' she said, smiling. 'Why don't you go and find him for yourself. He's in there somewhere but you'll need to be polite to him because he's very aristocratic, a real pedigree Maine Coon in more ways than one!'

As instructed I searched the downstairs rooms and came across two dark-grey kittens running about but intuitively knew that neither one was him. I had just begun to climb the stairs when I realized that I'd found him. Sitting upright on a stair looking down at me, with an adopted regal pose that belied his size, was a proud-looking little fellow with azure blue eyes. His gaze settled on me and mine on him and I believe that I was the one most impressed. He possessed that uncanny bearing that some cats have which can make a person feel inferior. In appearance he had a startlingly light-coloured chest. Its curly, silver-white fur gave him the distinctive air of a cavalier such as in oil paintings of the courtiers to King Charles II. The rest of his body was covered in thick silver fur and his bushy tail could have featured in a work of art. I admired his appearance but it was his stance and demeanour that spoke of the genuine thoroughbred strain of the nobility of Maine Coon lineage. Immediately, I was aware of the accuracy of Jane's description. He was exceptional – a fine little gentleman indeed.

As I picked him up he uttered a weeny cry, as if I should have first asked his permission.

'Oh, pardon me, your majesty,' I said to this baby prince. 'But you see we are destined to share life together and I promise to show due care and devotion to you.'

I carried the tiny mite into the garden with me and sat on a rustic garden seat at the far end with him cradled on my chest. In a way that only an animal can accomplish, his close presence began at once to ease and soothe the hurt I was feeling. I stroked his tiny head and body, and spoke to him gently about how I thought our life together might be, how I would take him for walks when he learned to wear a harness and lead, and how he would come with me in the car. Then he did a most extraordinary thing. He was facing away from me but instead of turning to look at me he bent his head back and viewed me from what was for him an upside-down angle. This move astonished me because it was exactly how Carlos had often looked back at me. No other cat I had known had ever done this and I felt that it was a good omen for our future. This kitten was destined to be with us.

I could see that my wife was in earnest conversation with Jane at the bottom of the garden, but she was keenly watching and had missed nothing of my interactions with the kitten.

'Well, your highness,' I said to him, 'please accept me as your loyal guardian and soon you will be welcome to share our wonderful cottage home.'

I needed him and would do my level best to protect him in ways which I was already thinking about, and which I should have done for Carlos. After a brief discussion in the car on the route home we decided to call him Luis, the Spanish form of Louis, in keeping with the Spanish names of the other cats. I also had in mind to pay a token of respect to the memory of the tragic French queen Marie Antoinette, without whose interest in breeding and decision to transport her cats to America Maine Coon cats would never have existed.

At this point I feel the need to express something regarding the sentiments that I hold regarding cats as well as other animals, which I'm sure are shared by many other animal lovers. When I relate to a cat, dog or a horse, for example, I am looking for what kind of personality the animal possesses and then I want to find out whether it is compatible with mine, just as I do when I meet a stranger. When an animal becomes my friend then I will treat it with the affection, respect and courtesy I extend to human friends. It is therefore abhorrent for me to hear other people judge my feelings towards my cats as ridiculously sentimental and out of proportion. As someone remarked to me when I recounted the death of Carlos, 'Well, he was only a damned cat, after all.' This statement implies that animals are not worthy, nor are they capable of sentiments such as love and caring, but the evidence from individuals who share their lives with animals overwhelmingly suggests otherwise.

I am aware that there is an entrenched attitude held by many throughout the world who evaluate animal life only in terms of its usefulness to humankind and who treat cats as vermin. Once I lectured to an industrial conference in Benidorm, Spain, and it was there that I encountered the latter. It was in the early hours of the morning as I went for a walk to clear my head after too much wining and dining that I heard gunshots. Curious, I investigated, and imagine my surprise followed by anger as I rounded a cove on the beach to find two police officers using the local feral cat population for pistol practice. A 9 mm bullet does not leave much of a cat's body intact and these officers were enjoying their sport. Incensed, I called on them to stop as I could hear the cries of wounded cats. One of the moustach-ioed officers confronted me with his pistol pointing towards me and barked in Spanish: 'Get lost. Do not interfere or it will be the worse for you.'

The next morning at breakfast I told the others of my encounter and was later informed by a member of the hotel staff that such shootings were commonplace, not only with cats, but with stray dogs, too.

'No one objects because these animals are a nuisance and a health hazard,' he said.

'Surely a more humane approach is needed,' I suggested. At this he shrugged his shoulders and commented that humane approaches cost money which the authorities do not seem to have.

As the weeks passed after the loss of Carlos I grew impatient to have Luis and so I pestered Jane to allow me to bring him home as soon as possible. Eventually, she acceded to my insistence and said that I could have him the week earlier as long as I brought him back for his final batch of injections.

It was wonderful to have a silver kitten in the cottage again and Luis's presence started a healing process both for Catherine and for me. He was a delight to have with us and we played the usual kitten games with him, dangling strings with bits of paper attached for him to jump at, but there was a marked difference in his behaviour from other cats we had lived with. For one thing he was so self-assured and independent-minded even at the age of twelve weeks. He was dignified to the point of appearing haughty. He gave me the impression that he was well aware that the Ancient Egyptians had venerated cats as gods and, indeed, believed the practice should be reinstated. I marvelled at his regal posture and worried that the way he looked denoted such a sense of superiority that I would never be able to get really close to him. The established *modus operandi* in his opinion seemed to be that we belonged to him rather than the other way around. I gathered that he had made up his mind to adopt us but only so long as he remained the Little Master.

'We'll have to see about that,' I thought, but then I have always believed all cats, even as kittens, come into this world with readymade agendas. Their willingness to modify their plans depends upon with whom they strike up a relationship. I would need to gently go to work on Luis as soon as possible or else I could envisage him becoming one of those lap-cats who take on the aloof disposition of a martinet who rules the roost – that would not permit of a fun, loving bond with a person. I was aware that some such situations had occurred with high-born thoroughbred cats, dogs and horses, perhaps through the emotionally negligent attitudes of the owners towards these animals, and I was determined not to allow this to happen with Luis or we would end up being treated as his servants. I was to learn more about this side to Luis' personality when we returned to Jane's home for his final injections.

We arrived early and Jane invited us to have some tea. Meanwhile, Luis was turned loose to rejoin the other five kittens in his litter. As usual Hamish came to inspect us but now that he knew us he was quite satisfied with just a cursory sniff at our shoes. Whilst Catherine and Jane chattered I watched the kittens. Seemingly the other kittens from the litter recognized Luis at once and treated him as something of a celebrity, which suited his ego no end. They gathered around him and gave him a good sniff all over, which was their way of saying: 'Where have you been these past ten days and what have you been doing?' After a while some of the kittens began to give him a tongue-wash, especially over his head and neck. I was intrigued to watch this behaviour because, whilst having this beauty treatment lavished upon him, he literally lorded it over the other kittens and adopted a pose which I can only describe as the 'Little Monarch'. The surprising thing about it was that the others seemed to accept Luis as their sibling superior.

Finally, it was time for Jane to take the litter down to the vet's for their final injections. The kittens were bundled into a secure carrying box and off she went in her car, accompanied by Catherine, while I stayed behind to 'hold the fort'. Soon I was surrounded by the mature cats of the household and I paid especial attention to Florence, Luis' mother, a beautiful silver she-cat who eagerly devoured some of the cat biscuit treats I always carry in my pocket. Then Hamish, the huge sable and brown tabby, the alpha male, ambled over to enjoy a handful. By this time the gang from the vet's arrived back in the midst of a drenching downpour and for a time there was a deal of fussing and disturbance until the adults dried off and the hungry kittens were released for a light supper.

We said our goodbyes and Jane told us to bring the car near to the gate and she would carry Luis out to us. It had grown dark outside and the pelting rain forced us to make a mad dash for our car, which I had parked further down the street. As I drove up the car headlights picked out Jane standing by her garden gate, a raincoat over her head and holding a wriggling kitten in her arms. Catherine opened her side window and took hold of the kitten from Jane. Then we were off homewards with the windscreen wipers on full power. In the faint light from the dashboard I kept shooting sideways glances at the kitten on Catherine's knee and I became increasingly disturbed. I could not recognize the kitten as Luis; as far as I could see it did not have such a light breast and there were no racoon-like dark rings on its front legs, which were a distinct feature on Luis. Convinced we had the wrong kitten I stopped the car and put on the interior light. Then, removing the kitten from Catherine's lap, I held it up for a closer examination. At this intrusion the kitten, which must have been afraid anyway, went berserk and raked my bare arm with its claws, drawing blood. I set it down and turning to Catherine said, 'This is not our kitten; I'm going back.'

'Are you really sure?' she said.

'Positive.'

Reversing the car I arrived back at Jane's house, where she was most surprised to see me.

'You gave us the wrong kitten; go out to the car and see for yourself,' I said, marching indoors. I looked around and began calling his name loudly. At once three kittens charged towards me with Luis in the centre. I picked him up and made sure that it was definitely him. All these kittens were due to go to their new homes on the morrow and if I took the wrong kitten home I would never see Luis again.

Just then Jane rushed in. 'The kitten in the car is definitely yours, Denis,' she cried.

'No, Jane, this is my Luis,' I said adamantly, holding him up for her to see.

'Oh!' she exclaimed. 'I must have given you the "she".'

'You'd better go and get her because she's not at all fond of me.' And here I proffered my scratched and bloodied arm for her to see. Of course, I did not blame the kitten. She must have been terrified at being taken away in the dark and manhandled by me, someone she didn't even know.

Jane soon returned, having retrieved the other kitten from the car. 'Sorry!' she murmured.

'Well, it's alright now,' I said, heading out to the car with Luis in my arms, feeling angry but vindicated.

The rest of the journey home was uneventful except for the atrocious weather. This time Luis sat on my knee and kept raising his head to look up at me as if to say, 'Why did you leave me and did you know my two brothers wanted to come as well?' I chuckled at my fanciful imaginings and found that my anger had totally dissipated.

Soon life at the cottage settled into tranquil bliss once more and my energies were focused on habituating Luis to our way of life. The heartache of the recent tragedy would never be forgotten but through time would be filed away in that special inner mind that helps us to cope with sorrows that would otherwise drive us mad.

During this time I was thinking carefully of what I could do to avoid losing Luis in the precipitous way that Carlos had died. Eventually, we decided that we had a large enough garden to build a compound wherein Luis and any other cats we acquired would be safe from killer traffic and yet be free to roam around trees and bushes in a limited area. Of course, I intended to train Luis to walk wearing a harness and lead like Carlos had done and would take him on excursions into the wilds of Northumberland. He would also spend an appreciable amount of time with us in the house. This was the best compromise I could think of to keep my cat safe and it matched the expressed current wisdom on keeping thoroughbred cats of any species.

To this end I contacted a man called Alan who worked as a carpenter for the Estates Office of the Duke of Northumberland. At that time he was a member of the team building a massive treehouse feature which was to enclose a restaurant in the

Alnwick Gardens Complex being developed by the Duchess of Northumberland. Alan proved to be a very great help and built a large square enclosure in the upper part of the garden, shielded by trees. Inside, the compound had high runs, balconies and shelves from which a cat could survey the world around him and feel part of the natural environment. A mature lilac and a bamboo tree, together with the grave of Carlos and his rosebush, were enclosed by the walls made from wood and chicken wire. High up in a roofed alcove, Alan built a long shelf which was protected from the weather. In this area I placed two large wooden hutches, one lying on top of the other. These had both indoor and outdoor compartments and were filled with cushion-beds and warm blankets to equip the facility with protection in cold weather. There was an outer and inner door for security and to prevent escape at our comings and goings with food and water.

All together it proved to be the ideal solution of where to house the cats when they were not with us in the cottage. It also afforded the cats with an exercise area and somewhere from which to view the garden and avail themselves of some fresh air in addition to their walks with us. It would provide a place of interest for Luis and we could also put Pablo inside as a precautionary measure to stop him wandering abroad and being at risk during the day, since he preferred that we let him out at night.

Now that the compound was built I could turn my attention to studying and befriending Luis. He really was a most interesting and adorable little fellow, entirely different from other cats I had known. Much in keeping with his aura of royalty, he was more than normally fastidious about his appearance, always tongue-washing and preening himself; he was also fussy about where he lay or sat. He preferred perfect conditions wherever possible and liked to sit on our chairs rather than the cushion-beds that we provided for him that smelled of the other cats who had used them.

My attempts to introduce him to wearing a harness and walking on a lead as early as feasible illustrated this aspect of his character. Pablo and Carlos had at first belligerently objected to wearing a harness. But not Luis. He stoically suffered the fitting around his body of the straps in dignified silence and trotted around the garden as if he had been born to it, almost as if it was beneath his high breeding to create a fuss. In this respect he reminded me of Toby Jug, who never fussed about wearing a harness and walking on a lead whenever I decided that it was necessary for his safety. It was at this point that I really began to be impressed by Luis and decided that this kitten was worthy of admiration.

As time passed we grew to know our new kitten better and to appreciate some of his foibles. For example, one day Catherine took him for an introductory walk around our garden with me trailing behind. Earlier in the day there had been a light shower and the ground was still damp. Luis did not like this at all and kept stopping to raise his paws and hind feet to shake off the moisture. When the walk reached the shelter of the gazebo

Catherine was astonished to observe Luis doing the exact same thing as Carlos had done in similar circumstances. He shook his paws, licked them clean and climbed on to the instep of Catherine's shoe so that none of his feet touched the ground, mimicking, just as Carlos had done, the image of the polar bear standing on top of a Fox's Glacier Mint sweet. It made us both laugh and also wonder at the power of the genes to affect behaviour in similar fashion to his half-brother. He then looked up at her and whined his irritation. We wished we'd had a camera to hand as it would have made an amusing picture. Luis' endeavours to remain not only high and dry but regal at all times gave us some hilarious moments, but he would glare at us with annoyance if we laughed at him too openly.

Alongside this princely air that Luis adopted there existed an attribute to his personality which was very reserved; he was a most introverted cat. I sympathized with him totally when I realized that this little cat needed quiet time to himself; he wanted to be alone. He reminded me of myself and he was most unlike Carlos. One morning when I had him on my knee and was quietly talking to him and gently stroking his fur he suddenly broke away and trotted across the room to where a small footstool lay underneath an easy chair. He climbed on to the stool and folded himself into a comfortable position with his front paws tucked under his body in the posture that all cats adopt, which we call 'Little Hen'. With his eyes wide open he sat there as if meditating on cat issues and other things.

I thought about it for a while as I silently studied him and began to understand that Luis craved the opportunity to be by himself as a necessary condition to enable him to cope with the world. This feature of his behaviour was repeated on many occasions over the weeks following his arrival at Owl Cottage, when he would secrete himself away somewhere, preferably dark and quiet, in a cupboard or behind the sofa, somewhere where he wouldn't be disturbed. When he'd had enough of this time on his own he would reappear and join our company. At first I played along with this, not wishing to aggravate him and lose his friendship, but then I began to think that perhaps he was overdoing it and it wasn't healthy for him. Whereas Carlos could rarely bear to sit quietly by himself without intermittently jumping into action, Luis liked attention but he preferred it to be his idea: he would choose the time when he would come to us to be fondled and stroked. His enthusiasm for life was muted and contemplative rather than the gung-ho approach displayed by Carlos.

In view of this I began to think carefully about how I could win his confidence and bond him to me like my other cats, because I needed to have a close relationship with any cat of mine or I didn't feel right. After pondering the situation at some length I made up my mind to employ the simplest tactic, one used for thousands of years as a means of taming and domestic-ating animals: I would feed him by hand. Since I am in the habit of writing late into the night and early morning it is usually Catherine who arises first and feeds the cats. I told her of my plan and asked her not to feed Luis with Pablo but to leave Luis for me. I thought that this would give him time to think and perhaps search me out for a solution.

The very first morning this happened I was awakened by a diminutive figure at my bedside making cries of protestation which I knew only too well from experience with my other cats. He was obviously worried and wanted me to do something about it. I walked downstairs accompanied by a small silver cat in a high state of panic who anxiously paced the kitchen and fretfully circled my feet making hoarse squawks of hunger as I brewed my morning cup of tea. Mug of tea in hand, I pretended to ignore him. His majesty was not accustomed to being treated this way. Seated at the table, having my bowl of cereal, I had to hide a grin as Luis scrambled on to one of the chairs and thence advanced tentatively towards me. Stopping at a respectful distance from my plate he gave me a fraught look that conveyed fully his dissatisfaction with events and he whined to my face.

'Sorry, Your Majesty,' I said, 'but you will have to make a much greater effort to be friendly if you want matters to improve.'

At this point Catherine intervened and stated firmly that she thought that I was tormenting the kitten and she would have nothing to do with it. I patiently explained that I wanted to win him over to become closer to me and to bring out his affectionate side. She looked at me disapprovingly, picked up the kitten and took him away to give him some comfort. But no sooner had she taken him into the study and set him on her lap then I heard her cry out and Luis came scrambling back on to the table and blankly stared at me. I knew that I had read somewhere that it is virtually impossible for a person to outstare a cat but I fixed my eyes on him and stared back. Then he did a surprising thing. He got up and came to me and purred. I then realized that he had shifted into manipulatory mode. I could feel his brain ticking over as he thought how best to relate to me in order to get me to do his bidding, which, after all, is what humans are for, only this one had not got the message. Therefore, he had to think again and try a little tenderness.

I reached out and stroked his elegant head and told him that I wanted us to be good friends. I continued staring at him and kept repeating the words, 'Luis, be my friend!' I knew that cats can pick up thoughts and I hoped the message would get through. Then I cleared away my dishes and left the cottage to go to the greenhouse and tend to my tomato plants. As I walked up the garden path I looked back and saw the figure of Luis gazing out from the conservatory door watching me intently. 'Well,' I said to myself, 'that will give him food for thought.'

Busy with my plants I was surprised to be interrupted by Catherine carrying Luis, whom she plonked on to the bench in front of me. 'He's been crying at the door for you so start making friends in here like you did with Carlos. And go easy on him – he's only a baby.' And with that she stormed out, sliding the door shut and leaving us together. Of course, she was right. There were other less harsh ways to break the ice between myself and an aloof and standoffish cat, as cats are traditionally accustomed to be, but not in my cottage and not with me. However, it often takes a woman to sort things out, so I took the hapless new kitten of mine and cuddled him to my chest and when he started to struggle to be free I continued to hold him until he sighed and just slumped against me. I did not get much work done on my plants but I felt that Luis and I were drawing closer to an understanding. I was seeking to arouse the powerful instinct for survival which is designed to make animals search for food and I wanted him to know that making friends with me was the path towards achieving what he wanted. I knew that very soon Luis would engage his super Maine Coon intelligence and figure out how he could get me to feed him. I desired our relationship to be warm and friendly rather than stroppy and distant.

Deciding that he'd suffered enough I took him with me into the cottage and under the critical eye of Catherine I opened the refrigerator and brought out some cold chicken. Meanwhile, Luis was circling my feet and brushing against my legs affectionately. Obviously he had worked out that I was the one to win over if he wanted to be fed. I lifted him on to the kitchen bench and, cutting slivers of chicken breast as I had done for Carlos, I offered to hand-feed him. He hesitated to take them from my hand. He could smell the chicken and wanted some but was baffled at my refusal to give it to him in the normal way, in his bowl. He looked up at me and whined. I gently encouraged him with soft words and dangled the chicken before him. Gathering his courage he lurched forward and snatched the chicken from my hand.

'Come on Luis, have some more,' I said and over the next few minutes he consumed all the chicken I had prepared for him, even forgetting to back away from me each time I fed him another piece. 'Good boy!' I called to him. When he'd finished he lay down on the floor not far from me and tongue-washed his paws and face and, now and again, shot a furtive glance in my direction, since I purposefully did not move but sat near him.

'Well, it's remarkable what a little psychology can do,' I thought to myself. Finally, I said, addressing him directly, 'I think, Your Highness, together we have made some progress today.' He stared at me for a long moment in the way that cats do when they are thinking hard about something, whereas I could not help being impressed at what a lovely little creature he was with his large bewitching eyes, huge for a kitten, and his coat of fur so strikingly marked in silky silver and grey. After that day's lesson had been learned Luis found no problem with feeding from my hand and to reinforce this behaviour I fed him a variety of cooked meats as well as chicken and departed for a while from the usual tinned cat food. Pablo received the same, his share in the normal way in his bowl. In addition both cats had access to a large bowl of dry biscuits. I continued to feed Luis in this fashion for the next month until I gauged that the intended bonding with Luis had been begun successfully, although there was still some way to go before we could be called friends and normal routine feeding procedures with him could be resumed.

During the hand-feeding period I was startled to be awakened early one morning by a robust small body treading my shoulder with needle-sharp claws. Strangely, it was Luis, come to give me a wake-up call despite the fact, unknown to him, that I had worked at my writing until after 4 a.m. Through half-closed eyes I stroked and welcomed him and then relapsed into a deep sleep. Awakening several hours later I felt a warm lump resting between my arm and my chest; it was Luis curled up against me inside the bedclothes. Immediately to my stupefied brain came the revelation that this cat, like all the others I had known and loved, was somehow making it all right. He wanted to show me that there was no need for extraordinary tactics to affect a relationship and that a cat will decide in its own good time when to bond to a human – that it can not be rushed, especially if it is Maine Coon cat. Of course, an alternative explanation could be that he was looking for a warm comfortable berth and my bed suited his purpose. Probably there was a little of both desires in his action.

There remained moments when I felt that I couldn't get close to him but I kept trying. He was still in the habit of sometimes retiring to his seat on the footstool under the chair. I decided to see if I could reach out to him with friendship at such moments. The tactic I adopted was to lie stretched out on the floor close to him and again sweetly to implore him to 'be my friend.' For a few days he ignored me but eventually he graced my efforts one morning by leaving his stool and coming close to me. He licked my face and began to purr as he rubbed against me and I felt elated that I'd made a breakthrough with him. But strangely he would not let me stroke him then nor when he was eating.

During this initial period of our friendship I made a point of taking him for a walk around the garden on his harness lead, encouraging him to investigate the different plants; this was the time when he showed me another aspect of his personality. He loved flowers. Whenever we came near one of the flower beds so carefully laid out by Catherine, Luis would bury his face, eyes closed in ecstasy, into the flowering blooms. Then he would flip on to his back and roll amongst them, which did not do a great deal for the flowers, though I did not stop him because he was so enjoying himself. After the walks I would leave him for a while shut in the newly erected compound so that he could acquaint himself with the area. He proved to be fond of the bamboo tree growing in there and he liked to hide himself within the dense foliage. I was glad for him that he could feel the breath of the breeze stirring his fur and that he could look out to the trees and the grassed areas and become aware of the massive, clear blue Northumbrian sky that overlooked his green space. I left him there for half-an-hour, then brought him back to the house.

Catherine met us at the door saying, 'I hope you're not going to put him through all those expeditions that Carlos had to suffer.'

In reply I could only say that Carlos gained many benefits from our forays into the countryside at large, which made him a more amenable cat with whom to live. Anyway, no matter how I tried I could not bring Luis to accept travelling in the car. He blankly refused to respond and simply moaned all the time. At that time I thought, 'Oh, for the adaptability of Toby Jug, who proved to be such a superior cat.' Although Luis and I gradually became closer I could never persuade him to retrieve objects thrown for him as Carlos had done. They had looked alike in colouring but they were obviously very different-natured cats.

Then all at once things changed for the better. After all my efforts to develop a close bonding with Luis, it happened. He began to accompany me wherever I went in the cottage and remained near when I was doing even mundane things such as hanging a picture frame or fitting batteries to remote controls or torches. He regarded it as a special treat to join me in my efforts at watercolour painting. He would position himself alongside me and all the equipment, and indicate that he wished to investigate every item that I was using. He did this by means of his nose, sniffing out the scents of both the delectable and the bland with equal concentration. He directed his curiosity to all the utensils I used: the paint blocks, the brushes, pens and watercolour pencils. Then he would explore the array of water jars, sometimes helping himself to a drink and occasionally stirring a jar with a paw, if the water had become coloured by washing brushes, to see if it contained anything interesting. During these painting sessions he would stay beside me, watching keenly my every move, apart from snatching a quick snooze when he felt that matters had reached a boring stage. I talked to him a lot of the time but we savoured the long silences together because, for cats as well as for me, silence is a prerequisite for thinking as well as being a personal indulgence. It felt grand to have his company and I realized with relief that he had finally and wholeheartedly adopted me.

He had learned by now that I favoured the rare times when he would join me in bed in the morning to celebrate the start of a new day together. I would tickle and stroke him and he would lie on his back in ecstasy and wriggle to prompt further attention. He especially liked to be stroked on his forehead and to have his nose rubbed. He was developing into a fun cat to be with and I began to feel for him a semblance of that love and true esteem which I had felt for his half-brother Carlos. What a shameful tragedy it was that I couldn't have enjoyed seeing them alive at the same time. Throughout it all Luis never lost the poise and grand look of being a royal thoroughbred of cats and it was heartening to be accepted as a friend of this noble and courtly feline.

He began to show me in numerous little ways that he appreciated my devotion to him by purring when we met, by licking the back of my hand and by making cat-talk to me, which consisted of a series of soft meows accompanied by much side-rubbings of his body against my shins. It was clear that our attachment was reciprocal. But it is strange to recount that I have never quite got rid of the impression that I am his subject, a sort of equerry, a courtier, although I admit that I have sometimes felt this with my other feline friends. Whilst Luis is a cat like any other cat, only more so, I am aware that befriending a cat is not an easy thing to achieve even though it has always been my aim from childhood onwards to relate in a friendly manner to any cat I might encounter in my travels. In the many houses that I visited as a child I chanced upon many house cats who were there to prevent the incursions of mice but although they were freely given a home to share with the family they were in fact strangers to each other and very few people seemed motivated to improve the status quo. What an opportunity they missed. To gain the love of a cat is a most enriching and uplifting achievement and not to be viewed lightly.

Now, there are numerous times when Luis would deliberately initiate contact with me. I may have been reading in the study or working on my laptop when he would suddenly appear and want to make contact. All cats are curious, it is part of their God-given nature, but I found that Luis increasingly directed his inquisitive senses at me. Sometimes he would stride up to me as I worked on my computer and he would, as my American friends are accustomed to saying, 'eyeball' me, probing me with his huge, beautiful, lucid eyes, trying to puzzle out in his cat mind what kind of person I am. He knew that I wasn't a cat and this perplexed him because I should not have been able to affect him in the ways that I had done. In his mind it was perfectly clear that cats, especially himself with a father as illustrious as Oscar, were far superior to humans and only deigned to allow them to serve all their needs. Yet somehow this man had found a way to manipulate cats and that should not be possible. Luis the Magnificent was being controlled and dominated by feelings of closeness to and for this human. It was very perplexing for Luis to work out even though he showed a degree of mental sentience beyond the usual level for a cat.

There exists a strongly held belief among travellers that cats possess psychic capabilities, can facilitate omens of the future and even have powers of divination. I have always felt that my cats have faculties of comprehension beyond my own, as well as superior senses, especially of sight and hearing. I feel a close attachment to cats but I am reluctant to boast that I understand them. Many of them I have loved as friends and in return been loved by them, but I have failed to figure out their precise place in the grand order of things, probably because I am simply human.

It would appear from an article in the *Daily Telegraph* (on Friday, 29 June 2007), which originated in the *Journal of Science*, that a genetic study has provided DNA evidence which suggests that cats probably became domesticated by farming people living in the Middle East around 130,000 years ago. They were attracted to human settlements because of the presence of rodents such as mice and rats which fed upon the farming produce. When some farmers migrated elsewhere they would bring their cats with them. In contrast, an earlier DNA study showed that dogs originated from Asian wolves a mere 15,000 years ago. This means that cats have lived alongside humans for a lengthy period of time in which opportunities to get to know each other really well have been abundant, and yet there still remains an unfathomable distance between the two. On the other hand a dog is much easier to know and to understand. Is this possibly why we regard cats as enigmas and have in the past raised their kind on a pedestal?

It depends on how far a person and a cat are willing to share life as to whether they will become close enough to begin to know each other and to develop a degree of friendship based upon the individual dispositions of both. But where there is determination, as in my case, and the motivating curiosity of the cat, as with Luis, then it is possible that a person and a cat can not only become friends but also end up devoted to each other. The relationship between Luis and myself reached that ideal stage at the beginning of May at the time of his first birthday which Catherine and I celebrated with him in true Owl Cottage fashion. It is interesting to reflect after all my efforts that Luis loves me despite his innate cat nature, which is profoundly committed to his own independence and only allows for contact of a mutually beneficial kind. Cats are instinctively programmed to be their own person, a singularity that permits no adulteration by other species. It required great emotional effort on my part to breach this implacable wall of self-defence against intrusion. In the case of Luis it was formidable, though with other cats of my acquaintance, less so.

After we had started to depend on each other for affection and day-to-day friendship, Luis began to reveal some intriguing aspects of his personality. For one thing he could move as swiftly and as silently as a ghost. When we were all relaxing by the fire in the sitting room of an evening, I might rise and head for the bathroom, only to be beaten there by Luis. He would get up from a state of deep sleep to outpace me so that he could be waiting for me, perched on the washing basket, before I had time to close the door. How he managed to get past me I shall never know. This incredible skill of being able to bypass me without my being aware led me to start referring to him as the Silver Ghost. But this skill of his was superseded by his ability to open doors. Cupboards, wardrobes, kitchen cabinets and kitchen doors left partially unlatched were no problem to this Raffles of a cat. Inevitably, this skill sometimes led him to become imprisoned and it was only after his high-pitched wailing penetrated the broadcasts of the radio or television that we grew aware of his predicament and could mount the rescue of a rueful cat who never seemed to learn his lesson. On one occasion this proclivity of his led to him being incarcerated all afternoon in a spare bedroom whilst we searched the garden and surrounds, thinking he had escaped.

Most of the time Luis was in the cottage, rather than outside, because he would join me in the study where I was writing at my laptop. His presence there became so regular that I bought him an extra cushion-bed and placed it on the shelf by the window so that he could snooze whilst I wrote, though I was aware that his attention always centred on what I was doing. If I left the room for a short while I would return to find him alert and standing, wondering what I had been doing and where I had been. Once a cat makes up its mind about something, nothing will change it. Luis had decided in his mind that he and I were bonded together now and it therefore followed that we would never be separated. Since Luis had abandoned his natural cat attitude of independence he could, and indeed did, demand all the love and devotion that I could give to him in return. I was very willing to do this.

The poignant nature of this relationship was illustrated one day when I drove off to do some specialist shopping and, because of circumstances beyond my control, returned very late. Catherine had brought Luis down from the compound into the cottage, which I usually did. When he could not find me he went berserk. Whining and wailing he paraded the cottage with angry outbursts of suffering at my absence. This behaviour not unnaturally alarmed and distressed her. She began thinking that the cat knew something that she did not and she worried in case something bad had happened to me. Meanwhile, Luis continued his agitation, running here and there in the house and checking all the rooms to try to find me. Cats are conservative in their habits and do not take readily to change; they like an established routine and become stressed when a pattern is not adhered to. Also, and this did not impress upon me until I thought about it later, Luis and I had become very close of late and the cat actually missed me because he had come to rely on me being there for him. Anyone who has viewed the desperate anxiety on a dog's face as they wait, tied to a rung outside the doors of a supermarket, will understand that animals are as vulnerable to feelings as are humans. It was a joyful reunion Luis and I had when at last my car drove up to the cottage. Catherine said that he appeared ecstatic with excitement when he saw me through the window of the conservatory and kept running along the window ledge uttering little cries of what she took for relief.

This episode touched me deeply and I made sure that I allowed time that evening to make a great fuss of him. I also coaxed Catherine to allow me to cut him a piece of her prized Welsh cheddar cheese, for which he'd developed a craving. In fact, he liked all cheddar cheese but Welsh cheddar was his favourite. His taste for food chiefly centred on what he saw me eating and he delighted in cadging morsels of meat from my plate and he was ecstatic when I shared a pork pie snack with him in the garden.

As we increasingly grew to know him, Luis revealed other traits of personality which showed the aesthetic side of cat nature. He enjoyed soft music but ran away from loud orchestral pieces. He dreaded the sound of the huge wagon which emptied the refuse bins and at the first sign of it he would go and hide in a dark corner. Once I followed him to give him comfort and was shocked to find him trembling fitfully. Maine Coon cats do exhibit a lot of delicate sensitivities. When I gave the matter some thought I began to empathize with my cat. While working at a university which was situated in the centre of a city, I became inured to the roar of heavy traffic and accustomed to wending my way though noisy crowds of people whenever I ventured out, but I never liked it. When I escaped through retirement to the sanctuary of rural life I became enamoured once more of waking up to birdsong and the sound of the breeze rustling through the trees. It was also a blissful moment when, on one of my first nights back at Owl Cottage, I saw the stars shining against a backdrop of black sky untainted by pollution. Thinking about all this made me realize how my cats felt. To a cat, sudden noise is an abomination and silence is not only golden, it is divine – a sentiment that mirrors my own feelings precisely.

After a while it became clear to us that Pablo and Luis merely tolerated each other, but sometimes not even that. The harmony of the home would be upset by spats of spitting, hostile cries and growls. While Luis did not appear to be unduly lonely, he did watch our departure in the car for an evening out with a forlorn look as he peeped through the conservatory blinds. We decided that we ought to have another cat to keep him company. And this is how it came about that we acquired Max.

MAX

Following the usual procedure when we wanted a new kitten, I telephoned Jane, the breeder, and asked her what she had available. Jane quickly replied with the good news that she had a pregnant tortoiseshell-coloured cat which had been sired by Oscar, the father of both Carlos and Luis, who was about to give birth any day now. However, her kittens would not be silver-grey but more likely red or pied in colour. She promised to ring and give us first choice when the litter arrived. Two days later she rang to tell us that a litter of two healthy kittens had arrived; one was a deep red with some white markings and the other was black with white mottling. Both kittens were male. We asked her to reserve the red kitten for us and arranged a date for us to see him.

Three-and-a-half weeks later we arrived at Jane's house to view our red kitten for the first time. The twin kittens were cuddled together asleep in a small cosy box, lined with a blanket, on the top of a pedestal. I lifted out the red kitten, which was just a tiny ball of red fur with minute white feet and a little white chest. I carried him into Jane's conservatory to show him to Catherine. Like all our kittens, he was perfectly formed and appeared so vulnerable and endearing as I held him close to my sweater. I stroked him gently with my fingers and he gave two faint squeaks as he viewed me apprehensively with his eyes sparkling like diminutive sapphires. Catherine was anxious to hold him so I laid him in her lap.

'We're going to call him Max,' she said, addressing Jane who had brought in two steaming mugs of coffee as warmers against the cruel January weather. Then a surprising thing happened. We suddenly heard a slight hiss, repeated several times, which sounded as if it was coming from the kitten, which Catherine was now holding up to her face in order to take a good look at him. Sure enough it came again: 'Pith . . . pith . . . pith.'

'This little chap is spitting at me,' laughed Catherine. 'And he's wriggling to be away,' she said as she set him down, only to see him run off. I followed him as he scuttled across the floor into the next room and clambered up the pedestal to rejoin his brother in their box. There they lay cosily cuddled into one another, reminding me of the story of *The Babes in the Wood*, so cute did they look. Catherine had followed me into the room and we both laughed at the sight of the comfy kitten twins soundly sleeping just like babies without a care in the world. But ominously in view of later circumstances we should have afforded these events more significance. If we had, we concluded with hindsight, Max would have had a much less traumatic life than he suffered. At the time we failed to realize, in spite of our experience, that cats, like many other animals, retain strong feelings of belonging to their family, especially certain siblings. It later transpired that in this case the twin brothers were emotionally bonded and as such were inseparable. They were Christmas infants, having been born during the night of 28 December 2002.

It seemed that the winter that year, although severe as always with heavy snowfalls and raging blizzards, passed us by so quickly that we were greeting the spring before we'd had time to prepare a welcome by organizing all the jobs we had to do in the garden and greenhouse. Spring happened so suddenly one golden morning that it seemed that nature had caught everyone unawares. Suddenly the flowers were blooming in plots of brilliant colour and the songbirds were frenziedly nest-building. It was also time to collect our fourth Maine Coon kitten, who had been given the quaint full name of Maxamillion. This is how Jane had printed his pet name on the pedigree certificate and we both laughed about the misspelling but inwardly hoped that it would prove prophetic. We arranged to collect him in the early afternoon. On arrival at Jane's house we were surprised to find her just driving up. As she got out of the car we saw that she was carrying a box and inside was Max. We followed her inside the house where she explained.

'I've had a really bad morning with this one. He's been crying and squirming about as if in pain so I rushed him down to the vet's but it seems as if there is nothing wrong with him as far as they could tell at the clinic,' she ended breathlessly. She went on to tell us that she had rearranged everything in the room where the kittens had been because Max's twin brother had gone to an owner in Glasgow the night before and she wanted to give the room a good cleaning. 'Perhaps shifting everything around upset him but I knew you were coming to get him today and I wanted to get on with reorganizing things.'

We nodded in agreement with her and gave her the cheque in payment for Max but not before thanking her for taking such great care of him. Jane is one of those dedicated breeders who give their all to raising magnificent kittens for the rest of us to enjoy. She coddles her female cats and acts as midwife during their pregnancy and delivery, for which she has all my admiration. We bade her a brisk farewell and, with Catherine cuddling Max on her lap, we drove homewards.

From that moment of departure, we started to develop an acute awareness that Max was suffering some deep distress. At first we put this down to all the changes over the past day or two and the trauma of a visit to the vet. But when we arrived back at the cottage he behaved as if everything was a threat to him and no amount of stroking and gentle talk made the difference. When we put him down on the floor in the conservatory to give him a chance to investigate his new home he withdrew to a corner and as we approached him he began to shake uncontrollably. As you might imagine, this behaviour by our new kitten really upset us and we wondered if we should take him back to Jane to ease his agony. We decided to leave him alone for a while to see if he would calm down. From a distance I watched him keenly for any improvement in his condition but all I could discern was a frightened and miserable kitten. I thought that if I put some food down for him – meat and biscuits with a bowl of water – it might help to comfort him, but he showed no interest in any of it. Eventually we left him alone, huddled in a corner under a chair in the conservatory, and reflected on the marked differences of our four Maine Coon cats. We left the door to the hall open for him to see if he would come and join us. I withdrew to ponder the situation, to see if I could find an explanation and a way to help him.

It was almost an hour later that we began to hear, from the hallway, a series of plaintive wails and cries that pained me to hear. I knew it to be a cat, or rather a kitten, sobbing his heart out. Catherine moved before I could and returned with Max in her arms, trying to mother him and soothe him as she would with one of her own babies. I looked on, feeling totally impotent and worried about how I could possibly relieve this poor kitten's anguish. The sounds emitted from Max indicated that he was consumed with grief for reasons we could not fathom. He shunned all my efforts to comfort him and I could see that Catherine was becoming weary with the effort of trying to ease him, like when all one's efforts to nurse a crying baby are to no avail. We sat with him in the sitting room of the cottage, wondering over and over again what we could do to relieve this lovely kitten of his suffering. At last, exhausted and tormented by his feelings, he fell into a troubled sleep in which he trembled and whimpered, lying with his head resting on Catherine's shoulder, facing her neck. When we were ready for bed we took him up to the bedroom with us and laid him in one of the cushion-beds used by Luis. He lay flat-out, totally comatose.

The next morning he took a long time to rouse himself but

would not move from the cushion, which we had carried downstairs with him in it, and he refused to eat anything even though we offered him every enticement we could think of. On the previous night I had deliberately kept the other cats apart from the kitten, but after Luis had finished his breakfast I brought him into the room where the kitten lay bedfast. I wanted to see if the presence of another cat would revive him and relieve his homesickness, if that was what was troubling him. Luis approached Max tentatively at first and there was a lot of cautious sniffing as the new member of the family was given a thorough appraisal. Then to my delight Luis began to give the kitten a fulsome tongue-wash. Interestingly, the tiny cat started to respond to Luis' persistent licking by moving his head and body around until he finally struggled to his feet and, watched warily by Luis, not to mention ourselves, tottered over to the water bowl. After a few timid sips he turned and began eating the dried biscuits we'd put down near him. I heaped praise upon Luis for working his cat magic in restoring Max to a semblance of normality and hoped that they would become good companions in time.

Max spent the rest of the day either close to or being carried around by Catherine, on whom he'd become fixated. Although his demeanour had improved somewhat he still indulged in bouts of mewing and whinging. This melancholic behaviour continued over the succeeding weeks and it all proved to unsettle us because we generally maintained a happy household in which our cats are afforded every care and indulgence. We were not accustomed to any of our cats showing a state of such wretchedness as we detected in our new red boy, Max.

Grappling for a solution I spent long hours in the conservatory with Luis for company whilst Catherine ministered to Max. Suddenly, the penny dropped: I knew, without a shadow of a doubt, what was causing Max to suffer those tortured feelings. I should have known earlier from my long experience in clinical psychology. The kitten was suffering from 'Separation Syndrome'. He desperately missed his twin brother. That explained his behaviour at Jane's the day we came to pick him up and it clarified the reasons for his subsequent conduct with us. I recalled my memories of the two tiny mites cuddled together in their box the first time we visited to see Max, and my heart bled with the emotional realization that it was I who had been instrumental in tearing them part when I could very easily at that time have bought them both. Me, who had lectured on the psychology of twins and tutored students at university on the insights culled from research on the subject. I felt ashamed and humbled. Now I would have to find a way to redeem myself and console a little being who had lost the other half of himself through my stupidity. But Max would have nothing to do with me. He cringed whenever I tried to hold him. Perhaps he knew who was to blame and could not forgive me. Cats never forget a wrong done to them.

A call to Jane confirmed my worst feelings. She described how the two kittens had always wanted to be together, with Max avidly searching out his brother if they became separated.

I asked her why she hadn't told me. She explained that she ran a business in which she raised kittens as well as she could, but then she needed to sell them to other cat lovers. To do so she had to mask her own feeling of love for them or else she would end up keeping every one of them herself.

'I understand and do not blame you but what can I do to help Max?'

'Time will heal him, especially with all the love that you and Catherine have for your cats,' she replied.

Meanwhile, back at the cottage we had to deal with the fact that Max not only had lost the comfort and companionship of his little brother but also had been deprived of his safety zone, because it seemed that his twin was the dominant kitten. We made up our minds that we would simply give him as much care and comfort as possible and try to involve him with the other cats as far as plausible. Luis willingly befriended Max and was content to lie with him in the various bed-cushions we provided for our cats but he drew the line at sharing his food bowl with the kitten, who received a few admonitory cuffs around the head for assuming he could eat with Luis. We sympathized with Max, who desperately needed to be close to another cat to fill the gap left by his brother's absence and we watched with compassion as he toddled round the cottage after Luis.

I thought it was also time to introduce him to Pablo but watched apprehensively as the big cat acted very much in the guise of the alpha male. Their first encounter was passably pacific; Pablo sniffed and licked the kitten's head, and then hissed and gently laid his huge paw on Max's head as if to say, 'Know your place and don't bother me!' Max cowered and trembled and didn't move for several moments. When it was over, he began washing himself as cats do when stressed. Then, in what seemed to be a delayed reaction, Max started to tremble and shake uncontrollably. Just as I was about to intervene, Luis, who had been watching, strolled over and lay down alongside Max as if to say by means of his body language: 'Don't worry about it; everything is fine.' It seemed to work because Max stopped shaking, cuddled into Luis and went to sleep, no doubt overcome by his emotions.

When I witnessed this it gave me hope that Max would perhaps soon transfer the attachment he had for his absent brother to Luis. Ever so gradually over the weeks and months that followed this appeared to be what was in fact taking place. Luis, however, remained undeniably the dominant partner, not averse to treating the newcomer to a cuff around the ears now and then to keep him straight. The essence of this relationship admirably suited Luis' lordly pretensions and Max's neurotic needs for comfort and protection. As far as Max was concerned, he was glad to be the follower and seemed to appreciate the developing bond with Luis, and yet his eyes retained an unfailing look of sadness. Only Catherine, with her bountiful show of affection, could put him at ease. Even so, during that first miserable year for him, Max never purred once. I was still very much sidelined by all that was going on with Max because he would have nothing to do with me. His rejection of me was most upsetting but nothing I did made an impression on him. No cat had ever failed to respond to my overtures of friendship like Max had.

Just when I thought that Max was improving we both noticed that he was beginning to lose his fur. The condition had probably been deteriorating for some time but it became unmistakable and we realized that there was something seriously wrong with him. We tried changing his diet to see if richer food would help him. To this end I bought him oily fish such as fresh mackerel and salmon, but to no avail. Then we spotted a number of little sores on his bare patches which could only be insect bites, though Max did not have any fleas on him. He fast began to assume the appearance of the proverbial scabby cat. We tried treating him with all kinds of home remedies, which included skin creams and saline sprays, but nothing seemed to work.

We hesitated about taking him to a vet because Max went into a paroxysm of terror if a stranger appeared anywhere near him, as we discovered when we enlisted the help of workmen for odd jobs around the house or garden. He possessed that haunted look of apprehension which meant that he was in a perpetual state of readiness to be alarmed. The sudden noise of heavy traffic, low-flying jet aircraft or knocks on the door would send him into such a traumatic state that he would hide away for hours until all was clear. Even if we moved suddenly or dropped something in the kitchen or exclaimed loudly it would send him into such a spooked state that he would crawl, bellyflop style, along the floor to escape. Perhaps the state of health he was suffering, I thought, was similar to humans suffering from alopecia (hair loss) due to nervous conditions.

After conferring with Catherine I rang the vet and described the condition Max was suffering. I told him that I wanted him to make a house call since our cat was too nervous for a visit to the clinic. He then advised me that if the cat was suffering so badly it might be sensible to 'have him put down to relieve his suffering'. I told him that it was out of the question and arranged for him to come the following day at 11 a.m.

The vet duly arrived with all his veterinary paraphernalia and examined Max, who was clutched tightly in Catherine's arms. After using his stethoscope he pronounced that Max's heartbeat was four times the norm, which I could see plainly enough from looking at one of his legs which was shaking wildly and thumping against Catherine's lap like a drumbeat. He said, 'I will give him an injection of antibiotics and another of steroids but if he shows no improvement after one week then my original suggestion to you stands because his immune system may be too poor to enable him to recover either from his physical allergic reaction to the bites, psychological condition of nervous response or both.'

Max closed his eyes and slumped against Catherine as the injections were administered.

Poor Max, I thought, after the vet had left and Max was once more curled as if in a coma in his bed-cushion. I posed the question to myself: 'Is he too vulnerable to survive in this tough world?'

He did not stir all that evening, not even when we stroked him and brought food in for him. Ultimately, we retired to bed, half afraid that he would die in his sleep. But a remarkable development occurred in the days that followed his treatment. Max began to improve. The changes were minute at first; then we began to detect fur growing on his body where formerly there had been a bald patch. He seemed calmer and developed a healthy appetite. After two weeks the changes were phenomenal in comparison to how he had been. He was still easily scared but his reactions were less extreme. The sores on his skin were beginning to fade and we decided to order another treatment session for him. This time a young lady vet visited and took an instant liking to Max. She fussed him and spoke soothingly to him as she administered the injections so expertly that Max hardly trembled. We were very impressed. She told us over a cup of tea that she specialized in clinical treatments for small animals, mainly pets, and that for her it was a childhood dream come true. On her advice we booked one further treatment in a fortnight.

After the completion of this course of treatment Max was like a new cat. No doubt the antibiotics had restored his skin to health but also the steroids had induced a placid effect to his manner and disposition. The medicines had 'done him the world of good', as my grandmother would often pronounce after seeing someone changed for the better.

Max continued to avoid me but was more responsive with Catherine and would spend hours on her lap in the evening or, if she stretched out on the sofa or by the fireside, he would lie alongside her. One morning at breakfast time he jumped onto her lap and as she stroked him Max began to purr loudly. It was the first of many such events. And so Max grew to be more firmly encompassed in our hearts and any thoughts of putting him down were summarily dismissed. To my mind this was unthinkable but I understood that the vet had made the suggestion out of professional consideration of our cat.

To his credit Max was growing into a most handsome cat, with a thick matt of vibrant red fur covering his head and back, which was given a vivid contrast by the pure white fur of his chest and paws. His tail was a magnificent upright long crimson plume of fine hair. And Max's eyes, deep golden gems, had lost the haunted look and they expressed devoted love to my wife Catherine. Following his own agenda and dispositions he would only sit on her lap and it was her alone he favoured with his purrs and from whom he accepted strokes.

I began to realize that for his own protection Max had made a deal with himself about the way he would relate to the world in which he found himself, and to preserve his independence he would restrict his trust and his self to Catherine and Luis exclusively. I understood the psychology of his riven emotions but felt hurt at being rejected. I hoped that in the future he would also accept me as a friend, though he most certainly was making me wait a long time for it.

Reflecting on the time when Jane rang to tell me that the red kitten had arrived, I remembered that I had been filled with excitement and when we first visited him I recalled that I had been the stranger who had plucked him out of his cosy box away from his little brother. I pictured in my mind's eye how the twin kittens had been cuddled into each other as if glued together. When I'd lifted him out, I now recollected, he had cried piteously at being parted from his brother. Perhaps from the time of that experience he had associated my scent and the sound of my voice with being parted from his twin and blamed me for the later separation.

It took a long while before he was ready to forgive and forget. It was only after two years that he began to give me some limited recognition for all my efforts to make friends. The curious, if not hilarious, thing about the whole affair was that Catherine had bought Max for me as a belated Christmas present.

It is an undeniable fact that nothing lasts forever, even the frame of mind of a large red and white cat called Max. The change happened one winter's evening as I sat alone in the sitting room reading a book. As I shifted around in my seat I realized that I had an empty paper packet in my pocket that I had meant to dispose of in the kitchen trash can. Taking it out I began absentmindedly to scrunch it in my free hand whilst reading. Suddenly, I heard a meow and on looking around I saw Max nearby giving me a fixed stare. Just then Catherine came into the room and, quickly grasping the situation, she said, 'He wants you to throw the paper ball for him.'

I looked again at Max, who was paying rapt attention to me

and at the rounded piece of paper in my hand, and understood what she meant, but I was still amazed when, as I tossed the paper to a far corner of the room, Max whirled and raced after it. He then picked it up in his mouth and jogged back towards me to drop the missive at my feet. Then he looked at me expectantly. That glance meant only one thing: 'Throw it for me again. I want to play.'

Catherine and I laughed. Max was showing us another facet of his personality; he knew how to retrieve. I was so elated at this development that I discarded my book and continued the game with Max. We must have played for nearly an hour, until we were both tired, and he lay down exhausted on the fireside rug. This welcome sign that he was at last ready and willing to relate to me both astonished me and pleased me immensely. I was reminded of Carlos and how he loved to retrieve and would initiate the playtime by carrying his cloth toy mice to me to be thrown; he was such a fun-loving cat and I still missed him sorely.

I began now to have high hopes that Max would take over this role so that we could enter into a new phase of having fun together that would build a friendship bond between us. The mechanism of our new game-playing took on a daily rhythm of its own: throw . . . run . . . catch . . . retrieve . . . return. As Max slowly began to acknowledge my part in his life as non-threatening, I was aware that he remained cautious if not jittery whenever I happened to enter his space and if I moved too quickly he would scoot away. But he was now, more often than not, ever ready to play 'Retrieve Ball'. It was clear that Max had chosen this method of relating to me as a way of breaking the ice and in due course other changes to our relationship began to emerge, but only in Max's good time. Luis looked on these games of mine with Max with a mild blandness which precluded his own involvement. Luis never did learn to retrieve. I expect he considered it beneath his dignity.

The way that Max's personality has developed is epitomized by the manner in which he plays. He developed a love of playing with his toy mouse. He has a large one, which I bought for him, that is his favourite, possibly because it squeaks when he bites it and tosses it around as cats do. If Max is in the mood he will hunt out this toy and perform acrobatic manoeuvres which defy gravity. He engages in leaps, mid-air turns and catches that leave him lying stretched out and panting for breath. Then he revives and the play continues a while longer. When the mouse is grasped in his mouth he makes a quick twist of his head and hurls the toy high in the air and then runs to make the catch, pouncing on it and batting it around with deft slaps of his paws until he is once more tired out and must succumb to a brief catnap, slumped in his cushion-bed. But this play activity is conditional upon it being solely for his own private enjoyment. He will not tolerate interference. If one of the other cats attempts to join in, Max ceases his play, looks upset and retreats somewhere to sulk.

Such behaviour from Max calls to mind a story that one of

the readers of *Paw Tracks in the Moonlight* related to me over the telephone when she was telling me about her Maine Coon cats. She also lives in a rural area and has a large garden. One day she caught sight of her cat called Barnaby playing indoors with a live mouse which he'd brought from the garden. Not wanting any rodents in the house she removed it and set it free outside, only to find that Barnaby had managed to slip out and once again returned with the mouse.

'No Barnaby,' she said. 'You cannot have a pet mouse!'

But despite her actions, removing the mouse several times, Barnaby persisted in finding and retrieving it to play with in the house. He obviously wanted the mouse as a playmate because he never bit it or hurt it in any way as far as she could see. Eventually the situation took a radically different turn when Claudius, the alpha male of her cats, strolled in and spotted Barnaby playing with the mouse. Without a moment's hesitation Claudius swiftly seized the mouse and with a single shake of his jaws killed it. Then with the mouse in his mouth he slowly walked over to the now distraught Barnaby, dropped the dead mouse in front of him and glared at him as if to say: 'Remember that you are a cat. Cats kill mice, OK, get it?'

My caller went on to tell me that Barnaby's response was to gently touch the corpse with his paw, all the while making whimpering cries over the dead body of the mouse he'd wanted as a friend. She said that if a cat could cry then Barnaby wept.

From my reading of the kind of cat that Max is, I believe him to be much like Barnaby because he has such a gentle and fragile disposition. This in so many ways renders him vulnerable and afraid of the world at large. He is moulded like those everywhere who suffer desperately with serious nervous conditions which make them much more sensitive to the feelings of others. Max is an extremely sensitive cat who wears his emotions very clearly on the outside for all to see.

Another aspect of Max's character is his intelligence in finding solutions to problems. On one of our infrequent trips with the cats to the local cattery so that we could take a short holiday, Max revealed a clever ruse to get himself back home again. When we arrive at the cattery we always take the time to introduce the cats to the environment they will be sharing and the people who will be caring for them whilst we are away. We try to make the experience as non-stressful as possible for our pets. On this occasion Pablo and Luis, ever the confident and self-assured ones, made a quick tour of inspection of the compound and settled on high wooden platforms from which they could survey the area without undue difficulty, especially the compounds housing other cats. Max timidly looked around, sniffed the floor and then disappeared. I thought he'd gone inside to hide in one of the beds. As we said our goodbyes we each carried a cat box back to the car but I noticed that Catherine was lagging behind me and having some difficulty carrying her one, which appeared to be lopsided.

'I don't know what's wrong with this,' she said. 'It's so awkward to carry and it feels heavy.'

I took the box from her and checked to see if there was

something wrong with the handle which was making it become lopsided, but the handle was fine. Then I opened the grill door at the front of the box and imagine my utter astonishment at seeing Max clinging to the back of the box with his claws fastened in the air inlets. He had made up his mind that the cattery was not for him and worked out that if he could stow away in the box that brought him he could return home but he needed to hide so that we wouldn't detect him. We burst out laughing at the sheer ingenuity of his escape plan, which mirrored some Second World War escape efforts, especially the one involving a 'Wooden Horse', of Allies held in German prisoner of war camps. We brought him out, congratulated him and Catherine gave him a surfeit of hugs. I saw that she was crying a little at her red cat's cleverness in arranging to get back home. Much to his dismay, and it took us extra time to settle him, we took him back to his apartment to rejoin Pablo and Luis. We then told them all again that we would soon be back. Hurrying away to the car we felt very guilty at leaving them even though we knew they would be very well looked after.

As I mentioned earlier, whenever we return from a holiday break we are not greeted with abundant friendliness by our cats when we fetch them back from the cattery. Our cats are enormously sensitive, some would say spoilt, and like their brethren worldwide are capable of sulking when events go contrary to their expectation and liking. This behaviour is meant to punish us for leaving them and it takes a while to thaw out. This time when we came back, following the escape ploy by Max, we were in receipt not only of the customary huffiness by our cats but also by a message that provoked extreme anxiety. The cattery manager informed us that Pablo had needed to be taken to the vet's because of an angry-looking sore on his right front paw. When we examined him at home we saw an ugly red blob between the toes of the paw. On contacting the surgery in Alnwick we were further alarmed by the prognosis that it was a tumour which required immediate surgery. An appointment was made in all haste and Pablo duly had an operation that necessitated the amputation of two toes in order to excise the growth, which was diagnosed as a 'spindle cell tumour'.

We brought him home with relief that it was all over but we were warned that it could recur. When he'd recovered from the anaesthetic he demonstrated just what a tough guy he was by wrenching free from the tight-fitting bandage which encased his leg and angrily demanding, as only cats can demand by means of piteous, hollow-sounding wails, to be allowed out. I opened the door for him, thinking that he would probably just want to sit outside on the patio to prove to himself that he was free again after all he'd endured. However, he proceeded to climb one of the highest trees in the garden and I could just make out his dark form resting inside the leafy foliage midway up. He stayed there for three hours before coming down to have his dinner.

Apart from hobbling slightly he appeared his old self and didn't even react when the two other cats spat at him because of the chemical smell on his fur. Later, they seemed to relent and, as he lay relaxed after his meal, they set to and gave him a jolly good tongue-wash. But both Max and Luis kept slavering and shaking their heads at the unnatural taste.

We pampered Pablo over the next few weeks to help to restore him to full health and hoped that he would make a full recovery without any recurrence of the problem. Meanwhile, we were enjoying a period of warm sunny weather and we took every opportunity to sit out in the garden and to bask in the glory that sunlight renders on the most ordinary landscapes. In our case we already have a beautiful garden but the sunshine makes it even more so. At evening time, for several days, the sunsets lit up the whole cloudless sky and made an eye-catching display of dazzling bands of red, orange, green and turquoise colours. During this spell we were pleased to see Pablo wandering less and spending more time with us.

Luis and Max were taken out separately from the compound and, wearing harnesses, were led around the garden for investigative walks. In truth, neither of them walks in the normal sense of the word. Luis likes to travel in accelerated spurts from one interesting area to another. He will stop and have a real good sniff at a bush or flower and then make a further spurt which would almost drag me off my feet. Then he might climb and claw his way up a tree, only to become entangled by his lead as he explores the branches. I have to go and get a stepladder to undo the muddle and coax him to come down, which is when I usually find my cat is at his most disobedient. Catherine has often found similar difficulties at times when she leads Max around. Max does not walk; he parades, delicately splaying his large paws in a stately fashion. He slowly proceeds with his head held high and his fluffy orange-red tail held aloft behind him like a banner. While on the whole it can be said that Max has the sweetest disposition, especially when he is in Catherine's company, he can also evince an intransigent attitude at times.

I remember one time when he was out in the garden being led along the paths and, as he meandered around the shrubs and trees, a slight difference of opinion occurred between him and Catherine with regard to the direction the saunter should take. Normally Max would be most amenable but on this occasion the situation developed into a full-blown dispute as Max dug his snowy white paws in the lawn and stubbornly refused to budge. Catherine was equally adamant, not wishing to have her clothes ensnared by rose thorns. The end result was that Max lost his temper and began furiously hissing. Having watched this pantomime with amusement from my vantage point in the greenhouse, I decided to intervene and to the surprise of both parties I strode out and picked up Max, divested him of his harness and lead and placed him in the compound. He set up an apologetic wailing intended to make Catherine come to his rescue but by this time she had had enough and left him to muse on his sorrows and reflect on his naughty behaviour. Later that afternoon Max showed in his attitude to both of us that he was thoroughly miffed over the incident, though when supper time came around, and Pablo and Luis were served their biscuits, Max began reviewing the cost his sulk was causing him and concluded that it was better to overlook the episode so that he could enjoy an evening snack.

Trying never to sleep on an argument was a maxim we tended to foster at Owl Cottag. Thus we made sufficient fuss of Max to yet again ease the troubled mind of our temperamental rouge cat and all calm and peace was restored to the happy home. Since it had been such a fine day, with clear skies, the stars shone down in all their splendour that night and I stayed late in the conservatory to view their brilliance in the company of Luis on my right side and Max on my left. Pablo, as was his wont, was out on the prowl. We saw no owls but spotted two red squirrels relishing a good meal at the peanut-feeders we hang for the songbirds. I left the room for bed, sonorously serenaded goodnight by the soft snores of my two boy cats.

Max is a remarkable cat, as I increasingly recognize now that I have been allowed to share his company more closely. It has taken fully two years for him to change his mind towards me and permit me to be his friend. He now competes with Luis for my attention and strokes. This sometimes causes trouble. Occasionally, Luis takes offence when he sees Max sitting anywhere near me for a head rub and caress, and then he will bully Max into a hasty withdrawal by growling and cuffing him across the face. Even though he is smaller than Max he can act the thug at times and he is especially possessive of me and my affections. I believe this attitude stems from his notion that he is personally descended from an elite line of royal cats who are superior to all other forms of life, including humans. Cats can display a remnant of the attitude of the Ancient Egyptian cat-gods, accounting for some of them to be viewed as snooty, aloof and even hostile.

But to return to Max: he is charm personified, at least most of the time. This genial feature of his character is revealed not only in his need for affection and harmony in his life but also because he wants opportunities to play. I have already mention-ed his ability to retrieve objects thrown for him as part of a game plan that is all his own, which he will happily pursue until he is exhausted. Further to this he will, when he is in the mood, seek out a toy of some sort. He also likes to dance. This is an activity he indulges by himself, for himself alone. In some respects this dance game could be described as akin to the antics of a whirling dervish in that he runs and jumps around whilst turning circles, coils himself into the form of a spring, and erupts into a gigantic leap, wherein he twists and flays the air with his paws. On landing he gallops off at express speed, upstairs and downstairs, and ends with a bound onto the top of some furniture. Dance finished, he will assiduously wash himself all over with his tongue. To witness this performance is to be enthralled and at the same time concerned for his safety, not to mention that of the furnishings. To date nothing has been broken, only scratched. If Carlos could have seen Max dance, I'm certain he would have launched himself wholeheartedly into joining him.

This amazing feat of creative gymnastics, or letting off steam, is not discharged regularly but it would appear to await the spur of an aesthetic impulse within Max. Whenever it happens the other cats are mystified, if not a little apprehensive. When we are privileged to view it we find it most entertaining and applaud heartily and loudly cheer him. This dance of his expresses what is singularly Max, much different from when he first came to us. At times he even displays a positively sanguine attitude to life and the universe.

One day Max discovered he had a taste for venison sausage. It happened one morning when, after a heavy bout of writing, I was relaxing in front of the television and Catherine brought me a plate of grilled sausage cut into small sections. Suddenly Max appeared at my side, licking his lips.

'You won't like any of this, Max,' I said, knowing that he had a fussy taste which I didn't believe would extend to venison and sage. But when he saw me enjoying the treat he leaned up and planted his two paws on my knee.

'All right, but I hope it doesn't make you sick,' I warned him.

Never doubt a cat's propensity to have what it wants. No sooner had I offered him a morsel of sausage than it was gone in a trice.

'Well, I would never have believed it if I hadn't seen it,' I said to no one in particular.

Thereafter, Max proceeded to eat several more pieces, relishing the taste with a purring accompaniment. Meanwhile, Luis wandered in, sniffed the piece I felt obliged to offer him and walked away in disgust. Pablo also gave it a cursory inspection but would not deign to eat it. I made a mental note to organize a trip to the rural market town of Rothbury and visit the self-styled 'Best Butcher in the World' housed at the foot of the main street. I would buy a supply of venison and sage sausage for Max and for me. Max and I were fast building a friendship bonded not only from playing games of retrieve but also by sharing the same taste in sausages. Whatever next? I thought. Aren't cats mysterious and marvellous to know?

We were about to go through a very difficult period at Owl Cottage, as the few thoughts I wrote down at the time reveal:

Bad news! Pablo has developed another tumour on his right foot. And so we have had again the collective trauma for our precious little family of having to subject Pablo once more to the surgeon's knife. He has come back this time with even less toes on the afflicted foot. The other two cats are seeking in their various ways, usually by licking his head and lying near to him, to show their concern and sympathy, whilst he is making the most of his life by still trying to act the big tough guy. Catherine and I are deeply troubled at what is happening to him.

Meanwhile, I am continuing to write this sequel to *Paw Tracks in the Moonlight*, spurred forward by a host of letters from my readers urging me to write the next book. I work at my laptop at my desk, adjacent to an upstairs window. I am still often visited by Luis, who has learned to sit and lie on his special bed- cushion on the window sill next to me so that I don't have to protect my keyboard from his intrusive paws. Luis may be my more frequent writing partner, but recently Max has shown that he will not be left out and demands his turn at my side. As I write this he is languishing on the window sill, making chittering noises at the birds flying around outside. Now and then he turns his golden eyes on me and I tell him that I am writing about him and all his doings. He yawns and rests his head between paws that are as white as snow and watches me intently until the rhythm of my typing mesmerizes him, and with a soft sigh he catnaps the afternoon away.

The problems with Pablo's paw have become worse and he has had to have the first three inches of his right paw surgically removed. He now really has to hobble around and my heart aches for him, knowing how much he misses his wild wanderings. He spends a lot of his time now in the company of the other cats as if he needs their fellowship in order to come to terms with what is happening to him. He responds joyfully to me when I spend time with him but I am deeply worried about the consequences of these tumours for him. The chief vet cannot help us regarding the reasons for these infections or how to treat them, except for surgical removal. It is frustrating for me to feel the impotency of not knowing what to do to help my beloved cat. He looks at me sad-eyed and I despair at the possibility of losing him.

The end came sooner than expected. Pablo was spending the night with the others in the conservatory, sleeping in his large cushion-bed. Sometime in the middle of the night I was awakened by a cat crying loudly. I hurried downstairs to find both Luis and Max grouped around Pablo, greatly concerned because he was faintly moaning. It was Luis who had cried and awakened me. I tried to reassure them not to worry even though I was worried sick myself. With Catherine's help I lifted Pablo onto a blanket we laid on the table for him. I could tell he was hurting so I crushed a paracetamol tablet in a spoon and mixed it with cod liver oil. Then, while Catherine held him, I managed to get most of it down his mouth. He seemed weaker than I expected and it shocked me to realize that our big loveable Pablo was suffering some serious pain.

We lit the fire and nursed him between us for the rest of the night, all thoughts of bed abandoned. In our anxiety we drank lots of cups of tea, kept Pablo warm and as comfortable as we could, and waited for the morning. Meanwhile, Max and Luis whined and wailed at the sitting-room door so we let them in. I was moved at the solicitude they were showing for Pablo as they insisted on being near him. The signals they were giving me would be a revelation to anyone in the strictly scientific world who regards any creature below themselves on the species scale as a dumb animal. Luis and Max were desperately trying to console and care for Pablo in his hour of need. After all, it was Luis who had alerted me to his condition.

As soon as we could we took Pablo to an emergency clinic and were told what we suspected and dreaded. The condition causing the tumours had spread to infect his whole body and his state of health was terminal; he was also suffering acute pain as his vitals deteriorated. At this forecast Catherine burst into tears and simply hugged Pablo. I gestured with a movement of my head for the vet to come into the corridor for a quiet word.

'I understand what you have told me but I beg of you to consider relieving his pain sufficiently so that we can spend a last day with him before you put him away. Can you do that?'

He replied, 'I should terminate him now to release him from his suffering and I'm not sure I can manage to do the alleviation of pain you want.'

'But you can try, can't you?' I burst out.

His face flushed red and he looked away from me. Then he turned and faced me with an icy stare. 'I'll do my professional best but you must bring him back in twenty-four hours, for his sake.'

I nodded assent and joined Catherine. We drove back home with heavy hearts and a heavily sedated Pablo. We spent the evening huddled together with our three cats, watching tele-vision and not watching at the same time. Luis and Max sensed that something final had been concluded and Luis in particular kept looking my way and making muted questioning cries. The following morning neither Catherine nor I could eat breakfast and made do with coffee. Pablo showed no inclination to eat but seemed surprisingly buoyant.

'It's the steroids keeping him comfortable,' I said to Catherine's questioning glances. We made him comfortable on a bed-cushion on the table between us and Pablo purred the morning away as we stroked and talked lovingly to him. Shadows of the last moments of Toby Jug's life came back as a kind of nightmarish déjà vu as we put Pablo in his box for his last journey to the vet's.

It was over very quickly and dealt with in a most clinically professional way, but we were in an emotional turmoil at the demise of our first Maine Coon Boy and we were very close to tears. The male vet and the nurse gently positioned Pablo on the bench. The vet took hold of his left paw began to inject an overdose of powerful anaesthetic into his bloodstream. Instantly, Pablo realized that he was dying and reared up out of the grasp of the young nurse. Urgently, I reached across and held his head to steady him just as the injection began to overwhelm him.

He then did a remarkable thing. He turned that big head I loved so much and looked directly at me: his eyes said goodbye to me. Then they clouded over and he slumped to the table and was gone. I hastened out from the clinic unashamedly in floods of tears. Catherine joined me in the car, equally distraught. On the way home she said the sensible thing.

'Remember we still have two other boys who need us and for their sake we need to act normal.'

I nodded and wondered how many times I could survive a broken heart. We didn't bury Pablo's body at the cottage. We had him cremated because I feared that whatever virulent virus had killed him might contaminate the soil and infect Luis and Max.

The night after the death of Pablo, I sat in the darkness of the conservatory and wondered how Pablo had become infected with what turned out to be such a deadly virus. Veterinary science could not offer an explanation and my thoughts were purely speculative. But I did wonder if Pablo's predilection for eating rabbits he caught on his hunting trips could have been a factor in his demise, especially since he seemed to like to eat the brains of his kills. I remembered the lethal virus myxomatosis, which was a manmade neural agent that accounted for mass destruction of the rabbit population in the 1950s. I wondered if some remnant had remained in the surviving rabbit population and had infected Pablo.

I missed him terribly and carved his name into the trunk of one of the trees he habitually climbed. I would never forget him. His photograph, mounted on the window sill in our bedroom, haunts me each morning as I open the bedroom window for air. He was magnificent. Catherine and I both loved him dearly. I never find it easy to say goodbye to a cherished and much loved animal friend.

It is some weeks since I wrote the above and during that time Max has matured to an astonishing extent. I find that now his behaviour is full of surprises. It just goes to show, I reflect, that cats, especially Maine Coons, are creatures of infinite depth and spread of personality. He has, to all intents and purposes, become a calmer, more affable and less troubled cat than he was. Also, he has become a true friend of mine and I feel most privileged at the welcome change in his attitude to me. The experience has taught me that one can never assume the love of an animal, especially a cat. One needs to earn it, to merit it.

When Max is taken for a walk around our large garden he parades slowly as if he is savouring every moment of the experience. He meanders here and there seemingly at random but I suspect he has his own agenda. He always inspects the barbeque and the bags of garden waste for any mysterious smells, he rubs his nose and head in the petals of any flowers he comes across in his path, just as Luis does, and he appears to delight in having a climb up any tree that takes his fancy. All of this is accomplished in an unhurried manner and he obviously enjoys it in a way that quite belies his former nervous rush down the garden to gain refuge in the sanctuary of the conservatory.

When I try to account for the difference in him I can only think that the tranquil ambience of the life we lead in the cottage has affected a change in how he identifies himself in relation to us and the world around him. I also believe that when he was treated with steroids a physical change was induced which allowed a change in his mental attitude. These reasons are speculative but something changed for the better, even if we cannot be sure what it was precisely. It could also be that he was able to change himself by an internal process of self awareness. Cats, like other mammals, are sentient beings and Maine Coons are reputed to be the most intelligent of all cats. In this respect I have observed Max behaving in a fashion very similar to Toby Jug's thoughtful pre-occupation with his own mental processes and feelings. I am aware that Max, in common with the other Maine Coon cats we have had, takes time out to have a think and I see him on the scratching post pedestal, especially in the moonlight, reflecting on life and the world as he sees it from a cat's perspective. At such times he is impervious to me, even though I am following a similar line of thought from a human perspective. If I then call to him when he is in this mode he doesn't respond because I am interrupting his mental flow. Sometime later, perhaps five or ten minutes after I have called to him, he will come to me with a friendly cry as if to say, 'What was it you wanted?' I will say, 'I understand, Max,' and he will then give me a throaty purr because we now comprehend each other. It is just like it was with Toby Jug. We are totally simpatico with each other. We often spend hours this way in the comfort of the conservatory, winter and summer alike.

There are also occasions when he comes looking to find me. Once discovered I am treated to a non-verbal display of curved back, upright and wavering tail, face-rubbing affection and stroking against the side of my chair or the lower length of my leg. This means in cat language: 'Hello. I've not forgotten about you and just wanted to keep in friendly touch.'

Such a demonstration of affection merits a stream of soothing and prizing words and strokes from me, after which, satisfied that our fellowship is in a good state, he will trot off to some other concern of his like having a game of chase upstairs and downstairs with Luis.

'Welcome to the world of free agents,' is my frequent plaudit to him as I congratulate him on his new found maturity. Now, whenever I settle down in the evening, Max comes to lie next to me, or as near as Luis will allow him since he usually takes pride of place on my left-hand side. If Luis challenges him, Max retreats for succour with Catherine and, if she is stretching out on the sofa, he will drape his not inconsiderable size over her like a warm blanket.

To my understanding, the way that Max has come to show love and affection for me after several years of ignoring me totally is nothing short of a phenomenon and leads me to realize that cats have profound and often latent attributes of personality which, as in Max's case, only truly emerge when the cat feels particularly secure in the love of those who care for him. It makes me wonder to see the astonishment which some of our friends show at the close bonds we have with our cats. They express views, which are not uncommon, such as: 'But cats are generally very self-focused animals and independent creatures, but yours are so different.'

I tell them that I believe that any animal, be it a horse, dog, cat, parrot or budgerigar, will always respond to kindly attention and caring affection, and that I know this because I've made good friendships with them all.

But to return to how I am with our cats, I can honestly state that quite apart from loving them deeply and being loved in return, I know them inside their minds and they know me; we are linked on a mental plane of mutual affection and understanding. They have even responded to my growing love of music, especially classical. One night as I was watching *Amadeus*, the story of Mozart's life, I was troubled to hear a discordant, rumbling interference to the soundtrack. I tried to find out where it was coming from until I realized that Max, who was lying behind me, was singing his purrs to accompany a piano concerto in the film. I was humbled by the discovery. Since then, we have found that Max is very fond of music and it was a revelation to both Catherine and myself to find that one of his favourite recordings is the soundtrack from the film *South Pacific*. Who can deny therefore that cats not only have mindful awareness and intuitive intelligence but also that they possess aesthetic appreciation of the creative arts? I often share appreciation of a beautiful sunset with my cats, in the same way that I did with Toby Jug and Fynn the horse on our camping trek into the Cheviot Hills one summer, some long years ago.

Max has now fully lived up to and deservedly earned the name that Jane mistakenly wrote out on his pedigree certificate: Maxamillion. He is truly one in a million.

ENDINGS

I am now near to closing this saga of our life at Owl Cottage with our four Maine Coon cats. But first of all let me back-track to the beginning to illustrate how we changed the cottage to become the very special Owl Cottage it is today. When Catherine and I first arrived, after newly acquiring the cottage and before we had any cats, we were faced with a place which had been severely neglected and which needed much repair and renovation. There were two stone outhouses which had become dilapidated with age and were now falling apart. I remembered them from my earlier time and had used them then as storage areas. One had also provided a shelter for Toby Jug in case of bad weather when I was not at home. We had these demolished and the stone was used again to build some low decorative garden walls. The residue was used with newer stone to build a garage, since the old wooden one was a ruin.

Further up the garden on the left-hand side, there used to be an unsightly horse paddock with a powdered grit base, partially surrounded by concrete. We dug it all up and, with the aid of several loads of topsoil, we were able to grass the patch once more and plant trees, lots and lots of trees, enough to turn the whole site into a woodland glade. Then we dug borders for flowering shrubs and flowers.

Next we turned our attention to renovating the inside of the cottage. A new bathroom and kitchen were fitted and given stone-tiled floors, while the old, ramshackle conservatory was replaced with a larger annexe, with wooden flooring, double-glazed windows and a glass door. We stripped the thick wallpaper from the room between the bathroom and the kitchen and installed a wood-burning stove within the arched fireplace. This is the living space we refer to as the cosy room. Painting and decorating followed until the look of the interior of the cottage was renewed and suited our taste.

It was at this stage that we recognized that the cottage would not be a home without a cat. Pablo came and took possession of us, the cottage and especially the garden, followed in fairly quick succession by those three other Maine Coon cats called Carlos, Luis and Max.

If I take an imaginary stroll down memory lane I become aware that the garden has figured as centre stage to our time at the cottage and has been the medium through which Catherine and I, and our family of cats, have lived our lives. Each tree, each bush and each flower is known personally to me and in turn to each of our cats.

In my younger life here at Owl Cottage my cat Toby Jug was fond of taking me on a tour of the garden to show me, for example, where the hedgehog hid during daylight, where a field mouse had built a nest of dried grasses in the compost heap which was now abandoned and where the grey toad had hibernated in a dank crevice formed by two ill-fitting stones.

These places are still there for the most part, but sadly Toby Jug is not. Yet I have found that my new cats have taken over this practice and on our walks around the garden they are anxious to point out to me the secret places they have discovered.

I will always revere the old gnarled apple tree with branches of thick rough bark which Toby Jug loved to climb and under which he is buried. Further up the garden there is a tall, green beech tree which bears the claw marks of Pablo's climbs. On his death his name was carved on its trunk by me and beneath the leaves of its branches his ashes were scattered to remind the earth that he, too, was once here. The trees growing in the compound we had built to house and protect our cats, with its runways and platforms, provide excellent shelter from stormy weather and also shade from the sun. If he is not relaxing in his hutch, Luis likes to hide in the thick stems of bamboo in readiness to ambush any hapless bird that might squeeze through the gaps in the chicken wire fencing; Max prefers, on fine days anyway, to settle high up in the canopy of the lilac tree. At ground level there is a flourishing rosebush, the white and pink flecked petals of which, when blown by the summer wind, may drop to adorn a flat grey stone, streaked with silver, that covers the grave of a prince of derring-do. On Midsummer's Eve, when wood nymphs, if such there be, are abroad and one chances by this stone, it might whisper the name Carlos in deference to the spirit of a fallen hero.

In a late autumn afternoon when I'm sitting at the top of the garden I'm sure to catch a glimpse of at least one bushy-tailed thief gathering a harvest from the branches of the hazelnut tree.

A stray sunbeam identifies the culprit as the red squirrel which lives with its mate in the plantation across the road. Gone now are the charming flowers of spring but the brief dalliance of white snowdrops, yellow and purple crocuses and golden daffodils remain painted on the backdrop of my memory. Summertime brings the brilliance of tulips from the vivid scarlet of 'Apeldoorn' to the vibrant yellow of 'Bellona' and the creamy white and green tints of 'Spring Green'. Then the season moves on to present us with the delectable sights and scents of the tea rose garden that Catherine and I hold most dear.

Here and there in our garden areas we have often found a single flower which is out of place, and we were at first mystified as to how this plant, be it daffodil or tulip or hyacinth, could have come to be planted where there are no others of its kind. One day in the local cafe at Felton we were remarking on this strange phenomenon when an experienced gardener enlighten-ed us. From his account, which I have no reason to doubt, the phantom planters are field mice which dig up some flower bulbs in autumn and replant them elsewhere as an emergency food store for winter. If the mouse forgets about them, or more likely perishes, then the bulbs will flower in the spring in their new setting. In this way, just as one example, the wildlife contributes to the natural beauty of our garden. I have even seen a coal tit planting sunflower seeds that I have put out for the birds to eat in container pots. Like the field mouse, he is helping with the gardening and nature is spreading and renewing herself with the help of her wild creatures.

There is also an abundance of small conifers and bushes in the flowering borders, which create dense and inviting areas of thick foliage for our two remaining boy cats, Luis and Max, to explore as they romp around the garden with us holding their leads. It is their practice to plunge their heads deeply inside some of the bushes they encounter, looking for birds and mice, but when this occurs in contact with a shrub called Choisya or Mexican Orange Blossom, as it is better known, the pollen from its star-shaped scented flowers causes an explosive fit of cat sneezes.

In Northumberland, autumnal fogs and drizzling mists are to be expected but this is also the time when hibernating animals need to stock up body fat to tide them through the winter. From my vantage point in the conservatory, my cats and I share a window on the world of the garden outside. We sit in complete darkness with the blinds open and we watch in silence. My cats, especially dear Pablo, taught me the cat skill of silent watchfulness. So we listen and observe. Our eyes cannot penetrate the misty curtains stretched before us outside until, that is, a pale moon illuminates white veils of a hazy vapour cloud. Then the boy cats and I lean forward excitedly as dark shadowy shapes can be seen secretly foraging over the grass for slugs, worms and snails. The moon brightens and casts a silvery translucent shroud over the dank foliage of bushes and trees, and suddenly we hear the muted scream of a little owl on the hunt. Then we dimly recognize a resident family of hedgehogs, a female and three piglets moving searchingly between the darkened trunks of trees. We watch in awe as this panoply of nature unfolds delightfully before us.

There is one exceptional feature of life at Owl Cottage which I must mention and that is the bountiful bird life which inhabits and visits our garden. During Pablo's time here I had to be cautious about attracting songbirds by hanging feeders out because he was an accomplished killer of wildlife; it was his instinctive drive, but since his departure I feel free to encourage birdlife to nest and raise their families in our garden. To this end I have placed bird boxes on the more mature trees, and on the wall to the left of the conservatory, where there is a heavy growth of greenery, I have inserted nesting boxes to encourage sparrows, titmice, wrens and finches to nest and raise their young.

Meanwhile, I make sure that the bird-feed station around the bird table is well supplied with sunflower seeds and dried worms, not to mention peanuts. During the day we are regaled by the sight through the conservatory window of goldfinches, nuthatches and great spotted woodpeckers availing themselves of the handouts freely given. Our resident pair of ring doves keeps us amused and enchanted each day by their obvious devotion to each other; they even drink from the bird bath together.

Now that I have almost reached the end of my tale of two people and four Maine Coon cats at Owl Cottage, I am suffering a state of denial about closing this account because it constitutes an ending of what I most treasure in my life. Yet I recognize that

Owl Cottage will always be here for future generations to enjoy and we still have two healthy and extremely happy Maine Coons who, beside their loving attachment to us, have the freedom to savour separate and sentient lives of their own and all that personally matters to them.

I yearn for what was and cannot be again, at least not for me. I know that there are still remote grassy meadows in the woods below the Cheviot Hills where skylarks nest and ascend to sing their throbbing hymns to life; I have been there and I have watched and heard them. I am aware that given a modicum of help the wildlife of this beautiful county can thrive and renew itself each year. I also know that when the winter comes again it will bring icy blizzards to cover the cottage and garden in a mantle of deep snow and I will look out on it in the company of my beloved cats and appreciate, as always, the sheer wonders of nature. But as I look out once more, in my heart I will be remembering a particular trail of paw tracks long ago belonging to a certain cat called Toby Jug, to whom my mind can never really say goodbye. Under the snow and ice the garden itself will be resting to recoup its strength for a new beginning of growth and floral abundance. Snow-covered Owl Cottage will also be resting, sheltering and preserving the life within it and everywhere around will be in a blessed natural state of grace before awakening once more to the hustle and bustle of the active life of flora and fauna.

When the winter goes and eventually summertime comes around again, Catherine and I will sit out in the garden with our cats Luis and Max and luxuriate in the sweetness of the air and the sound of vibrant birdsong. We will talk again of early times at Owl Cottage and pay homage to the many gifts it has bestowed upon us. Owl Cottage will remain forever as a celestially favoured site where elegance and grace are waiting in readiness to stimulate the creative mind to higher things and a profound love of nature.

HIGH CRIMES

JOHN WESTERMANN

POCKET BOOKS

New York   London   Toronto   Sydney   Tokyo

POCKET BOOKS, a division of Simon & Schuster Inc.
1230 Avenue of the Americas, New York, NY 10020

Copyright © 1988 by John Westermann
Cover art copyright © 1989 David Loew

Published by arrangement with Soho Press, Inc.
Library of Congress Catalog Card Number: 88-15771

ISBN: 0-671-67968-6

First Pocket Books printing November 1989

10 9 8 7 6 5 4 3 2 1

POCKET and colophon are trademarks of
Simon & Schuster Inc.

Printed in the U.S.A.

For Jessica

The author would also like to acknowledge the assistance and support of the following friends: Rhoda Keller, Mavis McIntosh, Rita Scott, Ray Powers, and Lisa Westermann.

. . . In the . . . black and bloody mire,
The dire wolf collects his dues
while the boys sing round the fire . . .
                    "Dire Wolf"

*Words by Robert Hunter,
music by Jerry Garcia*

HIGH CRIMES

1
Body Language

"What did we do now?" Jimmy Tibaldi wanted to know.

The window behind Lieutenant Cumberstadt's desk opened onto an airshaft shimmering with heat. Someone was laughing in another office. Detectives Nelson and Tibaldi stood on the carpet in front of the gray metal desk; they had not been invited to sit. Tree Nelson had long brown hair and a bandit mustache. The T-shirt he wore said FREE MUSTACHE RIDES HERE; it had been purple when he bought it in 1978. Tibaldi was less formally attired in jeans, pink polo shirt, and a 9-millimeter Sig Sauer. His lips were tightly drawn behind the navy-style beard. Lieutenant Cumberstadt sat upright, peeling an apple with his red Swiss Army knife.

"Ah. My two favorite crime fighters," he said. "Side by side like a pair of balls. Tanned, happy." The lieutenant shook his head. "You haven't done anything, Detective Tibaldi." He sighed. "Not a blessed thing. Which is exactly what I have to talk to you about."

Tibaldi smacked his lips. Nelson watched the apple skin fall to the blotter. They waited. Tree Nelson hated these moments of prolonged anticipation that were so much a part of a policeman's lot. Like waiting for a dentist to read X-rays.

"The goddamn stats for July," Cumberstadt said, "they just came in."

"Oh yeah?" Jimmy Tibaldi spoke with none of the deference a lieutenant normally expected of his men. "How did we do?"

"You just don't seem to be getting the hang of it. You two slackers have more sick days than arrests. Murder, gambling, prostitution, drugs—every vice known to modern man is flourishing in this fair hamlet. And yet I can open my office door almost any afternoon and find the pair of you rolling golf balls into aluminum ashtrays."

"We *have* had a run of bad luck," Tree Nelson said.

"Yeah," Tibaldi concurred. "Strep throats, sprained ankles, whatnot. We feel as bad about it as you do."

"You guys are pulling my chain," the lieutenant said, "which I find a rather unique approach to a career crisis."

"Me and Tree don't think of this as a career," Tibaldi said. He waved his arms in the air. "This is like driving a garbage truck, a garbage truck without a floor. You toss in the garbage"—he mimed the loading—"you drive away. And *voilà!*"

"Very amusing," Cumberstadt said. "The commissioner called a short time ago to express—how shall I put it—his displeasure with the low stats in my command. Your stats, Detectives."

Cumberstadt cored the apple.

14

"What I would like to be able to tell the commissioner the next time he calls is that the Rastafarian residents of this community are going to improve their behavior before the department's third-quarter figures come out. I'd like to be able to give him that nice warm feeling about us, instead of always more bad news about you guys."

Jimmy Tibaldi was steaming. "Easy to say. Easy to throw rocks at the man in the street from behind a desk. Who are we supposed to dump on? Tree and I aren't even married." Tibaldi was huffing. "Tell him we'll *all* have that nice warm feeling when he assigns more than *two* detectives to twenty career criminals who also happen to be witch doctors."

Cumberstadt interrupted his skinning. "You guys are unreal. Are you saying the assignment is beyond you?"

"You got some set," Tibaldi spat. "You'd think we *wanted* this gang war in the middle of golf season."

Cumberstadt's scalp grew pink beneath the light blond hairs on his head. "It's your turf! The Rastas became your beat when you changed your name from Officer to Detective. You and Nelson are supposed to watch Gladstone Lanier and his merry band, while Aviles and Gonzales watch the Spanish Brothers, and Hoskinson and Moses watch everybody else. My life is very fucking simple, fellas, and you guys are fucking that up."

"What Jimmy means is we need more men," Nelson said. "At least enough for all three shifts. Right now, when we go home these mothers start to howl."

"There's no more money. You two college boys are just gonna have to work a little harder."

"You should only know how little we learned," Nelson said.

Tibaldi spoke to Nelson as if they were alone: "Don't you find it strange how many bosses here quiver before the sheepskin?"

"We'll do the best we can," said Nelson to the lieutenant, as if Tibaldi wasn't there. "From now on."

Tree and Jimmy had gone to college together in that revolutionary time when schoolwork was optional. Their grade-point averages combined was less than 4.0. They succumbed to the police recruiter on campus when it looked like the only offer of gainful employment they were likely to receive. Since then their degrees had worked against them.

"Thank you, Nelson." Cumberstadt feigned a smile. "Now give me some status. What have you got going?"

"We . . ." Tree Nelson looked at Jimmy, who was suddenly examining his fingernails. It was true, he thought, you almost had to make an appointment with Tibaldi to get him to do police work. "We may have found a complainant with the balls to sign a statement: one of the factory owners sick of paying the Rastas for protection. He's supposed to call us sometime this morning. If that doesn't pan out, we'll bust another crack dealer and try to turn his ass around. What the hell, maybe we'll get lucky."

Cumberstadt nodded judiciously, as if he concurred. "We can always use a narc number."

"Big deal," Tibaldi said, under his breath. "Case dismissed."

Nelson smiled, because Jimmy was himself a weekend abuser, who loved nothing better than doing time with a bag of grass and a case of beer. "We do what we can," he said, assuming the guise of the hard-working cop who has heroically faced the bleak Big Picture. Nelson assumed the posture of spiritual exhaustion understood by all cops, that feeling that if you can't be everywhere, why be anywhere.

"We need a victory," Cumberstadt said as the phone rang. "Twelfth Precinct, Crime Prevention Unit. Yes, sir." It was the commissioner. Lieutenant Cumberstadt's expression was unmistakable. "We're doing the best we can, sir. If we had a few more men—" The guys in the precinct called him the Spaghetti Boss, because once you put him in a little hot water . . . "I understand what you're saying, sir. Yes sir." Cumberstadt hung up. "Body," he announced. "Crosse Forge Company, off Bennington Avenue."

It was the third in as many weeks. Tibaldi and Nelson exchanged glances and turned to leave.

"Before you go," Cumberstadt said, scratching an ear. "If you two wish to maintain your current status in this department, it would behoove you—"

"Tick, tick, tick," said Tibaldi, looking at his watch. "What's the take-home message?"

Cumberstadt's face went beet red, his lips chalky. "The commissioner is not pleased."

"Call him back and tell him you quit," said Tibaldi. "That'll cheer him up."

"Nice going," Tree said as they walked from the back door of the station house to the unmarked gray Chevy that had been their office for the last twelve weeks. "You're gonna talk us onto school crossings in Syosset for the next five years if you don't watch what you say to him. Asshole or not, he's still the god-damned boss."

"That little pussy hides all day and he wants to break *my* balls?" Jimmy's cheeks were flushed.

"Stroking the boss so we can do our thing is better than banging him," Tree said. "We're on Easy Street, my man. Let's stick around for more than a cup of coffee."

"At what cost?" Jimmy Tibaldi said, indignant. "Can't you tell when our dignity is at stake?"

"Usually not until you tell me afterwards."

"Your middle name should be Doormat."

"And yours should be. . . . You want me to drive?"

"No! I don't want you to drive."

Nelson half closed his eyes for the duration of the ride over to Bennington to protect them from the wind racing through the car as Tibaldi floored it, screeching out of the police parking lot and across the unincorporated village of Seaport.

Seaport, Long Island, ten miles from the New York City line. The northern two-thirds was crowded and shabby, a horizontal slum, the monotonous grid of level streets lined with rooming houses, body shops, small churches and less-than-exotic Arab delicatessens. The massive brick housing projects that break the grid are shared by the working poor with crack fiends, drunks, and hookers. Everything and anything is for sale or rent.

The southern third of Seaport, the waterfront, remains, like waterfront everywhere, precious. Except where marshland has been turned into industrial park, and dock space swallowed by trawlers. Four-story condominiums crowd the bay, but the young, predominantly childless, commuters who live in them have nothing to do with the northern sectors, unless they happen to use cocaine.

A decade earlier Sunrise Highway had been the DMZ, separating blacks and whites, but a new wave of Latin and Caribbean immigrants had totally confused the map and the rules.

Tibaldi stopped for a red light and a voice called to them, "Yo, Tree. Yo, Jimbo," and Nelson knew without looking that they had crossed North Main, the newest demarcation line: between the blacks on the east side and the Spanish neighborhoods to the west.

At the intersection of Henry and Plaza, in front of a closed-down movie theater, a small black girl skipped rope. "Ninety-eight, ninety-nine, a hundred. Hi, police!"

"Hi, darlin'." Tree waved.

A white-haired baglady, wearing gym shorts, high-top basketball shoes, and a cardigan, leaped from the roof of an abandoned car into the dumpster behind Dunkin' Donuts.

Jimmy laughed. "We shoulda filmed that in slow motion." He imitated an announcer's deep basso voice: " 'Air Jordans . . . are for *eve-ry-body!*' "

At the end of Bennington, in a cul-de-sac by the Long Island Railroad trestle, drab factories pumped smoke into the hazy sky—Nelson shaded his eyes with his hand. We were here yesterday, he thought, pretending to protect life and property.

Jimmy pulled up in front of Crosse Forge. He and Tree got out and pushed their way through the crowd of people standing behind the sawhorses. They flashed their gold shields at the uniformed cop standing guard at the door.

"Get masks, guys. This one's funky."

"Old?" Nelson said.

"Naw. Used and abused."

Nelson and Tibaldi donned breathing apparatus from the Crime Scene van and walked inside the shop. The machines were silent, the benches and tools inert, because the man who brought all this to life was naked, hanging by the neck from a hoist in the middle of the shop, his waist eye-level to the masked and rubber-gloved detectives gathered around him with cameras and clipboards.

Gummy strands of blood hung from his crotch to a pool beneath his feet. The body was naked and mis-shapen, a pewter ingot, solid and permanent, extrud-ing from the corpse's hideously swollen lips. The air the mask supplied Tree was not enough.

Tibaldi nearly gagged. He looked at his brother officers, wondering why there wasn't a more visible effort to right these monstrous wrongs. A touch made him flinch. It was Gallo, a sergeant from Homicide.

"What?" the sergeant said with exaggerated sar-casm. "Was it crowded on the back nine?"

"Sorry," Nelson said, grateful for the excuse to look away. "Cumberbutt had us kissing his ring."

Gallo grunted and nodded, and he began reciting the particulars. "Mr. Georges Crosse. He was shot in each kneecap. Over here"—he pointed down the aisle between the workbenches—"by the bloodstains. And they poured the boilermaker down his throat over here. We found hair and skin samples in that vise. I expect we'll find his dick when the medical examiner takes that plug out of his mouth."

Gallo motioned for them to follow him from the work area to the small paneled office. Inside, he closed the door and pulled off his mask, then sat in Georges Crosse's high-backed leather chair.

"So," he said, "you recognize the work?"

Nelson pulled off his mask; the inside was slick with sweat. "We knew the victim," Nelson said. "Talked to him yesterday. He was ready to drop a dime on Gladstone Lanier."

"Anybody see you workin' him?"

"Of course," Nelson said. "We stop and talk to lots of people. Everybody knows us."

Tibaldi was looking at the Japanese tool company calendar on Georges's desk, the twenty-four smallest tits he had seen since high school. He looked up now. "What are you getting at? You think we tipped our mitts and got him minted?"

"I think somebody came in here last night and fucked that nigger where he breathed. That's what I think. And work like they done is meant to leave a message. So maybe running his mouth to you two wasn't an inspired idea. Hot tips sink loose lips."

"Why say something like that?" Tibaldi said. "Nobody knows what we talked about."

Gallo lifted his chin. "Because I don't like empty suits, who don't give a fuck, running around my zone getting people wasted."

"Okay," Tibaldi said, nodding vigorously. "Fuck it then! We're wasting our time. You're the only one who cares. Okay?"

"How are you gonna collar anybody if you don't even try, Tibaldi. Ever think about that?"

"Hey," Nelson said to both of them. "Come on. We're all a little pissed we haven't nailed these pricks, but that's no reason to start on each other."

Gallo wasn't buying. "People are starting to talk funny about you two."

Now Nelson bristled: "You think we're on the pad? Is that your allegation, Sergeant Gallo?"

"Take it any fucking way you like."

Nelson looked down at the grimy linoleum and shook his head. Then he looked Gallo straight in the eye. "You're wrong. Way the fuck off base."

"Just a word to the wise," said Gallo.

Jimmy Tibaldi said, "Save your breath."

Nelson and Tibaldi went back to the shop floor. A cop on a stepladder was cutting the corpse down with a blowtorch. A cart had been jerry-rigged underneath, with nothing to cushion the imminent descent. Tibaldi motioned that he and Nelson should go and they retraced their steps to the door. Outside, they couldn't turn in their air masks fast enough.

Tibaldi ran his fingers through his hair and beard. "I know it's early, but I sure could use me a cold one."

"Not till my stomach stops turning."

"Actually, I feel more like driving past the Blake Hotel and blowing a couple of those scumbags away."

"You think it's the Rastaman?"

"Who else?"

In the car, the first blast and smell of the air conditioner gave Nelson a chill. He shuddered, as if someone were walking on his grave.

"So what do we do now?" Tibaldi said, as they drove away. "Start a canvass? Buy a bag of birdsong? I still say we could save ourselves a whole lot of trouble by waxing that prick one night on our own time."

Tree seemed not to hear him. He winced. "How could they mutilate a guy like that?"

"Like Gallo says, it's a message to somebody. Anybody, everybody—mind your fucking business. Shit, if we could only catch him doing anything."

We couldn't catch a cold, Nelson thought. The truth

was, they had no idea what to do. They had been uniform cops too long. Uniform cops rarely saw things through to the end. They called the doctor, wrote the report, stuffed the body in a bag, and notified the next of kin. When they were handed the gold shields, nobody had said anything about anything like this. Some detectives.

Tibaldi turned onto the Strip. Two skanky white hookers and a beautiful black transvestite were working the last of the morning's city-bound commuters. Every lady had her spot, every dealer had his own doorway in the open-air market along Main Street. Life was normal, profitable. Sweet. For everyone except Georges Crosse.

They cruised past the Blake Hotel, the run-down rooming house where Gladstone Lanier and his associates bedded down.

"Merrick Road," Nelson said. "Maybe he's down there spooking the bodega owners."

"Right."

There was no sign of him downtown. Tibaldi parked in front of a florist shop. A line of people waited under its yellow canvas awning for the bus. The door to the shop was closed, they noted, the blinds drawn.

"We ought to let the man know," Tibaldi said.

"You sure we aren't the kiss of death?"

Tibaldi cut the engine. "Paranoia strikes deep."

Inside they found Jensen Macomber sitting behind the counter on a stool. He held a shotgun in his hands.

"We come in peace," Nelson said and laughed weakly.

Macomber nodded and leaned the gun against a shelf. Metallic balloons floated above the cash register. Like ingots, thought Nelson. "Hey, Jensen," he said, "what about some bad motherfucker comes in here and shoves that gun up your ass?"

"Not bloody likely," Macomber said.

Macomber was in his fifties but trim, and Nelson did not doubt that he would be a problem for the unsuspecting robber. Would that Gladstone Lanier were an unsuspecting thief, and not the local Prince of Darkness.

Tibaldi said, "I take it you heard about Georges Crosse?"

"Everybody heard."

"Lanier?"

Macomber sneered. "I'm sure he has heard, too."

"I mean, was it our friend at the Blake who did it?" Nelson said.

"Not by his own hand, you can be sure of that. He's got plenty of mates more than willing to savage his enemies." Macomber walked to the front of his shop and peered out between the blinds. The back of his neck looked like a Labrador puppy's. He had sweated through his tan knee-length smock. Nelson doubted that it was just the heat.

"Me and Jimmy don't have a thing we could use."

Macomber nodded absently. "We can talk sometime, but not here. Not now. I don't relish the thought of that creature stopping by to stuff a rosebush down my throat. Georges was a friend for most of my life. We were boys together in Jamaica."

Tibaldi nodded. "You tell us when and where. Say, in a couple of days."

"I'll call you," said Macomber.

"Make it Monday," Nelson said, "if you can."

"Georges was holding back," Tibaldi said. "He should have spoken up, fought back."

"Be kind to the dead, Detective. He has family in Jamaica he couldn't protect. He has family here, as do I and many of the other shopkeepers around here. Perhaps he did his level best for you. He may have even died with your names on his lips."

"Yeah," Nelson said, avoiding Macomber's eyes.

"I tell you, get out of here. I will be in touch."

Nelson and Tibaldi returned to their car, and Nelson entered Macomber's name into the Witnesses Interviewed list. One was better than none, if Cumberstadt asked.

"So," Jimmy said, "do we report back to our favorite lieutenant?"

"And tell him what—that they even snipped his johnson off?"

For a moment there was silence in the car as the radio served up dead air. Then the calls began again, a static wailing: stolen auto, family fight, missing kid. Another body. Tibaldi and Nelson turn instinctively toward the sound. Homicide. Victim: Angel Rodriguez Colon. They know him, everyone knows him. The Cock is a man about town. Was. He has been found in a dumpster, a bullet behind each ear, his throat slit and his tongue pulled through the opening. A Colombian Necktie. They look away. It's unrelated. It's not theirs.

Tibaldi said, "I just want this day to end."

"Okay." Nelson wiped his face. "Okay. We'll get some lunch, then figure our next move. Only, when we call in, it's your turn to jerk off Cumberbutt."

Tibaldi squinted against the light. "What we want is cocktails—big ones. With little umbrellas and pieces of fruit. Down by the water."

"When the going gets tough, the tough go to lunch."
Nelson shook his head. "We eyeball the corpses and
jerk off the bosses."

People disappear, bodies send messages, and we
make a pit stop. Gallo was right, he thought. What a
couple of empty suits.

2

The Lost Boys

Trevor Nelson is napping in the passenger seat as Jimmy Tibaldi parks his black Corvette next to Tree's old Volvo, in the slot marked PENTHOUSE—T. NELSON. Tree's father owns the waterfront condominium but does not live here. Tree pays him a minuscule rent for the suite overlooking Baldwin Bay.

Jimmy Tibaldi lives alone in Garden City, but he tries to spend as little time as possible in his one-bedroom walk-up.

They climb out of the car and walk unsteadily into the lobby, singing, "Weekends were made for Michelob."

"Ah, oh," Jimmy says, stopping short. "There's Annie. We're bagged."

"Steady now," says Tree. "Make yourself invisible."

Annie Sutherland is checking her mailbox. Ozone, her gray-striped alley cat, is trying to tie himself around her ankles.

Annie is thirty-five and pretty, with long blond hair and an athlete's body, a holdover from the seventies.

She would make a perfect surfer, thinks Jimmy, if there were still some surf about on Long Island.

Annie pumps gasoline at the local Getty station, today in a tight white halter (which she has miraculously kept clean), cut-off jeans, and hiking boots. Besides serving on the condo board, she also works nights for a caterer. She used to teach art. She says she likes doling out food and fuel.

Her parents live next to Tree's father in Westhampton Beach, which is not to say they are of equal caste. Her folks are year-rounders by necessity, professors at a local university. Annie's mother's mother had built the house after the hurricane of 1938, and then resisted Alistair Nelson's efforts to buy her out during the forties and fifties. He finally gave up and erected a high brick wall, the very first wall his son was to scale. She has known Tree since childhood, Jimmy since college.

"Are you two drunk again?" she says, seeing them slinking by. "Who the hell is minding the store?"

"We had a grisly day, woman," Jimmy says. "Cut us some slack."

Tree kisses her lightly on the top of her head. "How'd you do?" he says.

"Mediocre," she says. "I got a couple of good tips."

"Wiping down windshields again?" Jimmy chortles.

Annie's real smile, her crooked grin, appears on her well-tanned face. "Just the classy ones. Mercedes and Jags. No Vettes, or anything tacky like that."

She pushes the elevator button and then holds the door for them while Tree reads his envelopes and throws them away. "Today," she says, tapping her foot. "I have to go out later."

"Where?" says Tree.

"Out."

From the look on her face that is all they are getting.

"Are you mad that we're drunk?" he asks.

"You're not that drunk. Jimmy's still dribbling from the side of his mouth. Drunk is when he dribbles from the middle of his bottom lip."

Tree is about to say hello to the guard at the desk as they pass, but he can't remember his name.

The elevator door closes and they ascend to the second floor, where Annie's one-bedroom faces inland. "You guys want dinner, or what?"

Tree says, "Sure." Jimmy wants to know what she has.

"Broccoli quiche and everything bagels. Some wine."

"We'll be down in an hour," Tree says. "I'm going for a run."

"Good," she says. "I'm going with you. Come along, Ozone." The cat obeys—like a dog.

Tree and Jimmy shake their heads in disbelief.

Tree and Annie are making the loop around Hempstead Lake, running side by side on the bridle path. The air above the picnic grounds is filled with charcoal smoke and Frisbees. "Let's pick it up a little," Tree says. "I gotta elevate my heart rate."

"I gotta get out of this rut," she says.

"What rut?" He resents her discontent. As far as he's concerned, things are going good, if she'd just leave well enough alone.

"The mundane jobs. Our mundane relationship. All of it, I guess. . . . We could move away," she says. "I'd like to live somewhere else, somewhere warm.

You don't have to be a cop. Just because you fell for that campus recruiter doesn't mean you owe them your life."

"I'm not going anywhere, sister. I've got it made here. Five more years and they can kiss my ass forever. Besides, what would Jimmy do? We're both ruined for regular jobs."

"I don't care about Jimmy Tibaldi. I'm not in love with Jimmy Tibaldi. I can't wait that much longer, Tree. Every day puts me further into the red zone on having a baby."

"What do you want with a kid?"

She stops running abruptly. Two strides later he does, too.

"I'm saying if something doesn't happen soon, I'm outta here. Okay? You understand, knucklehead?"

"Split? Load up a van and head to California? We're too damn old for that, Annie."

"Too old for this, too young for that. What if I said I want to put this half-assed love affair on paper?"

He doesn't answer. He doesn't know anything where she is concerned. He runs with her, they swim, they lift weights, they make love. And yet he lives on her periphery, what he believes to be her periphery.

"Well?" she says. "Say something. You always used to give such good advice."

He looks at her rosy face, her nipples against the nylon singlet, the sleek wheels and hard ass. "Maybe we *should* get married," he says.

"We're not even going steady."

"You're absolutely right. Forget I mentioned it."

"Let's think about it," she says, pushing past him, running away.

The thought of loving her forever fills him with a

sudden saving grace. He ducks his head and takes off in hot pursuit. But by the time he catches up with her, and times his stride to hers, his confidence is mixed with tired doubts.

She pulls ahead and he finally slows to a jog, feeling the alcohol careening around in his system and smiling at Annie sprinting back to the apartment house. In no time at all she is out of his sight.

"He's out running, Mona. Why don't you try again later?"

"When?"

"I don't know. Fifteen, twenty minutes."

Jimmy is sipping Chivas and smoking a joint on the balcony, getting specially affected, herbally refreshed. He has the munchies, and, like a starving child, beyond filling his belly there is nothing on his mind.

"Half an hour, then," he says.

"I wish he was more reliable."

"You ought to work with him," Jimmy says. "You don't know the half of it . . . Hey, wait a minute. Here he comes." From his perch on the balcony, Jimmy sees Tree walking toward the building with his hands on his hips. "Yo, Tree. Telephone," he bellows down.

"Who?" Tree yells up, wiping the sweat from his mustache.

"Mona."

Tree flinches, ever so grateful that Annie's windows are on the other side of the building. "Tell her I'll call her later."

"He said he'll call you later, babe."

"I'm going out later."

"Later's no good," Jimmy calls down.

"Tell her to call again when she can, then."

"Mona, Tree says to try him again when you can."

"Well, you tell him once a month ain't making it for me. I get that kind of attention from my ex."

Jimmy knows that this is all Tree will give her: slide-by quickies when he's had too much to drink. He says she gives him the Mozambiques, that syndrome deadly to relationships that occurs the moment after orgasm, when he wishes either he or she were in Mozambique, and it doesn't matter which.

"So why don't you put more men on the job?" Jimmy says to Mona.

"Meaning you?"

"Now don't get me wrong, I mean, you're a fine-looking lady, but Tree's like a brother to me, and if there's one rule I—"

"You got handcuffs too?"

"And leg irons."

"How would you like to take me to an X-rated motel?"

He met Mona once with Tree, quite by accident, at the Walt Whitman mall. She was wearing skin-tight blue jeans and Candi boots, and her T-shirt said KEEP YOUR HANDS OFF MY EARS, I KNOW WHAT I'M DOING. It wouldn't be the first time, he thinks. Tree only bangs Mona to get back at Annie anyway.

"Then again, he's not my biological brother."

"When?"

"I'll call you next week. We'll talk dirty to each other."

"I love it!" she says. "You're such a prick."

Jimmy hangs up as Tree comes in. "Hustle it up, willya. Annie said one hour. I'm starving. And horny. Your little tart, Mona, just gave me a raging woody.

You don't mind if I let her ease the pain, do you, partner?''

"Not at all," says Tree. "It gets lonely in Mozambique.''

"Have I told you lately that I think you're a helluva guy.''

"I want to hear you say that after you've spent more than an hour with her.''

"Let me make my own mistakes," Jimmy says. "Please.''

"Haven't I always?''

Annie, her damp hair wrapped in a towel, glides about her well-lit kitchen fixing dinner for her "Lost Boys." The rest of her apartment is cool and dark. Her balcony offers only the northern vista of small houses, and children on Big Wheels; she keeps the drapes closed most days and all nights. Her rooms are smaller than those of the penthouse though she has too much furniture and bric-a-brac scattered about— an abundance of clutter from a life compressed. The couch, the bar, the cocktail table, the loveseat: all are slightly worn but expensive Early American, solid, comfortable relics from her days as a doctor's wife. She got it all in the end, everything he had. But then, one need hardly dicker with a corpse.

An album from the sixties, *Workingman's Dead*, plays on her stereo. It seems to spark her; she dances around the kitchen, the refrigerator door her partner.

The guys walk into her apartment without knocking. They take their regular places at the dining-room table, where Annie has laid out steaming pans of quiche and a pile of buttered bagels. Their plates are paper, the forks saved from McDonald's. They eat in silence.

Nelson looks over her turbaned head to the mantel, where, trapped in a gold-leaf frame, reposes the image of Doctor John Sutherland, killed in a senseless accident. It seems to him like only yesterday . . . when Annie became again her parents' daughter—much too young to be a doctor's widow and no longer soon-to-be-rich.

She rises from the table, wiping her mouth. "Help me with dessert," she says to Jimmy. He grumbles something about woman's work and follows her into the kitchen.

She says softly, "There's been a little change in the weather. You were so snotty before, I wasn't gonna tell you."

"You got the blow?"

"I got the blow." She slips two small amber vials filled with cocaine and a tiny silver spoon into his hand.

"Ah," Jimmy says. "The days of lines and noses. Thank you, condo-mommy. Thank you. I'll pay you at a more convenient time."

Jimmy goes into the bathroom and locks the door, digs out a pile of snow, sniffs, snorts, secures the load. He smiles to himself about sneaking on Tree, who also did his share of shit way back when. But Annie doesn't want him to know anymore, like he's on a health kick or got religion all of a sudden, which Jimmy knows just isn't true. And even though Annie stopped packing her nose in April, she still has her connections. She is the only one Jimmy will ask to score the occasional social gram for him, the only one he trusts.

The coke connects. Jimmy smiles. He runs the water in the sink and stares, remembering.

He met Tree at Trinity College in Hartford the week

of freshman orientation, and they lived together all four years, first in a dorm, then an apartment off campus, then in the Presidential Suite of the Sigma Nu fraternity house on Vernon Street.

Sigma Zoo everyone called it. Now sadly defunct. Jimmy sighs with nostalgia. There were the unpaid bar bills, the annual Rites of Spring Riot with the Hartford Police Department, and those scandalous public accusations that the frat had become nothing more than a hostel for boozing, doping, and whoring.

Jimmy had warned his parents before heading off to school: "Where else can I do for four years what those people are going to let me do?" And he was right. Most of his friends were trapped in dull careers or their father's footsteps. Some already had 2.5 children. "A wonderful opportunity," his father had argued. "Moe Drabowsky went there, for Christ's sake. Charlie Sticka, George Will—"

"Listen, Pop. I've looked at life from angles you wouldn't believe, and it's come to me that on the average, people only get about fifteen years or so to really fuck around and enjoy themselves, and that only when they're too damn old and sick to appreciate it. I just thought I should tell you—I'm taking mine now."

The day after graduation, while everyone was still in town, Jimmy married Stacy O'Brien, his on again–off again college sweetheart. The union lasted three and a half bitter years, and gave issue to a child named Susan, now twelve years old, who lived with her mother in Wallingford, Connecticut.

It wasn't all Jimmy's fault the marriage failed. Stacy hated sleeping alone when Jimmy worked midnights. So she stayed up late and read romance novels. She hated his new cop buddies, whom she found crude and unsociable. Even Tree was better company, and she was already sick to death of him. So she took some courses to find herself, then took a lover, a professor in the economics department.

They went to a marriage counselor, who suggested a trial separation. Jimmy suggested he separate the professor's head from his shoulders. Stacy grabbed her bag and walked out.

"That fucking nerd," Jimmy was screaming while he pounded the hood of her Jeep with his fists. "That pencil-neck fucking geek."

When he got home from work that night, his clothes, his stereo and his golf clubs were boxed and ready to go.

The counseling continued. Jimmy learned about Quality Time and Autonomous Adulthood, Distance and Desolation, New Beginnings. But Jimmy spent very little time at his new apartment, very little time on self-repair. He hung around his ex-house on his days off, playing Chutes and Ladders with Susan, and he followed Stacy on her dates at night. He threatened to kill the marriage counselor, who he felt had sided with Stacy's need to be free of him, probably because the guy was doing her, too.

Stacy notified his superiors at the police department. He slashed her tires. He tore up her best dresses. Stacy ran for her life.

"It's not worth all the heartache," she told Jimmy before driving away in the Ryder rental truck. "You don't love me. You don't trust me. You'll never respect me. I'll find Susan another playmate, hopefully one more her age."

"You're a bimbo, Stacy. I can't believe I was dumb enough to marry you."

"Then you won't miss me."

"Of course I'll miss you . . . I'll miss the baby. You're killing me," he told her.

Susan comes to Long Island every year for the month of July, but you wouldn't call father and daughter close. He has, over the years, gotten over her. He doesn't speak of her daily activities any more, doesn't bother with the long-distance runaround. Camp, school, riding, skiing . . . he couldn't say where she is or what she's doing. And, of course, Susan worships the ground her father walks on, her faraway knight who would be with her if he could.

Jimmy does however complain with some regularity about the monthly checks he addresses to Stacy the Slut Sponge.

"What are we doing tonight?" Tree says to Annie when she returns from the kitchen with three bowls of ice cream. The towel is off; her damp hair hangs to her shoulder.

"I told you," Annie says. "Make your plans without me."

"Why don't you meet us at the bar later," Tree suggests.

"Because I've got things to do."

"What things?" Tree asks her. "It's Friday night."

"I got another letter from John's parents. I want to answer it tonight. They want me to fly out there again," she says.

"Let the poor bastard rest in peace, willya," Jimmy says, sitting back down at the table.

"They're good people, Jimmy. They care about me."

"Only because you help them remember their son."

Annie sits down slowly, in sections, like a crane collapsing. She looks across the table at Tree.

He shakes his head and says, "Whatever." He can't believe Jimmy said that to her, again overdoing his backup act, his women-suck-and-no-one-fucks-with-Tree routine.

"Don't worry," she says to Tree. "That's why me and Jimmy get along. You always know where you stand."

"You thinking of going out there?" Tree asks.

"They want me to live with them. John's dad can get me a pretty good job."

Tree says, "If you leave me, can I come too?"

"I'll give it my serious consideration."

After dinner Tree and Jimmy drive to Jimmy's apartment in Garden City. Tree watches *Wheel of Fortune* while Jimmy showers, dresses, and splashes on the Turbo cologne. Vanna looks hot tonight, and Tree wonders if Pat Sajak is getting some of the good thing from her. He smiles grimly. Sex and death are all he thinks of. Sex and death. And golf, thank God.

He ponders the quicksilver changes in his life since making the change from uniform patrol, those endless, blameless hours of slogging about in life's muck, to detection, where the sense of searching for solutions is relentless; he ponders the changes in Jimmy; the changes in Annie, the greater arc in her mood swings. She loves him madly. She's splitting for the coast. " 'There's something happening here,' " he sings softly. " 'What it is ain't exactly clear. . . .' "

They prowl the singles clubs in Jimmy's Vette, making cameo appearances at Whispers, Fridays, and the G Club, then the Barbary Coast.

A DJ in a sound booth pumps Top Forty tunes

through the smoky darkness like it was still 1979. The tables are filled with pretty women in cocktail dresses, and at the circle bar the crowd of men—in business suits with mousse in their hair—is at least two deep. "There's enough beaver here to dam the Hudson," Jimmy says, as they stroll across the dance floor. "We died and went to heaven."

"Yeah," says Tree. "Of Herpes Duplex Twenty-five, or some other sleazy disease." He snorkels his way to the bar and orders a beer for himself and a Beefeater's martini for Jimmy. The drinks cut in half the twenty he hands to the bartender, wearing a Mr. T starter set, but then, at the Barbary Coast, so much more than liquid refreshment is promised. There are Ladies' Nites, Singles' Nites, monthly meetings of Parents Without Partners, and tonight, the aftermath of an all-male nude review. So, he figures, for the investment of ten dollars American, they have purchased alcohol, air conditioning, and proximity to fifty preheated members of the opposite sex, two of whom already have Jimmy cornered near the plastic palms that separate the dance floor from the bar. A pair of fives, he guesses, grading on that generous curve, semidarkness. Naturally, their glasses are empty, as Tree suspects are their heads.

"Yo, Tree," says Jimmy, taking his martini. "This here's Sally and Eve. They said they had their eyes on us from the moment we walked into the bar."

"Hello, girls," he says, happy to be the object of almost anyone's adoration. "Can we buy you a drink?"

The little brunette with stumpy legs speaks up first. "Sure," says Eve. "Black Russian. On the light side."

"Kir, on the rocks," says Sally, the one with whom

Tree has decided he would like to spend a minor interval of time. She is long-legged and chesty, and a redhead, which is something he has never had. He turns to fight his way back to the bar, while Jimmy starts their tag-team rap: "Man, me and the Tree, we've been partners since the dawn of time. . . ."

Tree tunes him out, already very familiar with Jimmy's hardball pickup line that only goes over with drunks or degenerates. He can only hope the bartender will fill his order quickly, before the damage is irreparable, the horror all too real. But when he returns with the drinks, he sees that Sally and Eve are attentive, even interested. Or wonderful actresses.

"Here we are," says Tree, sounding to himself like his grandmother as he passes out the drinks. "No shop talk, eh partner?"

"Let me finish this one story."

"You do," says Tree, "and you'll be telling the next one to just me."

Eve and Sally giggle, then clink their glasses together in a silent, private toast.

"My man's a pisser, ain't he," says Jimmy, snaking his arm around Sally's white, freckled shoulders.

"He's not the only one," she says.

Jimmy puts his other hand on her waist and steers her to the dance floor. "Hey, Red," he says into her ear. "I hope you don't mind beard burns."

Tree shrugs and takes a long swig of his beer. It seems he has drawn Eve by default as his companion for the night's activities; watching Jimmy nuzzle Sally's neck, he remembers when they used to talk these things over in the john.

Then the DJ spins a mellow tune that is obviously one of Eve's favorites, for she parks her glass in one of the planters and drags Tree by the arm to the dance floor. He feels sad and foolish with her head resting on his sternum during the Willie Nelson ballad. He considers faking an ankle sprain and slinking away like a dog.

" '. . . Maybe I don't love you . . . ,' " Eve sings to him.

Please, God, make her stop, he thinks. This is Annie's song. She'd roll over and die if she could see him now.

"Do you come here often?" Eve asks, looking up his nostrils.

"No. I live in Seaport."

"Really?" she says. "Good. I love fresh meat." She snuggles closer, purring.

Oh God, he thinks, here come the bumps and grinds. I hope I don't see anyone I know, or worse, anyone who knows Annie. "Do you come here much?" he asks the top of her head.

"Only when I'm looking for some action . . . like tonight."

He coughs to cover an oh-well-what-the-hell smile. Short and fat can be nice, he thinks. And she's probably not anywhere near as ruthlessly straightforward as she seems. The construction crew in his pants erects a girder, which seems to please the smiling Eve very much. "We gonna do it right here in front of all these people?" he says.

"A girl like me needs her creature comforts."

"Oh," he says, still dancing in stupid circles, the blood rushing out of his brain. "I see." She wants to rent a room. Let's see . . . that's sixty-five balloons at the minimum for the chance to bang old Eve. He figures in Time, Cost of Capital, and the lost opportunity at all the other girls he might meet should he turn the offer down. He waffles: "You think they have vacancies on a Friday night?"

"Stick your hand in my pants . . . pocket."

This girl is good, he thinks. So playful, so lusty. The five I gave her was a trifle hasty. She's a dead solid six if ever I saw one. We're not that far apart.

"You'll find a key in there. Room 204."

He removes the key and runs it up the inside of her thigh.

"You want to go straight to the room?" she says. "No more drinkie? No more flirtie?"

"Yeah. You go on up." He drops the key into her décolletage. "I'll be right there."

She smiles and slips away, grazing his arm with her breasts as she passes.

They push through the crowd back to the bar. The lady vanishes. Jimmy has Sally in a headlock, her face as red as her hair.

"Let's book," Tree says.

"You got it, brother."

Jimmy drops Tree off at the condo at the end of what has not been what Tree would call a banner day.

Tree steps out of his clothes in the middle of the room and flops on his bed, naked. Annie's windows were dark as they drove up, and he doesn't think she'd appreciate a drunken, horny visitor, much as he'd like to drop on down.

Lying in bed, he remembers his first time with Annie, before she met John Sutherland and was suddenly a woman and temporarily out of his reach—the summer before John's parents bought the new house on Dune Road, when Tree was still the village prince.

His father was sailing with a friend. Annie's folks were playing tennis at the club. Their idle offspring broke into the Adams family's liquor closet and swilled Southern Comfort for the better part of an August afternoon. They were sixteen and he was a virgin.

Annie said she had some pot. Tree said he'd always wanted to try it. Afraid to leave odors in the house, they took the joint into her backyard and sat against the wall that separated their parents' homes.

Tree felt nothing at first. And he'd heard so much about the wonders of weed. Annie swore she got off, and that it was very good stuff, and that all he needed was to practice holding the smoke in his lungs. They burnt the roach between two matchheads and snorted the smoke because Annie said this would help. When sin is the subject, Tree remembers, pretty girls find tutors sooner than skinny boys.

The sun rose higher and hotter, and soon they were kissing and giggling. Annie let him touch her taut stomach, her shoulders, the sides of her tiny breasts. "Trust me?" he said. "Now? . . . Now?"

Annie kept drinking and trusting. She let him run his hand up under her shirt to her nipples. He moved to kiss her and missed.

"You're stoned!" she said, laughing, satisfied with the job she had done on him.

"I thought that was the idea." He tried to kiss her again, and she rolled away.

"Aren't we forgetting someone?" she said, meaning Ginny, his high-school girlfriend, who lived in Hampton Bays.

"With all due respect—"

"Ah, ah, ah. A stiff prick has no conscience."

"Who said anything about my prick." He had not

dared to hope. The very thought of her thinking of it first.

"It's just not right," she said.

He sat up and wrapped his hands around his ankles. His head was beginning to spin. But Tree was an athlete: He knew how to play with pain, to take the shot that wins or loses the game. He understood persistence. "What about what we already did? That's okay?"

"I didn't say that."

"Hey, this is Tree you're talking to, the boy next door."

"Ginny's boy."

"Now and then," he allowed.

"Like when she was wearing your letter sweater at the Desmonds' pool party."

"She was cold. Her nipples were erect. All the guys were staring."

"On the hottest night of the year? Forget it, Tree."

He reached under her shirt to rub her back, from the nape of her neck to the waistband of her tennis shorts. "Ginny can't feel this," he told her. "She has no idea this is happening. It's just you and me in our own little world."

"Uh-huh."

"She occupies an entirely separate reality. She's vibrating at a different speed. Operating on a parallel temporal plane."

"Uh-huh."

"Besides, I think she let Joey Walsh feel her up."

"This isn't fair."

"You want me to stop?"

She turned to face him, to press her complaint. His

head rose again to her breast. "Don't take advantage," she said. "You're the best friend I've got."

"I want to kiss it."

"Oh, God," she said, lying down on her back, letting him slide her shirt up.

It was warm on the grass, with the smell of pine needles and old bricks in the air. His hand dropped to her hips, slowly, like a burglar trying not to trip an alarm. Her fingers went for the zipper of his jeans. He had trouble tugging her shorts over her hips. And she was more intent upon playing with his length than allowing him her depth. His concentration wavered. Pornographic pictures flashed in his head. His fever spiked. All fluids came to a boil. "Annie, wait," he said. Too late.

She sat up quickly, her face hidden by her hair.

"Uh, I said wait?"

"Right," she said, standing and straightening her clothes. "My fault."

For years she must have thought him quick on the draw, a lousy lay. It drove him crazy until he had a second chance, then a third. Sometimes he still thought he had to prove himself.

Tree gets off the bed and walks to the bathroom at the end of the hall. When he opens the door the light is on. Annie is on the bowl, reading *Money* magazine. She looks at his erection and smiles.

"I saw you pull in, so I decided to come up. I see I got here just in time."

3

Cheap Talk

The street stools aren't talking, and no one is home to their calls.

They drive back to the precinct house and head for the squad room. Tree has paperwork to finish and Jimmy wants to call in his pre-season football bets for the weekend's card. Jimmy is holding on the phone and bragging to Detective Edelson about one of his latest conquests. "We go up to her room, right? She tells me to get naked and . . ."

Detective Wilfredo Aviles is on him and Nelson the minute he walks into the bullpen, yakking at them about opening lines of communication and sharing sources of information, working together for the good of the cause. But he is wasting his breath. Jimmy hates his guts. A month ago Aviles ratted them out to Lieutenant Cumberstadt for leaving a senseless stakeout ten minutes early. Tree smiles at him; Jimmy, sitting on the desk, ignores Aviles and the color shot of the corpse he is holding, the Colombian Necktie job.

" 'Wait in the bed,' she says."

"A promising beginning," Edelson agrees.

"She was a little plump," Jimmy expounds. "And wacky, too. I figured it was a lock she'd make me spank her, or something equally appalling."

"I love it," says Edelson. "You're giving me a semi."

"Hey," says Aviles.

"She makes her grand entrance, complete with a coy little peek around the door first. Then she sprints across the room and dives on my belly. She sticks her tongue so far down my throat I almost gagged."

"Aggressive. I like that." Edelson nods.

"That's when I made my big mistake. Don Juan here starts rubbing her saggy butt, and she starts breathing funny, telling me her tush-tush is her numero-uno erogenous zone. Then she turns around and hikes up her tu-tu, hanging her dumper an inch from my nose. I gotta tell you, I damned near puked. She had an inoculation scar the size of a pancake, and that's the good news."

"So what'd you do?"

Aviles, too, was listening now.

Jimmy shakes his head. "First I gave the old blank stare."

"The one where you look like you're brain-dead?" asks Tree.

"Exactly. Then I told her that I didn't believe in anal sex on the first date, and just what kind of man did she think I was."

Edelson and some of the others laugh. Aviles proffers the photo again.

"Wrong gang, thank God," Jimmy says to Aviles, handing him back the Polaroid of the body in the garbage. "Take a hike."

"You think dissension has reared its ugly head among the Spanish Brothers?" Tree asks him, if only to spare the cop's feelings.

"Who gives a flying fuck," says Jimmy.

"I give a flying fuck," says Aviles. He is dark and dapper, and terribly serious about his career as a law-enforcement professional. "I will not be made a fool of by these lowlife punks. Very soon there will come a day when I lock away Victor Guardina forever. And I hope that you will do the same for Mr. Lanier."

Tree shrugs. "Maybe Crazy Victor didn't do it." Tibaldi gives him a wary look. "Maybe Lanier turned up Angel Colon to make it look like the Brothers did it." Tibaldi shakes his head. "Maybe someone new is moving in that we don't even know about."

"Maybe this is all a fucking hallucination," says Tibaldi.

"I would know about it." Aviles sniffs. "I keep my feet on the street, where they belong."

"We're all very proud of you," says Tibaldi. "I'm putting you in for Cop of the Month."

"And I am putting you in for wop of the month."

Without another word—the argument apparently over and decided—Detective Wilfredo Aviles throws on his sport coat, stuffs his walkie-talkie in one pocket and his partner's walkie-talkie in the other, tucks his clipboard under his arm like a swagger stick, and marches from the bullpen.

Tree and Jimmy amble over to the window that overlooks that back parking lot and separate the blinds. "There he is," Jimmy says. When Aviles gets to his unmarked car, he kneels down next to the driver's side door, and checks to see if someone has again stuffed dogshit in the space behind the handle.

Three times they've got him so far. And once with his private car. But not today.

Lieutenant Cumberstadt watches Ashti crush Lendl in the semifinals on a television being held for evidence in his office.

Cumberstadt looks at his watch. "This is right away?"

Jimmy says, "Yes."

Cumberstadt says, "Fine." He throws them a fat manila folder. "Odds are good your boy just removed another competitor." He ushers them out of his office, then stands over their desks as if to make sure they open the files.

While Jimmy makes humming noises, Tree reads.

Wilson Bermudez: born San Juan, Puerto Rico, a.k.a. Wild Willy, Freddy Fire. Arrests for arson, possession of a deadly weapon, burglary, attempted burglary, robbery, attempted robbery . . . Former member of the Savage Skulls, a Bronx-based gang. Current member of Spanish Brothers. Dead of gunshot wounds to back and head. See DD-12-9763. Detective Alvin Baumgarten assigned.

Tree and Jimmy know Wild Willy as a laid-back ladies' man and part-time torch. A nuisance. A coke freak. What Jimmy calls a bebop spic.

Cumberstadt sits next to a wall poster for abused women that says IF YOU'RE BEING BEATEN, WE CAN HELP. Someone has painted whiteout over most of the B in BEATEN.

Jimmy takes a look at the body. Both shake their heads.

"Make copies or take notes. The Bureau wants the files available to their narc agents this afternoon."

Jimmy picks up a file and hands it to Cumberstadt. "It's all yours."

"We'll go after this through some of Crazy Victor's people," Tree says. "We'll put it together."

"When?" Cumberstadt asks.

"Real fucking soon, I suppose," says Jimmy.

Cumberstadt doesn't know whether Jimmy is mocking him or not. He gets out of Jimmy's chair, goes into his office, and closes the door. By the clock on the wall it is two fifteen. Tree spends three minutes making copies of the files, fifteen minutes reading *Penthouse* in the john, one minute getting Crazy Victor Guardina's last known address from the Rolodex on Aviles's desk, and one minute waiting for Jimmy to get off the phone with his bookie. At two thirty-five they stop at Cumberstadt's door. Tree leans his head in. "We're on the road, if you need us."

"The world's a safer place."

Jensen Macomber stands by his locked front door, peeking past the shade into the street. He might be expecting someone he loves, or perhaps waiting for a delivery, or then again very frightened, this strong black man in his shop of delicate flowers.

A smaller, darker man with dreadlocks steps through the curtain at the rear of the shop. A man Macomber knows the cops can't touch.

Gladstone Lanier is wearing fatigue pants and a yellow tank top; the gun in his hand is a Colt .38. He points the barrel at Jensen Macomber's face. "Now, what am I to make of that?" he says. Macomber knows he is referring to the police who questioned him.

"They were checking on my health."

"Oh?" says Lanier. "Do they think you're in some danger?"

"Not any longer."

Lanier smiles, showing his chipped front teeth. "You learn well, old mon. You may yet be of service."

"You frighten me. That's no secret."

"But I am your friend, your protector, and you are my wise and ancient adviser. Your fears are groundless. Jah protects us all."

Macomber nods, his gaze fixed on the front sight of the revolver. Lanier steps around the counter and picks up Jensen's shotgun by the barrel. With a one-handed baseball swing he demolishes a line of purple ceramic vases. Then he hands the shotgun to Macomber, its barrels loaded. "How many times do I have to tell you, your guns are unnecessary, an insult. So is crying to the police about matters that are none of your concern."

Macomber places the shotgun behind the counter. "I wouldn't worry," he says. "They're all just street cops, screwing around. They wouldn't know a truth if it hit them on the ass."

Lanier cocks his head slowly to one side, holding in his hand the longest of his dreads, fondling the end of it. "They'll know it when it's me."

Macomber nods and his visitor slips away. Macomber doesn't bother to lock the door behind him. Instead he sits on a high stool and tries to compose himself, but he can't help thinking about Gladstone Lanier, and remembering what he has heard about the man.

GO ABROAD TO IMPROVE, the posters in Jamaica read, COME HOME TO HELP. Stop the brain drain.

Slogans. Government propaganda, about the road to prosperity and growth. Bullshit on the wall.

You wanna buy some sinsemillia? Another Kingston slogan, one that made more immediate sense and delivered more immediate results.

Gladstone Lanier and his brothers Pansy and Roland worked the Kingston streets whenever they could lay their hands on some ganja. And, as their customers were largely tourists—rich, young American know-nothings—Pansy argued that they were doing their bit to right the unfavorable balance of trade under which Jamaica perpetually labored. The ganja you're smoking's no good, they would tell potential customers. Too damn old, from the shady side of the tree. As long as you're here, sir, you ought to try the best.

Pansy was the oldest, the most experienced. A hard case from a hard place. Gladstone and Roland were just boys, their futures still in doubt.

Gladstone's mother could readily guess what her sons were up to when large amounts of American dollars miraculously appeared in the house. Many of the children from West Kingston sold ganja, making more in a month than their parents could in a year. She blamed the Americans, who, she said, really ought to know better.

When Gladstone was fifteen she got him his first real job, working nights with her at one of the large hotels, sometimes as a bellhop, sometimes as a room-service waiter. The work was clean and easy. He shared his salary and tips with his parents.

One night he brought a large tureen of potage St. Germain and a platter of hors d'oeuvres to a party of middle-aged Bostonians. The man who answered the door wore a kelly-green jacket and pink pants. "Bring it in, boy, right away. We're absolutely starving."

Gladstone set out the food as fast as he could. The man in the pink pants was delighted with the service. He said, "Marvelous. Wonderful." He put his hand on Gladstone's shoulder and walked him to the door, digging deep in the pocket of those silly pink pants. He pulled out the largest roll of bills young Gladstone Lanier had ever seen. Dimes and nickels and quarters, all the coins of the realm, fell from that head of cabbage to the floor. Gladstone dropped reverently to one knee and started to pick up the loose change. "Perfect," said the man. "It's all yours, son, whatever you find. Come," said the man to his guests, "someone help me out with the tip." And then the other white men started tossing coins down to him, until someone hit him in the cheek with a Kennedy half dollar, and the room grew suddenly silent.

He remained on one knee, ice cold and motionless. He thought about how his mother loved her job in the laundry, how she loved the idea that she made as much money as her husband. He stood up and squared his shoulders, looked pink pants in his pale blue eyes, and then slowly, a few at a time, dropped all of the coins into the soup.

A complaint was made. "He looked like he wanted to cook us in that bowl and eat us," the shaken guest reported.

The hotel manager explained to Gladstone and his mother that giving bad service was the one unforgivable sin a colored boy could commit. They both of course had to be terminated.

Then Pansy was killed by an American tourist,

stabbed in the chest with his own knife by the wrong kind of guy to hold up.

An inquest was held, apologies were made, the government paid the American's cleaning bill and put him on a plane. And a few months later Gladstone moved out of his father's house and into a Rastafarian commune in Trench Town.

His parents were heartbroken. The boys had been baptized. Now one son was dead and the next thought the late Emperor of Ethiopia was God.

They find Crazy Victor Guardina sitting in a dark corner of the Stadium Bar, checking yesterday's receipts, sipping a beer and smoking a cigarette. The fat white barmaid is watching *Card Sharks* and balancing her checkbook from a stool on the customer side of the bar. She says, "five-o," and rolls her eyes at Victor when Tree and Jimmy walk in, but he doesn't need the high sign. Detectives Nelson and Tibaldi are the least of his worries.

"What's happening, amigos," he says. "Welcome to my humble if empty inn. Please, join me in a drink to Wild Willy. A loco motherfucker who didn't have the sense of a rock."

"Sorry about your friend," says Tree.

"Thank you for coming to pay your respects. His mother will be pleased."

"*De nada*," says Jimmy.

"She will be even happier if you two gringos get off your lazy butts and do something about Lanier."

"What'd you say, you little piece of shit?" Jimmy steps toward Victor, stroking his beard, and Tree is momentarily concerned about personal liability in brutality cases.

"Jimmy!"

"Relax, Detective Tibaldi. Your temper is showing."

Jimmy stands there smiling at Crazy Victor, who does a very good job of appearing unafraid. He is wearing blue jeans and a leather vest; his dark arms are muscular and covered with tattoos.

"I am not a piece of shit, Detective. You would know that if you knew your turf. Besides this bar, I own a beauty parlor and a health-food store. I am fluent in two languages. People around here are happy to see me—"

"You're a freaking prince, Victor, everybody knows that," Tree says.

"You really think so?"

"Whatever you want to hear," says Tree.

"So why don't you guys help me out then. Get this Rasta madman off my ass."

"That's why we came to see you."

"Will wonders never cease. Mary Ann, bring my two new friends glasses and a pitcher of our very best beer."

Tree and Jimmy sit down and big Mary Ann waddles over with a tray and sets them up. Tree is not really ready for a beer, but it's plain Crazy Victor wants to talk, as long as it appears to be on his terms.

"What's going on?" Tree says. "Why have people started to die?"

"In a word? Crack. Too many people bugging out on it. Too much easy money to be made. Used to be you could talk to Gladstone Lanier about certain things, or at least I could. But crack never misses, my friends. That nigger is over the edge."

"What exactly," says Jimmy, "did you guys talk about, back when you used to be able to talk?"

"You guys are beautiful," Victor says. "I would have given my left nut to have you guys put on my case instead of those two assholes, Aviles and Gonzalez."

"They break your balls?" Jimmy asks, lighting up a cigarette.

"Wilfredo Aviles thinks God put him on earth to write me traffic tickets, and Gonzalez doesn't even speak Spanish. They follow me to the Little League games I sponsor, and on Sundays we all go to church; but where the fuck are they when my friends are being killed? Eh? Nowhere to be found. So while my guys are taking it up the ass, you two don't even open Lanier's mail. That's fair? That's America? The citizen gets his balls crushed while the foreigner sucks up the benefits."

"I never looked at it quite like that," Tree says. In truth, he frequently forgot that Puerto Ricans were American citizens. And to him the Rastas were like visitors from a faraway planet.

"Well of course you didn't. You guys think I'm a piece of shit."

"I try not to form opinions," says Tree.

"But that's your job, no?"

"Give us some help and we'll take him down for God and country," says Jimmy. "We can call it Operation Joint."

Victor waves his hand and frowns. "Gladstone Lanier is doing what he's doing because he thinks he can get away with it. That or someone big is helping him. Like the Cubans. He doesn't need me anymore."

"What Cubans?"

"The Cubans. From Havana. Mother of God, don't you guys know anything?"

"What was Willy up to last night?" Tree asks. "What the hell was he doing that far away from Sunrise and Main without backup?"

Victor drinks some beer. He looks older than his thirty-nine years, showing the scars of time in prison and too many lines of cocaine. "He went after the white guy who did Angel and then cut him up like a pig. Him and Angel had been following the white guy to and from the Blake for the last couple of days, something you guys would've known if you ever staked the fucking place out. They were just looking to lighten his pockets, nobody was gonna get hurt. All of a sudden the white son of a bitch pulls a piece and shoots Angel in the head. Willy ran away, and then I guess the white guy did his thing. The next night Wild Willy disappeared."

"Another case solved by Twelfth Precinct Anti-Crime," Jimmy says. "Cumberstadt will be happy as shit."

"We're on a roll," Tree agrees.

"Lanier is on the roll," says Victor. "You guys better get busy or soon your friend Victor Guardina is gonna be run out of town or dead, and poor Mary Ann will be spending her mornings all alone."

4

The Redeemer

They finish the eighteenth hole at Crab Meadow by the last light of day, with Jimmy taking the match one-up. Jimmy then suggests they do something for which they possess some talent—like getting drunk—and soon a sunburned self-satisfied exhaustion weighs them down in the corner of the clubhouse bar.

The bartender brings them iced mugs of Beck's, a round Tree pays for, as he will all the rest, the cost of losing his patience in a bunker on seventeen. "So what do you think?" he says, after slugging back the top half of his beer.

"About what?"

"Me and Annie getting married."

Jimmy lights a cigarette.

Tree takes another slug of beer and wipes the foam from his mustache. "I asked her in a fit of passion . . . God knows I know better."

"And?"

"She wants to think about it. I said, that's cool. It's the same old story: I'm soft when I'm hard and I'm hard when I'm soft."

"Bullshit," says Jimmy. "Don't waste your time talking tough around me. I know better, my man. Annie head-fakes to California and you crumble."

"I love her," he admits. "I really do. I don't trust her much. But then I don't trust anybody much. Maybe I'm just afraid I'll get like she is. Can you imagine the attitude on this kid she wants to have? I can already see myself doing his homework."

"What if she says yes?"

"You and me get tuxedos."

"No?"

"You and me party back. Nude beaches, Club Med . . . a smorgasbord of sin."

"Something new," Jimmy says, laughing.

"Borrowed and blue."

Tree swallows the last of his beer and waves the bartender to refill their mugs.

"What's the big rush?" Jimmy says. "Girls like Annie keep guys like us single."

"I'm thirty-five years old. You call that rushing?"

Jimmy sighs and pats him on the back. "Okay then, that's it. I'll call the hookers for the bachelor party when I get home."

"Get nice ones, willya. Even if I have to kick in the extra bread."

"For you? A pair of tens."

"There are no tens."

"Sure there are," Jimmy says. "They just don't hang around with cops."

The following evening, on a regularly scheduled day off, Tree and Jimmy are trapped in their unmarked car.

They pass the Blake Hotel three times before turning onto Fulton Avenue, in what used to be the heart of town. Within a mile there are shops still open for business, and trees, that have not yet been cut down for fuel, line the sides of the road. They stop in front of a smoke shop, make sure they haven't been followed, then drive back to the Blake and park beneath a yellow canvas awning that says OLLIE BASON'S FURNITURE.

"Why," Jimmy says, half his face visible in street light, "in God's name, did we suggest staking out the Blake Hotel?"

" 'We'?" says Tree. He slumps in the passenger seat, sipping coffee and eating an Entenmann's chocolate-covered doughnut. *Newsday,* the *Post* and the *Daily News* have been consumed and lie scattered in the back seat; he is trying to decide between *Golf* magazine and the coverless *Penthouse* Jimmy keeps rolled up under the driver's seat.

"I didn't think Cumberstadt would ask *us*."

Tree says, "That's the problem with good ideas."

"Fucking Victor," Jimmy says. "Imagine the nerve of a crook like that asking for equal treatment. I say we give him one night and that's it. If Lanier don't stick his dread-head out the door, we're wasting our time."

"I just wish he'd ride around in the same car more than once. I wish he'd get himself a shiny jig-rig, something all pimped out so we could find him. A dealer of Gladstone's stature shouldn't be seen in the back of no Pinto."

"You racist pig," says Jimmy. "I thought they taught you better than that at the Academy."

"They tried."

Tree clears his throat and reads aloud for the first

time from the police information bulletin, Ethnic Series #18, that Cumberstadt had given them the day they began their current assignment.

" 'The cult of Ras Tafari had its beginnings in 1927, when Marcus Garvey was returned to Jamaica from the United States. Garvey continued to work for the repatriation of Africans to Africa. He told his followers, "Look to Africa, where a black King shall be crowned, for the day of deliverance is near." ' "

"Jesus," groans Jimmy.

" 'In November 1930, Ras Tafari was crowned Emperor Haile Selassie I of Ethiopia, and soon after several preachers in Jamaica proclaimed Ras Tafari the returned Messiah. One of them, Leonard P. Howell, was found guilty in 1934 of sedition for his preachings, and for distributing pictures of Selassie which he claimed were passports to Ethiopia.' "

"Give me a break."

" 'When Howell got out of prison he purchased an old estate. He was joined there by hundreds of the faithful. The estate was raided by police in 1941, and Howell went back to jail for two years. He then returned and lived quietly with his followers until 1954, when the place was raided again and permanently dismantled. Howell's followers emerged from isolation. Word of the Rastafarian movement spread rapidly.

" 'In 1958, a twenty-one-day convention of the brethren was held in Back 'o Wall, a Kingston shantytown. Three thousand Rastas fought with police.

" 'In 1959, thousands of people believed cards given to them by a Rastafarian preacher named Claudius Henry guaranteed passage back to Africa. They sold all their possessions and waited at the church for ships that never came. Claudius Henry was charged with treason and sent to jail in 1960. His son then arrived from New York City with several American blacks. They set up a guerrilla base in Red Hills and made plans for armed insurrection. Most were captured and executed.

" 'But the movement grew. The black man in Jamaica had a living black God calling him home. A Redeemer.

" 'Thousands took to the streets in April 1966, to welcome to Jamaica the King of Kings, Lord of Lords, Conquering Lion of the Tribe of Judah, the Emperor Haile Selassie of Ethiopia, who brought with him as a gift to Prime Minister Michael Manley a beautiful staff called the Rod of Correction, a symbol of Jamaican solidarity with Africa.' "

Tibaldi groaned again and leafed through the *Penthouse*. Nelson ignored him and read on.

" 'The Rastafarian considers ganja, marijuana, to be a gift from God, a sacrament, and necessary to complete understanding of the ways of the world, a concept which places the cult in direct opposition to U.S. criminal statutes.

" 'The movement numbers approximately one hundred thousand practicing members, predominantly male, ex-Christian blacks. They can be found in every major city in the Western hemisphere. The dreadlocks and beards are a sign of their ancient covenant with God. A Rastafarian has no use for razors. To fight against the hair is to fight against the self.

" 'The Rastafarian wants to go home to Ethiopia. He has been too long here building the West.' "

"I am going home, I am going home," mocks Jimmy. "Glory be to Jah in Zion."

" 'He dreams of universal repatriation—' "

"Doo da, doo da." Jimmy mimics a minstrel.

" '—not just the return of the blacks to Africa, but whites to Europe and redmen to America. Jah did not intend the different races to live together; each was given a continent to develop in peace. For the world to be at peace, every race must return to its own land.' "

"You done?"

Nelson nods yes. "You don't appreciate the Rasta culture."

"On the contrary," says Tibaldi, "if I were black, poor, the descendant of slaves, with no hope for a comfortable life in Western culture, and you gave me a God that looked like me, that I didn't have to wait for, who told me I was one of the lost tribes of Israel, one of His Chosen, and that I could smoke dope and lay out in the sun and that everything would turn out fine, I might be wearing a set of dreads myself."

"That's true," says Tree. "You would."

Just then they hear a radio notification for a robbery at the Citibank in Hempstead. Shots fired, cars wrecked. The suspect (male-black, twenty, dreadlocks, armed with a semiautomatic pistol), who bungled the holdup and then blew away a cop, is chased south on Nassau Road into Seaport and then lost in the ghetto darkness.

The airwaves fill with the assignments, acknowledgments, and conjectures of frantic uniformed cops, scouring the precinct for the yellow Datsun B210 with the murderer behind the wheel.

"We stay right where we are," says Jimmy, checking the magazine. "We got the best seats in town."

At nine thirty-two they see the getaway car roll into

the alley next to the Blake Hotel. Jimmy keys the microphone.

"Twelve-seventeen to Headquarters. Request assistance at the Blake Hotel. Suspect in Citibank A and R observed exiting vehicle in south alley and heading behind the building. My partner and I are in foot pursuit."

"Roger, twelve-seventeen. Command advises you proceed with caution."

Tree and Jimmy don't hear that last piece of news. They are already sprinting across the street with their guns drawn and their eyes wide, making sweeps from the windows to the roof to the alley to the car, the back seat, under the car.

They hug the side of the hotel, scraping paint from the rotting wood as they make their way into the darkness.

"Ssh," Jimmy whispers. "Listen."

They hear the scrape of shoe leather on rusty iron; the bad guy is climbing the fire escape. They peek around the wall and see him tap on a third-floor window with the barrel of his gun. "Gladstone. It's me. Open up the damn window."

They point their guns at him. "Freeze!" they cry in unison, in spite of the fact that in all their time on the job neither one of them can remember a perp pulling up short on command, unless, of course, he planned on shooting back at them.

The bad guy scrambles up the ladder for the roof.

"I said freeze, you son of a bitch!" Jimmy screams. He debates with himself the pros and cons of shooting the kid in the ass, just long enough for his target to vanish.

"Fuck," Tree mutters.

They follow him, covering each other's upward forays. Jimmy's heart is pounding from anger and fear. Tree has to grab Jimmy's shoulder to slow him down, to keep him from diving recklessly onto the roof.

On the top step of the fire escape Tree holds his Winged Foot Country Club golf cap up before he risks a look over the edge. He sees the guy kneeling on the ledge at the front of the hotel, looking down, trapped.

"Let me see those hands in the air," he calls to him, pointing his revolver at the boy's black mane of dreadlocks. "Cover me," he says to Jimmy. Jimmy does.

Tree sticks his gun in his belt and hikes himself onto the roof. Sharp pebbles stab his palms and knees. He springs to his feet and draws his revolver again.

The kid slowly stands and turns to face them, his pistol held low in his hand. "Go ahead and shoot, mon. I've used up all my luck."

Tree keeps his sights on the bad guy's head and fights the tremor in his knees. Please, God, he thinks, if he gives up his gun and lets us cuff him, I'll never, ever, even think about Mona.

The kid tosses his 9 onto the hot tar roof. Tree almost shoots him, right then and there, a mere boy giving up his weapon. Probably an honor student Eagle Scout. He imagines the scrubbed-face, clean-cut photo *Newsday* would have produced, the bleeding heart editorials about the boy's commitment to his religion and the need for more tolerance among the nation's white police officers.

"Come on, little Rastaman," Tree says. "Get away from the edge and assume the position. There ain't no reason for anybody to die up here."

"Come and get me."

Jimmy calls for assistance on his portable radio; sirens fill the warm summer night. "Help on the way, Tree. Let's not lose him now."

"You know," the kid says to Tree, "I'm going out of here right past you, guv." He rocks from side to side, as if he is Yannick Noah waiting to receive serve.

"You're going to jail, scumbag!" Jimmy says. He walks across the roof, getting closer, moving into position. "The only other way off this roof is in a bag."

Tree sees an audience of black faces pressed against the windows of the housing project across the street. "He's not a scumbag, Jimmy. Just a little bit confused. Right, kid? I mean, everybody makes mistakes."

A voice cries up from the alley, "Nelson. Tibaldi. Where the hell are you?"

Jimmy runs back to the fire escape and calls down to Sgt. Robert Allison, the uniformed supervisor on duty. "He's flirting with the ledge, Sarge. You'd better call for negotiators. The prick might try to take one of us with him."

"Negotiators, my ass." Allison hauls his heavy body up the ladder, his equipment banging on the railing. He steps around Jimmy and marches to Tree's side. "Keep your gun in his face, Nelson. If he so much as farts, you blow his fucking brains out. One shot cop's enough."

Allison is winded. Tree can smell the booze on his breath.

"Check it out, kid," Allison says. "You get your black ass over here right now before someone hurts you bad." The beam from his flashlight dances on the kid's sweaty face. "Someone like me."

This is hardly, Tree thinks, the recommended procedure for talking down barricaded suspects or jump-ers—not that kissing their butts and bringing them pizza works all the time either.

The kid takes one step forward. There seem to be tears in his bloodshot eyes, a look of distance. His thoughts of escape have evaporated.

"That's a good boy," Sergeant Allison says.

The kid laughs in Allison's face. "Babble on, Baby-lon. I've heard it all before . . . I'll be going now, Mr. Down-pressor, but I will be right back. There's noth-ing you can do."

Tree is beginning to find him amusing, spunky be-yond reason. This Mexican standoff with a Jamaican in America could take a while. He says to Jimmy from the side of his mouth, "You want pepperoni or mush-rooms on that pie?"

Allison says to the kid, "You think the laws of gravity don't apply to hairy spades?"

"They apply to all men *equally*."

"Is that really what you think?" says the sergeant.

"It doesn't matter what I think, now does it. Only what I do." The kid looks over his shoulder at the darkness behind him, the street down below.

Allison gives a sickening laugh and his face turns icy cruel. "Nigger," he says, "you ain't got the balls."

"Nigger?"

"You heard me, asshole. Stupid fucking nigger."

"Wrong, Satan. Behold . . . the Lion of Judah." Before anyone can move a muscle, the kid takes two steps back and one more little hop, and disappears over the edge into the vaulting darkness.

Tree blinks twice, hoping that what he has just seen is an illusion, or a fantastic escape, and not what it feels like: an unrestricted, held-upside-down-by-the-ankles view of the abyss. He has the sudden sensation of losing his balance, of spirits dragging him after the boy.

Jimmy Tibaldi says, "I think I'm gonna puke."

They look at Sergeant Allison, who hasn't moved, hasn't changed expression.

"What?" he says. "Now you see him, now you don't. End of fucking problem."

The television crews already have the front of the old One-Two lit up by the time Tree and Jimmy return from the scene. An angry mob has Cumberstadt pinned against the front doors, demanding answers to questions the reporters have fed them.

"Yes, it was a fine piece of police work . . . No, we don't know that the John Doe wasn't thrown to his death . . . Highly unlikely. I can't imagine it . . . Well, yes, stranger things have happened. I'll know when I've spoken to the detectives involved in the . . . incident. *Tree. Jimmy,*" he yells over the heads of his inquisitors, pointing out the pair sneaking in the EMPLOYEES ONLY side door with Allison.

Tree and Jimmy and Sgt. Robert Allison stop in their tracks. The cameras swing around and close in on them. "What?" says Jimmy.

"In my office. Forthwith. You too, Sergeant."

Jimmy gives the swarm of reporters and the New York television audience his hard-guy look, and sneers, "He jumped on his own, sir. Don't make something out of nothing."

Inside Cumberstadt's office, Allison is furious with the lieutenant for not backing his boys to the limit.

"Why, you fucking moron, would we throw the

splib to his death and miss out on all that overtime going to court? Alive, that kid was worth thirty bucks an hour to us. Probably for years.''

"Oh," says Cumberstadt, gesturing broadly. "I'll just tell that to the district attorney and *everyone* will understand.''

"The truth usually is stranger than fiction," says Tree.

"You guys are killing me," says Cumberstadt. "You know that? I'll be lucky to get a job washing cars if you murdered that kid.''

"We didn't," says Tree. "Put the thought out of your mind.''

"That crowd outside is calling for your scalps." Cumberstadt massages his eyes with the heels of his palms. "One of the reporters called this a landmark case.''

Tree shakes his head sadly, as if Cumberstadt is an awfully slow learner. "Do we look like killers to you, Lieutenant?''

Cumberstadt searches their faces for signs of guilt or conspiracy, and finding no more than the usual amount, concludes his initial investigation. "Make out your reports, and get the hell out of here. I'll handle things on this end. And oh, yeah. Nice job. But don't even think about calling in sick tomorrow.''

The following morning at 6 A.M. they park at the curb in front of the Blake Hotel. Baumgarten and five other policemen are standing in the lobby, wearing flak jackets and holding shotguns. "You got your vests?" Baumgarten asks them.

"At the precinct," says Tree. It was all he could do to slide on a pair of jams and a T-shirt. Jimmy is wearing an operating-room scrub suit and his shoulder holster. Wednesday morning coming down.

"Good place for them . . . Here, wear these." Baumgarten hands them each a bulletproof vest. "You guys'll go inside with me and Tommy Winters," he says, waving at the tall blond cop in a police jumpsuit. "I've got three guys out back, and the rest of the boys will stand by in the hallway."

Tree adjusts the Velcro straps on the front of the vest and says okay.

"About the search," Baumgarten says. "The nice lady judge—who thought our reasonable cause sucked eggs—was most explicit in her instructions: She said if we trash the place and come up empty, she'll hang us by the balls. So be thorough but neat, okay?"

Jimmy says, "Ten-four." He racks one into his Sig and grins. "We won't ruffle slimeball's feathers."

They follow Baumgarten up the narrow wooden staircase. At the third-floor landing, the backup team spreads out along the wall opposite Gladstone Lanier's apartment door. Tree and Jimmy each take a side of the door; Baumgarten crouches low next to Tree and raps high with the butt of his revolver.

They hear feet scurry, and whispers. Tree expects high-speed projectiles to rip through the wooden door, or worse—splinter the wall against which he leans. Baumgarten moves a step back. "Police," he says. "Open up."

"Where are your manners, white man?"

"Down at the morgue," Baumgarten says to the closed door.

"You wouldn't want me coming to your house, would you now?"

"I'd blow your fucking head off in the driveway."

"And well I know that."

"I believe a friend of yours was killed downstairs. I was hoping you might be of some assistance to the police department."

"I don't know nothing 'bout that, mon. The dead can take care of themselves. I've been sick in my bed since Thursday."

"I've got a warrant, Lanier."

"But I do not recognize your authority."

"Would you recognize a sledgehammer breaking down your fucking door?"

Bolts slide, chains clank, the door swings slowly open. Gladstone Lanier, frail as wrought-iron railing, stands inside in dirty white painter's pants, smiling, instantly the magnanimous host.

"Come in, come in," he says. "Welcome to the bowels of the skyline city, the shrine of Ras Tafari. Let me close the door. I'd hate my neighbors to think this call was social."

Baumgarten stares into Lanier's face and kicks the door closed with his heel. "Where's the rest of your rat pack?"

"Two doors down, Satan. In the living room. Sitting peaceful and pretty, contemplating Jah the Protector."

"Check 'em out," Baumgarten says to Tree and Jimmy. "Carefully."

"Yes, Mr. Nelson . . . Mr. Tibaldi. Do be careful."

Tree stops short in the doorway. "Listen, asshole," he says to Lanier. "The days when we could talk nice to each other have come and gone. Keep in mind that what goes around comes around."

"I don't know what you mean, Trevor." Lanier gnaws on one of his dreads and shrugs.

"I mean Georges Crosse, Gladstone. The night you crossed the line."

He shakes his head of dreads in confusion. "I?"

"Get going, Tree," says Baumgarten.

Tree is hard pressed to tell the difference between the room in which is huddled the rest of the clan and the rooms they've come through to find them. All have mattresses on the floor instead of carpets, and the smell of smoke and sweat is uniform throughout. No VCR, no television, no personal computer, no stereo, no microwave oven, no clocks. We're the Jetsons and they're the Flintstones, he thinks. It's almost not fair.

Giving credit where it is due, Tree notes that the rooms are fairly neat, for the Blake Hotel. A framed photograph of Haile Selassie is on the wall, above the silver spray-paint message JAH LIVES. Four men in dreadlocks and one young light-skinned woman, in a dress of bright orange and black, stand in front of the couch, saying nothing, like prisoners of war.

Baumgarten and Winters bring Lanier in after them, and while Tree watches the occupants of the commune, the other cops search the place like men looking for their car keys. Every inch is inspected, rapped on, sniffed: the toilet tank, inside the vacuum-cleaner bag. All those mattresses are laid upon and fondled.

Lanier sits on the arm of the couch, scratching his crotch, holding about himself an air of smug superiority, as if he and his followers were beyond the reach of any secular power. His hate is hidden well, a silver sword concealed in a black ivory cane. All of them appear as carefree and confident as lawyers. And why not? For all the havoc Gladstone Lanier has wreaked upon the already destitute inhabitants of Seaport, his rap sheet is shorter than the owner of the New York Yankees'.

They are finding absolutely nothing to connect Gladstone Lanier to the violence on his doorstep. No drugs, no weapons. Three thousand dollars in cash, but not one spent shell, not one burnt roach. Every piece of incriminating evidence has obviously been passed from the apartment through trapdoors in the floor and walls, and carried away from the hotel by the other tenants.

The lone woman smiles at Tree and shrugs, as if to say this oppression of poor black people is unnecessary.

"We're looking for the guns," he says to her softly.

"But you are standing in a cathedral."

5

HEAVEN'S DOOR

That morning Tree runs for his life, moving freely on feet that are light and quick, past charter boats tied up in their slips, crab shacks, gin mills, then a row of yachts registered to corporations in Delaware. Wearing only red nylon shorts and a pair of running shoes, his silhouette in the dawn light is that of a thin student-athlete. There is a visible calm to his efforts, a sense of floating, that is in keeping with his belief that God does not deduct playtime from the total allocation. He picks up his pace, racing hard for every other telephone pole along the canal, flushing himself as he alternates the exertion of the sprints with the punishing recovery from oxygen debt.

It is within these margins that the job becomes a dream, and the hanging man a grainy black-and-white photograph on the front page of the *Daily News*—something that happened to somebody else far away. Like the unreal vision of an ebony boy stepping lightly into oblivion.

* * *

It is early morning and still dark. Except for the twinkling light from the solitary beach shack on the opposite side of North Cinder Island, Annie sees no sign of human habitation. The only intrusions are the faraway sounds and feeble lights from Lido Beach. But Annie has been here often enough over the years to find the rickety dock and secure her dinghy without light.

The house is small—little more than a bungalow. Reeds threaten to one day overgrow the front porch as they have the barbecue pit and picket fence. A very large American flag flaps in the darkness overhead.

"Maria?"

The door opens. Maria steps onto the porch. "I was sleeping. I didn't hear you until you were halfway up the walk." She looks ill. Her skin is pale, her dark brown hair is matted to one cheek, and the T-shirt she wears is much too big. She hugs Annie, kisses her cheek.

"I brought food. It's down on the dock."

"What about money?"

"Twenty?"

"That's all?"

"I called Geoffrey on the Coast. He said he didn't want you to have any at all. The temptation to spend it on drugs, I guess. He said to tell you he'll keep you supplied with food."

"That righteous prick. He sneaks off to L.A. for a week of rehab, and I can't go to the drive-in at Burger King."

Annie shrugs and pats her on the back. Together they lug the packages into the shack. With the flashlight Maria keeps by the door they find space on the kitchen counter for the bags.

"What goes where?" Annie says.

"Everything goes everywhere. Just leave it."

Annie can see where Maria was sleeping; the old red velvet couch still holds her shape. A kerosene lamp, about which are scattered playing cards and books, burns low on the floor.

"What did you get me?" Maria asks, ripping into the bags.

"Tuna, grapes, oranges, powdered milk, beer, pretzels . . . oh, yeah, and some M & M Chocolate-Covered Peanuts."

"Vitamin M's," Maria says. "May the road rise to meet you. How many days' worth do you figure?"

"Maybe a week if you don't pig out."

Maria starts in on the grapes. "Care to join me?"

"I already ate."

"Want some coffee?"

"You have gas?"

"Sterno."

Annie pulls two cups from the drying rack loaded with mismatched silver and china. Maria takes the coffee from the shelf.

"Fresh well water's in that enamel pan."

"Got it."

Maria leans on the counter, munching, visibly grateful to have someone to talk to. "You gonna spend the day, honey?"

"I have to get back."

"What's the matter?"

"Not a thing. I've just got to get back."

"I see." From the tone of her voice and the look on her face, it is plain that Maria is hurt. But Annie doesn't care. Maria was always far too much into drugs and the life for her taste. A day in a cold-water bay shack couldn't be less attractive. As usual, Maria will try to seduce her, and Annie will politely turn her down.

Annie doesn't do anything romantic or exotic anymore. Not really. Even her love affair with Tree was an act of preemptive divestiture, designed to preclude the possibility of large losses. Until recently.

"I thought we could be together this time," Maria is saying. "So much is happening to me. . . . It would be wonderful to have someone to be with."

There is too much tension around Maria, too many errands, too many lies. Annie figures a week of baby-sitting Maria would be like a month of taking care of Tree.

The pot of water is still cold on the stove, giving her the sense of being stuck in an unfortunate time and place. "Look," she says, "forget the coffee. You're gonna need it."

"Where are you going?"

"I can stay a few more minutes and then I have to split."

"Already?"

"Jesus Christ, Maria."

"Go," Maria says. "You've done more than your share. I can make it the rest of the way without you."

Annie nods. Maria has not been near drugs for two weeks. Another week stuck on the island and she will have beaten her habit, perhaps.

"I'm worried about you," Annie says. "I had a dream last night that you got caught."

"Really . . . I'm okay as long as I can call you. I've stayed in worse places than this, believe me. As long as I can call. But I freak when strangers answer."

"I wish you'd lighten up," Annie says.

"I'm in deeper now than ever before. You don't know."

"I don't want to know . . . How much longer do you think you can last?"

"I can last until it's over," Maria says. "Till I'm rich. You could get into it, Annie. Because this time we've got a beautiful idea."

"Forget it."

"It's business."

"Everybody's but mine."

"Nelson?"

Tree grunts into the phone.

"Lieutenant Cumberstadt here."

"Good morning, Lieu."

"It's nearly afternoon . . . and I guess I should tell you it's Saturday, too."

Tree opens his eyes. "What's up?"

"I don't want to take up too much of your precious time off, but I thought you ought to know about something the uniform guys ran into last night . . . a dope deal that turned shitty in the lobby of the Blake Hotel. We really don't know for sure what happened yet, but somebody hit somebody good. We got one dead so far—an unidentified white guy. Looks like mob. A Rastafarian named Moffitt was shot in the face. He's at the medical center on machines."

"No name on the white guy?"

"Not yet. Does the Rasta mean anything to you?"

"These guys change their names like we change our socks. You gotta know his street name."

"We don't have that."

"That's too bad."

"It's a crying fucking shame," Cumberstadt says,

"because he was carrying pictures of you and Tibaldi in his wallet."

"Say what?"

"You heard me. Thirty-five-millimeter color prints, taken with a telephoto lens, the lab guys tell me. You and Jimmy are sitting at a table, sharing a pitcher of beer."

"Are you going to be in the office later?"

"In and out."

"We'll be there as soon as we can. Do me a favor— try to find out the white guy's name and leave it on my desk. Me and Jimmy will hit the hospital later on and see if we know Moffitt."

"I'll be expecting you."

Tree hangs up and rolls out of bed. His joints crack as he walks stiffly to the living room. Bright sunlight fills the room, and Tree can smell coffee and bacon and the Third World odor of marijuana burning.

Jimmy and Annie are at opposite ends of the couch, watching Abbott and Costello. Annie is dressed to run. Her hair is limp and unwashed; the tips of her ears peep out below her headband.

"You up to an easy five?" she says to Tree.

"No, I ran this morning."

"Runners," Jimmy sneers. "You all don't know when a fad has come and gone." The only exercise Jimmy gets is hitting Tree's shag golf balls from a mat on the balcony into the bay, and the weekly eighteen holes, for which he always takes a cart. He is wearing only black swim trunks, which droop from his behind as he crosses the room to get his breakfast. "Who was that with the nerve to call you before cocktails?"

"Cumberbutt."

"You chew him out?"

"He stands properly scolded."

"Yeah, sure," Jimmy says, returning to his position on the couch near the portable command box. "You probably gave him your Anything We Can Do to Help line of shit." He scoops a load of scrambled eggs into his plastic spoon and shovels it into his mouth.

"They had a shootout at the Blake Hotel last night. One dead, one vegetable."

"Lanier?"

"No such luck. The veg is a Rasta named Moffitt. He had pictures of you and me in his wallet."

Jimmy frowns and thinks this over, then whips through a channel-scan from CBS to MTV before deciding to stick with Bud and Lou. "Well," he says finally, "either we're such lousy cops the bad guys have formed a fan club, or somebody is very interested in what we're up to, which is kind of surprising, considering what we're up to. Any time you want to go back to uniform, you just let me know."

"I told Cumberbutt we'd come in and check it out."

"I got us a starting time at Crab Meadow. Three forty-eight, I think."

"Hey, Jimmy, I mean, if they think we don't care about something like this . . . What do you say we give them a couple of hours overtime."

"God, you're a wimp."

For half a block on each side of the faded red hotel, yellow crime scene tape, strung from parking meters, flutters in the warm summer breeze. In front of the hotel the chalk outline of a man starts on the sidewalk and ends on the street. The blood is already dry. Richie Hartmann, the cop who found the body, is sitting in a patrol car parked on the sidewalk. Tree and

Jimmy say hello to him, and he adds their names to the crime scene time log.

"What happened?" Jimmy asks him.

"Man, I just walked up to him, face down in the gutter with a crater where his chest shoulda been . . . I wouldn't have even noticed the other mutt if this radio they give me wasn't a piece of shit. So I went into the hotel, looking for a phone. Which was real fucking smart. All I found was lots more work."

"Where's the squeal man?" Tree asks.

"Baumgarten's on the roof."

Tree is glad it's Alvin Baumgarten. They've always gotten along. He's honest and thorough and thinks like a crook. They climb the stairs to the roof and find Baumgarten standing at the front of the building, looking over the edge.

"Hi, boys," he says, turning around and stepping toward them. "How's it going?"

"Not so good, I guess," says Tree. "We saw the mess downstairs. This hotel is a horror show."

Baumgarten nods and shrugs. He has receding gray curly hair, and a bit of a paunch protrudes from the front of his unbuttoned jacket. He looks like he's been up all night, which he has.

"Fucking lovely, right?" he says, lighting a cigar, staring at the Abraham Lincoln housing project rising four stories above the roof of the hotel. "This might as well have happened in the Arctic Circle for all the help we've gotten from the folks across the street. Goddamn Third World sons of bitches have turned this town to shit and nobody gives a damn . . . or everybody's scared."

"You blame them?" says Tree. "These fucking guys use a different rule book."

"My folks used to live around here," Baumgarten says, "but they had the good sense to move before the stores became sweatshops and the parks became private hunting preserves. But that's all eyewash. Come on."

Downstairs, behind the service desk in the lobby, where marijuana, crack, and smack are sold when the cops aren't around, Baumgarten shows them another cartoon outline of a former human being on the worn wooden floor. The normally vile smell of the Blake Hotel, of dirty laundry, sweat, and urine, has been accelerated by the lingering odors of death.

"Fifty bucks says the bellhop did it," Jimmy says. "Him or the tennis pro."

"But the point is why?" says Tree. "And why the hell is a lily-white mob guy hanging out with trash like this?"

"Who knows?" Baumgarten says. "I mean, did persons unknown take off these people, or did one guy bang the other and get wasted himself. Was the white guy robbed after he was shot? Before? By the guys who shot him or passersby who thought it might be fun to loot the body? We thought the one in here was unarmed, but when we picked up the body I found a twenty-five caliber automatic in the white guy's windbreaker. It looks like it's been fired recently, but I don't know if it was fired here. We didn't find any spent brass."

"Could you tell what the deceased got hit with?" Tree asks.

"A fucking bazooka," Baumgarten says grimly. "Actually, he was so mangled I couldn't tell."

Tree looks up the center hall staircase that leads to Gladstone Lanier's floor of rooms.

"I know," says Baumgarten. "That skinny little cocksucker. He's been waiting hours for me to knock on his door again. We talked to everybody else who was here at the time. Nobody saw nothing, of course, but most of them have packed a bag and made plans to spend the night somewhere else."

"What, are you making Lanier sweat?" Jimmy asks.

"Oh, I certainly hope so, but the real reason I'm waiting is for a search warrant. I'm having trouble getting another one so soon. What's he gonna tell me anyway: 'Gee, Officer, I'd like to help, but I didn't hear a thing. Sorry.' "

"Shit," says Jimmy. "The reggae bastard sits up there with an arsenal—and no one can touch him."

"I can wait," Baumgarten says. "No big deal. I've got a guy outside his door and one on the fire escape. Hell, he can't even smoke a joint. He's probably going nuts."

Tree asks, "Is there anything we can do? Do you want us to wait around for the warrant?"

Baumgarten shakes his head. "I probably won't see that until tomorrow, the way things are going. I'll keep a couple of uniforms hanging around. You guys can breeze."

Tree writes his home telephone number on the back of their business card and hands it to Baumgarten.

Tree and Jimmy leave the hotel and cross the street to where the Vette is parked. Perhaps twenty-five residents of the Abraham Lincoln projects are standing around the courtyard, drinking, gawking, smirking, having themselves a grand old time. Jimmy and Tree walk into the middle of the crowd, and Jimmy raises his hand. The good times stop.

"Last night being a Friday night," Jimmy says, "I figure maybe half you folks were cracking it up out here when the shooting went down across the street. Now we don't need statements from all of you, maybe just say five. So why don't those of you who were around last night line up right here in front of me."

People chuckle. No one moves.

"Not all at once, please. We only need a few."

They remain rooted and mute. Someone in the back of the crowd turns his blaster box back on, and heads start bobbing, feet start shuffling.

"Thank you, good citizens," Jimmy says, and he leads Tree back to the car.

"You're a cynical bastard," Tree says affectionately and slides in the passenger side.

"No one can say we didn't try."

"Sure they could," says Tree.

Lieutenant Cumberstadt leans out of his office with a cup of Sanka in his hand. "Nelson, Tibaldi, get in here. The boss is on the line."

"Good afternoon, Commissioner," Tree says when he and Jimmy are inside.

The intercom squawks: "I'm a little concerned about that Rastafarian having your pictures. Never mind the fact that you're drinking beer in them."

"Yeah," says Jimmy. "Isn't that great? They've got us under surveillance. No budget problems at the Blake."

Tree sees in his mind's eye the camera lens, like a scope centered on the bridge of his nose, and he for once doesn't care what Jimmy says to the commissioner.

"No, I guess not, Detective Tibaldi. The question

is, though, what are we of so limited resources going to do about it? Short of throwing in the towel, that is.''

"I talked to another one of the merchants earlier,'' Tree says. "I think he's ready to get real with us on an extortion complaint. But we're gonna have to protect this one, maybe call in the Feds.''

"If needed. But call me before you book a suite at the Marriott. Detective Tibaldi can fill you in on my budget problems. And for God's sake be careful. The next thing, these creeps will have voodoo dolls of you.''

The intercom snaps off. Tree and Jimmy turn to leave, but Cumberstadt coughs and shuffles his feet.

They stop and look at him. Jimmy sniffles like he's caught a summer cold. "Well?'' he says. "Tick, tick, tick.''

"Look, I don't like to break your balls on the small stuff, but yesterday afternoon I tried calling you on the radio for the better part of an hour.''

"So?'' Jimmy says. "What did you want?''

"So—you said you'd be on the air, staking out the Blake. I've got your overtime slips right here. I'm wondering whether to sign them.''

"I had a headache,'' Jimmy says. "I shut the portable off because the buzzing we told you about a month ago hasn't been fixed yet, and it was driving me fucking nuts.''

"Yeah, right. What about the car phone you had me install at department expense? I called that number twenty times if I called it once.''

"What number?'' says Jimmy.

Cumberstadt reads off the number they gave him.

"That's not it. The last digit is wrong.''

Tree has all he can do not to laugh out loud. Jimmy

has now given Cumberstadt three slightly wrong numbers to a phone that the lieutenant is paying for.

"You guys must think this is 'Miami Vice' or something. I give away the store so you can be heavy, and all you gotta do is jack me off now and then."

"Don't sign the slips," Jimmy says. "And don't call us on a day off again, either."

Cumberstadt smiles. "You know, I think it's time you boys went back in the bag . . . back on rotating tours."

Jimmy shows Cumberstadt his middle finger. "Rotate on this, sir."

The color drains from Cumberstadt's face. This time Tree's sure, Jimmy has gone too far. It's back to the graveyard shift, and the trancelike separation from regular folk, or worse, to a clerical unit at Headquarters. The Bow and Arrow Squad. The Rubber Guns.

"Get him out of here, Nelson. Before his smart mouth costs him his job."

"Is he kidding?" Jimmy says, after Tree pulls him from the office. "The most dangerous thing that prick does is sharpen a pencil, and he wants to know where I was?"

"Jimmy, he was right. We played golf on company time."

Tibaldi is indignant. "*He* doesn't know that."

By the service entrance to the Abraham Lincoln Housing Project, Jimmy Tibaldi locks his car door and says to Tree over the hood of the gray unmarked, "What a dumb place to meet. We stand out like rabbis at Club Med."

"I told you, he's afraid to go to his shop."

"Typical florist."

"Yeah, right. How anxious were we to go to our shop this morning?"

"Different story," says Jimmy. "Jensen's job ain't life-and-death and lawsuits."

"Actually," says Tree, "we made out all right this morning."

Al Baumgarten, conducting the preliminary investigation of the Blake Hotel suicide, questioned each man separately. The stories they gave matched the statement taken from an eyewitness at the housing project. And Lt. Anthony Lee, the designated hitter over at Internal Affairs, was unable to keep his noon appointment with them, which suited the accused just fine. The case would remain open until the autopsy report on the as yet unidentified body was completed.

They walk up the concrete ramp, past the graffiti-covered garbage compactor, through the dented, heavy metal doors. Half the lights are out in the filthy stairwell, which they climb to Jensen Macomber's fifth-floor apartment. At the top of the stairs, Jimmy has to pause to catch his breath. "Damn," he says. "I've got to quit smoking."

"Smoking what?"

"Or only talk to people on the ground floor."

"If you mean that rhetorically, I think we're already there."

Jimmy bangs on Jensen's door. It swings open freely, its deadbolt smashed.

"Not again," Tree says. "This is getting ridiculous."

They draw their guns and leap inside, sweeping the barrels of their weapons around the room in search of targets.

The apartment is in ruins, the drawers all pulled from the dressers, the mattress slit open, the phone ripped from the wall; Jensen's groceries—Wheat Chex, goat's milk, and eggs—are spattered across the walls and floor of the kitchen.

"You calling Lanier every morning with our schedule?" Jimmy says.

"Funny. Close the door."

"Fuck that noise. Let's get the hell out of here and call for uniforms."

"Could we at least check the closets, Jimmy? It wouldn't look too fucking swift, us not finding a body."

But Jensen Macomber's body is not stuffed in one of the closets, nor is it hidden under the bed, or hanging in the shower. Jimmy lights a cigarette and kicks around some of the clothes on the floor. "What do you think?" he says. "Straight burglary? Or a side show?"

"Who the hell knows." Tree is on his knees in the kitchen, going through a box of papers he found under the sink: leases, bank bonds, his passport. "Jensen was scared shitless when I talked to him this morning."

"Jesus. Are we as bad at this as I think?" Jimmy asks.

"A man does begin to wonder. Come on, let's get back to the car and call in our latest fiasco."

They jam the broken door into place and head back down the stairs. The hollow smell of garbage and urine is strong in the gloomy dark. Neither one of them uses the handrail. "These splibs are incredible," Jimmy says. "Wild animals don't foul their own nests."

Tree cringes. "I do hope no one heard that."

By the service doors, Jimmy gags and pretends he's going to throw up. He pulls open the heavy metal door and gasps for what he hopes will be fresh air.

Tree laughs and shields his eyes from the glare of the sun; and because his vision is obstructed, he is not at first sure what the whipcrack explosions and whining ricochets around them are all about. Jimmy's body slams heavily backward into his, pressing him against the side of the door, and for a moment he is tempted to laugh. Jimmy has fooled around like this before. But the sound effects are wrong. Jimmy's "guns" were never this loud.

Tree's neck is stung by pulverized brick. He cries out and turns his head away from the blasts while Jimmy tries to tackle him. Then Tree feels something rip his right buttock, as if Jimmy is biting him, holding on with his teeth like a fish on a hook. He falls back inside the door, and pulls Jimmy in after him, then kicks the door shut on the maelstrom. A heavy hand pounds a moment longer, then stops.

Jimmy groans. "Someone heard me. God, I take it all back." He is lying on his side, his head on the floor.

Tree can't believe he is cracking jokes. "Are you okay?" Please, God, let him be okay.

Jimmy doesn't answer. He rolls onto his back and stares at the concrete ceiling, making up his mind. Tree hikes himself up against the door, leaving a thin trail of blood on the concrete floor, like a slug. Jimmy tries to raise his head and cannot. "I think I'm fucked," he says finally. The front of Jimmy's white tennis shirt is torn and red. Blood spills from the waistband of his nylon windbreaker, where it's been pooling from more holes than Tree has fingers.

"We're going to a hospital, buddy. Toot sweet."

"I'm hip," Jimmy says, and a frothy pink fluid spills from the corner of his mouth across his beard to his ear. His hand, as Tree lifts it to check his pulse, is shaking.

Tree pulls his revolver, opens the door a crack and looks outside. The vacant lot is empty, the street deserted.

"Call the cops!" he screams, hoping his voice will hook around to the front of the building and fall on the ears of someone who cares. "Call an ambulance. Help!"

"If Aviles were here, you could use one of his two walkie-talkies," Jimmy says dreamily.

Tree remembers that their walkie-talkie is on the front seat of the unmarked car, where it does not belong. And then it occurs to him that they are both going to die. Here, on the loading dock of a housing project. And that when they are finally found, their bodies will have been stripped of weapons and valuables, and abused, their heads carried away on spikes.

"I want you to talk to my kid . . ."

"Lie still, Jimmy. I hear sirens. Help on the way, man."

More blood dribbles through Jimmy's beard, yet there seems to be none of the pain associated with shredded organs and severed arteries. Tree knows Jimmy is long past pain. He lies down on the concrete next to him.

"We're gonna make it," he says into his ear. "We always have."

But Jimmy has nothing more to say. No more wisecracks, no more tantrums, no more baffling bullshit. Tree puts his arm across Jimmy's bloody chest and kisses him on the ear, then finds himself mindlessly reciting the first prayer he was taught as a child.

"Bless us, O Lord, and these Thy gifts, which we are about to receive . . ."

6
Hail Mary

Tree wakes up on his stomach with the smell of over-cooked towels in his head. A nurse stands beside him, changing an IV bottle. "Good morning, Detective Nelson," she says. And then before he can ask what's going on, she leaves him alone in the small private room.

He hears bells ringing in the hall outside his door, and the hospital operator paging Dr. Klein, Dr. Irving Klein. He struggles onto his good side, feels the pain in his right buttock. He is about to roll out of bed to his feet when Police Officer Luke Cromarty pulls back the curtain and gently but firmly says, "What are you, nuts?"

Tree hasn't seen Luke in years, not since Luke broke them in after their training at the Police Academy. He thought Luke had pulled the pin and gone to Florida.

"The doc said if that slug had hit you five inches closer to center, you'd be singing in the heavenly choir." Luke holds up his hands to show him, a man complaining about a fish or the size of his wang.

Tree nods and rolls back on his stomach, exhausted.

"I gotta let Headquarters know you're awake," Luke says. "The Uh-Oh Squad wants to talk to you right away."

"Do me a solid?" says Tree. "Get them all down here at the same time."

"You got it, kid, and anything else you want, too. They said the sky's the limit."

Tree can't think of anything else he would like at the moment, at least anything the police department would provide.

"Remember, kid. Don't fucking dwell."

Tree remembers a lot of things Luke said. Such as . . . a good cop is never hungry, horny, cold, or wet. And that no one prays for peace like the beat police. And the priorities: your partner, yourself, the union, the public, then the care and feeding of the dumbass bosses. But first, your partner.

"Got it," says Tree.

Luke pats him on the shoulder and leaves.

The nurse returns to sedate him. She says he needs rest, he's lost some blood. She hopes he won't mind feeling drowsy. Tree assures her that he doesn't mind at all.

The shot works wonders. While those who wish to interview him are racing to the hospital, he is floating out of their reach, untethered by earthly concerns. The silly word *hero* sneaks into his consciousness, where he savors it for a moment as he might a delicacy on his tongue.

Nah, he thinks. Anybody can get shot in the ass.

He can already hear the locker-room jokes, the innuendoes.

He'll get a guinea bar, one of those tricolor combat

medals with a golden star, and his picture in the paper. Jimmy'll sneer and tell the reporters the wound is just another knot in the Tree. Get a load of these, he'll say, pulling up his shirt. Talk about battle scars.

Then Tree remembers that Jimmy won't do diddlyshit . . . and the bottom drops out of his heart. His best friend is not dead a day and already he's forgetting, already not taking it seriously, figuring the angles on his own behalf. He takes small solace in the notion that Jimmy would have felt the same way.

When Tree wakes up again the drapes are open. The parking-lot lights are on outside his window. A basket of fruit from Nelcorp International crowns the table at his feet. Colored envelopes on the nightstand await his perusal. Later, he thinks. His wound is on fire. He rings the buzzer for the nurse.

A foxy blonde appears, Ms. Sommers by her name tag.

"I have some pain," he says, twisting his neck for a better look at her.

"That's to be expected."

"The day nurse said to let you know if I needed more painkiller."

"Did she now?" Ms. Sommers checks the chart at the foot of the bed. "Demerol, eh?"

"Whatever. I'm easy."

"A little too. You know it's not a good idea to grow overly fond of that stuff. You should really only take it if you need it."

"Trust me. I need it."

"You have visitors downstairs. Why don't we wait until after they're gone."

"They're the reason I need it."

"Come on now."

"Who's downstairs?" Right now he'd trade an audience with the pope for the mellow warmth of Demerol.

"Your brother officers, I suppose. No one else is allowed in to see you."

Cops, Tree thinks. What marvelous people. Downstairs giving blood for him, in the chapel making novenas. The thin blue line closing around one of their own. Luke Cromarty steps into the room and motions at Tree, who feels suddenly like an exhibit in the Police Museum.

Then Jack and Colleen Tibaldi walk into the room, holding hands. God, he had completely forgotten about them. Susan, too. And Stacy the Slut Sponge. All those unresolved relationships. All that emotional baggage left behind.

Lt. Anthony "The Hitman" Lee from the commissioner's office is with them. He clicks his heels together and throws Tree a smart salute. Lieutenant Lee has foresworn his usual crisp blue uniform today for a plain black business suit, black police clip-on tie with handcuff tieclip, and factory-buffed oxfords. He's tall, dark, and solemn as an undertaker.

Jimmy's folks look small and out of place with him, leaning on each other for support. Jack Tibaldi tells Tree that they drove down last night from Oneonta. Jimmy's younger sister Melanie can't make it; she's expecting her first child any day now. And Stacy doesn't want young Susan brutalized by the newspapers.

"We had a chance to see Jimmy," he says. "Lieutenant Lee here has been kind enough to coach us around the bases. I don't know what the missus and I would have done without him.''

Then the small-time broadcaster can say no more. His nose is running, and tears leak from his red-rimmed eyes. Mrs. Tibaldi hands him Kleenex tissue from her pocketbook and keeps some for herself.

"My God," he croaks, wiping his face. "What they did to him."

Tree remembers how Jimmy always used to say what a pain in the ass the old man was (at football games cheering louder than the other fathers, selling booster buttons, taking movies), how embarrassing his enthusiasm could be.

"Did he suffer?" she wants to know. Her voice is upstate twang, without guile or subterfuge. Her bone-white hands work a set of black rosary beads.

"He told me to tell little Susan that he loved her."

She turns to the window and leans on the sill. The room grows so quiet they can hear distant voices rising up from the Emergency entrance. Lieutenant Lee shakes his head, and Tree wonders what he can say to ease their pain, now that it's too late to throw his body in the way.

Jack Tibaldi asks, "Is there anything we can do for you, son? I understand your dad is out of town."

"I'm okay."

Still staring out the window, Mrs. Tibaldi asks if Jimmy had time to make his peace. Jimmy's father looks at Tree in a way that says, Humor her, boy, no matter where the truth may lie.

"We said our prayers."

"What prayers?"

Tree wonders if Jimmy even remembered any prayers. He knows he can't tell her the truth, that she'd fling herself out the window if she knew that Jimmy'd made no Act of Contrition, and that all he had been able to manage was Grace. "The Our Father," he says.

"He was a good boy, Colleen," Mr. Tibaldi says. "He's with God."

When she turns around her face is a mask of desolation, the lips pinched together, the eyes downcast and narrow.

"He was a heathen, Jack. There's no point kidding ourselves anymore."

She nods slowly at her husband and then glances at Tree, and then walks quickly out of the room. They listen to her heels click down the corridor, past the nursing station to the waiting room by the elevator.

"Don't mind Jimmy's mom," Jack Tibaldi says, scratching his head. "She had a son, then a grand-daughter, and now she doesn't have either one. It's the hardest thing to bury a child, even one as much trouble as Jimmy was. She don't blame you, and I sure don't either . . . I didn't think she'd act like this."

"No apology necessary, sir."

"Jim's mom is understandably upset," Lieutenant Lee says. "As we all are."

The phony bastard, Tree thinks. No one ever called James Colin Tibaldi Jim. At least not to his face. "Yes sir."

"I think you'll be pleased to know that we've closed our investigation of that rooftop suicide, Trevor. There will be no charges filed by our office."

"Yeah, that's great news all right. I was really worried."

Lee narrows his eyes and stares at Tree, a flash of anger visible in the set of his jaw.

Mr. Tibaldi shakes Tree's hand with both of his. "We'll see you real soon," he says. "You'll come up and visit us sometime."

"I'd like that, sir. I want you to know how much I cared about Jimmy. How much I'll miss him."

Mr. Tibaldi is again unable to respond.

Lieutenant Lee puts his hand on Mr. Tibaldi's arm. "The Homicide boys are here, Jack. . . . Why don't we let them go to work. We can run over to Jim's apartment now and collect his things."

"Whatever you think is best."

Jack Tibaldi pulls free of the lieutenant at the door and looks back at Tree. "I'm glad it was you that was with him, Tree. Somehow it don't seem quite as bad. Like he wasn't so alone."

"Yes, sir."

Al Baumgarten squeezes past Mr. Tibaldi in the doorway and then settles into the chair at the side of the bed. He has a clipboard and a case folder on his lap, a Styrofoam cup of coffee in his hand. "How you feeling?" he says.

"Like I lost my best friend, what did you think? . . . What's happening with the case?"

"Not a whole hell of a lot. Mostly I've been waiting to talk to you."

"Great."

Tree is enormously tired; his neck hurts from twisting to see visitors. Since he woke up alive, it's been all downhill.

"I'm thinking that Macomber set you up for Lanier," Baumgarten says.

"Don't waste your time on Jensen Macomber. He's as straight as the day is long."

"You say that now," Baumgarten says. "What if he didn't want to do it but had to? What about that?"

"If that's the story, I shoulda been a janitor."

"What else can you tell me?"

Tree twists his head away from Baumgarten. In his professional monotone he says, "We went to meet Macomber at the projects. He wasn't there. The door to his apartment was kicked in and the place had been ransacked. You'll have to ask Jensen what was taken."

"One of many things I'd like to ask Jensen."

"What do you mean?"

"I mean he hasn't been seen since yesterday morning."

Tree closes his eyes. "Then he's dead."

"That's very possible."

"Jesus, we fucked this up."

"Let's just say that you underestimated your opponent's capacity for violence."

"When our pictures turned up in that guy's wallet, we should have paid closer attention." We should have paid closer attention all along, he thinks. Police work is a contact sport. "Anyway, we went back downstairs and opened the door. Jimmy walked out first."

"You see anybody?"

"No . . . I was blocking the sun with my hand and looking down, then I was looking at Jimmy. Then the floor, the door, Jimmy. They coulda rode by in a stagecoach for all I know."

"They?"

"It sure sounded like more than one gun." Tree replays the ambush in his head, but there is nothing in this painful memory that will help them solve the case. "You want me to say I saw Lanier?"

"I'd love it, as long as it's the truth. But maybe he

didn't do it, and then maybe a cop-killer gets away with it.''

"Like who?"

"Like Crazy Victor Guardina."

"Come on, willya?"

"Aviles thinks Victor did it to warn him off. He also didn't think Victor appreciated you and Jimmy getting on his case.''

"That's beautiful," says Tree. "Victor hit me and Jimmy to warn off Wilfredo Aviles. Hey, I love the little fanatic, but with all due respect, Sarge, that's like slapping Michael Tyson to put the fear of God into Pee Wee Herman."

"He says he's close to putting Victor Guardina away."

"What? For traffic violations?"

"Possession, sale."

"He's pulling your prick."

"Cumberstadt agrees with him."

"I rest my case."

Baumgarten smiles, then mimes smashing his head with his clipboard several times.

"That's quite a precinct we've got down at the old One-Two, isn't it?" says Tree.

"Even a stopped clock is right twice a day."

"Find Jensen Macomber," says Tree. "Everything else is bullshit."

There are the sounds of another day in the room when Tree awakes. The day nurse is rattling around at the end of his bed.

"Good morning, Detective."

"Is it time for my shot? My ass is killing me."

"But you were barely nicked," she says.

But the pain is enormous, he thinks, watching her leave. And so is the fear, the paralysis of the spirit, the temporary death of the soul. He knows because he's had it once before . . .

. . . when the mental patient snatched that third-grade girl from the playground of Saint Anthony's and put a revolver next to her pretty little pigtail. He wanted an audience with the President, right there by the swings, in exactly ten minutes, or he was gonna shoot her. If they came any closer he would shoot her. If they reached for their guns he would shoot her. Jimmy relayed their predicament to Headquarters on his walkie-talkie and was ordered to maintain the status quo. "He's on his way," Jimmy said. "Good," said the nut, a grizzled white man in his forties, wearing flannel pajamas. "The clock is running."

For the first two minutes, everybody stared and wondered what would happen, what the hell was going on. Then the little girl started crying, so the nut covered her mouth with his hand.

"What you're asking for is impossible," Tree told him. "There are better ways to make your point."

"What point?"

"I don't know."

"Don't bother me with your stupid advice. The girl has five minutes left."

"Hey," said Tree. "That's not fair."

"Two minutes."

"Will you please stop pissing him off," said Jimmy. "Even the President needs a little time to get from place to place."

They had to buy time, to allow the precision rifle teams to respond and set up a kill shot. If it looked like the nut would go through with it. "One minute."

He was crying; his nose was running. The hand squeezing the pistol grip was white with strain, and shaking.

Tree begged him not to do it. He offered to exchange himself for the child. He offered him money. Jimmy promised to forget the whole damn thing, just everybody turn and walk away. "Some day we'll laugh about all of this," Jimmy said.

Then time ran out and the President wasn't there and the nutjob pulled the trigger, just like he said he would. The little girl's other pigtail blew away from her head, and she dropped to the grass like a broken puppet. Jimmy snapped to a point-shoulder shooting stance and emptied his revolver into the nutjob's chest before Tree could even think of revenge . . .

"Luke?" he calls out over his shoulder.

No answer from the hall. He wonders if Luke is asleep in the chair outside, his spirit paralyzed too.

"Luke?"

"What's all the racket in here?" A white-haired, pink-smocked volunteer sticks her head into the room. "You want a magazine?"

"I want the cop."

"What cop? What happened?"

"The cop who's supposed to be guarding my door."

"Are you a celebrity?"

"Hardly."

"A criminal?" she says, suddenly excited, turning the handle on her cart.

"Just a guy who's supposed to have a twenty-four-hour guard on his door. Sorry to disappoint you."

"I'm sorry, too," she says, "because there hasn't been anyone guarding your door all morning. I wouldn't pay the bill if I were you."

He reaches for the phone on his bedside table and calls Cumberstadt's office. The lieutenant is out, he is told. No one else there wishes to speak to him.

Tree wonders if the security perimeter has been expanded to include the entire hospital, requiring squadrons of officers, sharpshooters on the roof, helicopters. He wonders if things have gotten that bad in his absence.

When he looks up again, Annie is standing next to the bed, and with her is Francis Brophy, his father's best friend and closest business confidant.

"How'd you get in?" Tree asks them.

"Walked," says Annie. She holds up her pink visitor's pass for his inspection.

"Good morning, Trevor. It's good to see you looking so well." Brophy retired from an illustrious career with the New York City Police Department when Tree was five years old. He was hired by Alistair Nelson for his loyalty and his savoir faire. And his connections. He was, in many ways, Tree's boyhood idol, after Mickey Mantle and Whitey Ford.

"What do you say, Broph? Hey, Annie. It's good to see you."

"Hello, Tree," she says, bending to kiss the back of his head. "I tried to see you last night, but they wouldn't let me in. I wasn't family," she says with a pout.

"All you would have seen was me cutting z's."

"I figured as much. How do you feel?"

"Okay, I guess. I'm dreading my first dump."

"I've a telegram here from Dad," Brophy says. "We reached him last night in Bonn. It says, 'Son: Heard of your tragedy. Cutting trip short. Ask Brophy for anything you need. Love Dad.' "

"Bring me the head of Gladstone Lanier."

Brophy laughs. "Hey, I was good, but maybe now a little old for that sort of work."

"Yeah," says Tree. "I think I am, too."

"If it's any consolation, it sneaks up on you quick and you cannot do a thing."

Like death, Tree thinks. The unexpected ending of life. He is remembering the last time he and Annie were in a hospital room, when their positions were reversed and she was the patient and he the awkward visitor. She'd had a difficult abortion, undertaken without the father's knowledge or assistance. She'd talked about killing herself, saying she might "end it all with Tylenol." Ancient history, he thinks. She looks beautiful today, solid and sensible. This time it's his ass in the sling.

"I'm gonna pack our stuff for the beach," Annie is saying. "We can hang out there until my parents get back." Doc and Betsy Adams teach at Stony Brook University, and are on holiday in Ireland until—as they would say—school reconvenes. "I'll get someone to take my hours at work."

"Fine," he says. "The farther away from here the better."

"In the meantime," Brophy says, "until your father gets back, you let me know if there's anything you need. I'll be around the office or the club, or Martha will know where to grab me. Annie, you take all the time you need with Tree. I'll wait in the coffee shop to walk you out."

"No," she says. "I'm ready to book. I've got tons of things to do if we're gonna move out east. Laundry and whatnot."

"I'm tired anyway," Tree says, disappointed, but in

a way relieved, not yet ready either to discuss with her the future or the past.

Annie bends over and kisses his cheek. "The nurse said you'll be going home in a day or so. We can talk then . . . much more comfortably."

Comfortably numb, he hopes, though he doubts the hospital will pack him a Demerol doggy bag.

He grunts and turns his face to the pillow, his back to the world. He pulls the phone over from the nightstand and punches in a number. The lieutenant is still out.

Ten minutes later Lieutenant Cumberstadt returns his call. "What's the matter?" he wants to know. "Why are you bothering my secretary?"

She must have been screening his calls. He's nervous, worried about something. "It's probably just a fuckup, but there's no one on my door."

"It's not a fuckup, as you put it. The commissioner determined that you were out of danger."

"Wonderful. You picked up Lanier?"

"What do you think—he mailed in a confession?"

Tree knows that was wishful thinking, as he knows that when you start providing plausible explanations for the most unlikely occurrences, you are just about to get screwed. "How did the commissioner decide that I was safe?"

"Input from several sources, me not being one of them."

"Who, then? Al Baumgarten?"

"I wouldn't know."

"Thanks for looking out for me, Lieutenant. Thanks a hell of a lot. My partner's dead and I'm hurt, and my people don't want to know me anymore. Something about this sucks."

"I wouldn't worry."

"You sure as hell would. You get scared when the guys won't listen to you at roll call."

Cumberstadt doesn't answer.

"Listen, I can get out of here in time for the funeral. Do you think you could at least have one of the guys pick me up and drive me down there?"

"No."

"What are you talking about, 'No.' You're lucky I'm stuck in this hospital room, Dwayne, because you're really starting to honk me off."

"I'm talking about whether you should go to the funeral. Trimble had some very definite thoughts on that at last night's staff meeting. He said it wouldn't look right, you being there."

"Jesus." Tree is stunned. "I'm gonna get even with you, Lieutenant."

"This wasn't my idea, Tree. I don't know why I should be jammed up in all this. I'm getting it from both sides."

"Jimmy Tibaldi was my partner. I have an obligation and a right to be there. I should be one of the fucking pallbearers."

"I understand all that. Still . . . if your career means anything at all to you—"

"Forget it. I'll go as a private citizen. You tell Commissioner Trimble I said he's a douche bag."

"I wouldn't, Nelson. The commissioner was adamant. He also said that you and Tibaldi really let us down."

"*What* are you talking about?"

"Yes," says Cumberstadt. "Indeed. What am I talking about?"

Click.

Tree sees what's coming. His superiors are maneuvering—coordinating their disavowal of him. Good riddance to bad rubbish and all that. Just a couple of rotten apples. Defectives. The high muckie-mucks think we brought this on ourselves, the way white folk assume Negroes broken down by the side of the road have neglected their autos.

7

Flying on the Ground Is Wrong

Immediately after the funeral mass for Detective James C. Tibaldi, cops in and out of uniform from all over the tri-state area gather in Garden City gin mills to swap war stories and guzzle beer. A fine turnout, they say, with tears drawn from their eyes by the pipe band; and Jimmy flying home with his parents, so no burial, no thud of earth on wood. Better that way for all concerned. Easier on the living.

A damn shame, he was so young. A damn shame, he was so close to retirement. Shots are tossed back for Jimmy Tibaldi. Glasses raised.

Annie Sutherland is in Leo's Midway, watching the funeral crowd work all-world bartender Danny Patterson to the bone. She is hanging on the arm of Francis Brophy, doing her best to take Tree's place in this small affair of state, all the while fending off politely the sexual advances of the bereaved. She tries several times to buy drinks for the mourners, but her money's no good here. The drinks are on the house.

Dr. Charles Canavan, the police surgeon who was ordered to order Tree Nelson to remain in his hospital bed until after the funeral, is down the block in Sweeney's, knocking back double martinis with Commissioner Trimble and his closest advisers. They are discussing the miracles of forensic medicine, and its role in the detection of crime.

Several miles east Detective Trevor Nelson is discharged without fanfare from the Nassau County Medical Center.

"Don't forget now," the candy-striper carrying his fruit basket tells him, "today is the first day of the rest of your life."

"Uh-huh."

Most people leaving the hospital have someone waiting for them. That someone has a Big Mac, small fries, and a Coke, and some idea of what to do next; and waits patiently beside a station wagon, ready to lift the healed from the wheelchair.

But nobody is waiting for Tree, almost as if no old and trusted friend exists. He is on his own, like a man leaving prison, the world made over fresh without him. Without Jimmy.

They roll him through the doors and down the ramp, order him to have a nice day, and then dump him on the sidewalk without a compass or a map. He has his fruit, a Hefty Bag filled with his bloodstained clothes, and a *Newsday* under his arm. Annie brought the charcoal pin-striped suit he's wearing because she thought he'd go directly to the services, but she didn't think to include money in her Care Package, not even bus fare. And who could blame her?

He limps to the bus stop on Hempstead Turnpike and joins the black people climbing on board, thinking that he could tin his way into the bus if they hadn't taken his gun and shield for safekeeping. Maybe the driver will have a heart. Maybe the rest of his life will turn out okay, after all that's happened.

The bus driver laughs in his face.

Tree makes a mental note that not having money sucks, on the first or any other day of the rest of your life.

"Trevor Nelson!" a voice calls as the bus pulls away.

"Hey, Broph. What's going on?"

He limps to where Brophy has double-parked his BMW, and he stands next to his window as if he's about to give him a summons.

"Get in," Brophy says. "Get off your feet. You look like hell."

"Thanks."

"What in God's name is going on?"

"Not a thing," says Tree. "We're talking Day One."

"Yeah, well I just left a funeral that seemed to be for two. Everybody there was using the past tense where you were concerned."

"Out of sight, out of mind, I guess."

"Have you read today's paper?"

"Not yet."

"Page three."

Tree climbs into the passenger seat, and finds a way to balance himself on his good side. Then he opens the paper and reads aloud the smallest article on page three:

MURDERED COP LAID TO REST TODAY

Homicide investigators in Seaport remain puzzled by the conduct of the two detectives ambushed here Monday. "We have many unanswered questions," said Lt. Dwayne Cumberstadt of the Twelfth Precinct. "The investigation is continuing."

Interest in the case is furthered by the fact that neither officer was to the civil service born. James C. Tibaldi, the dead officer, was the son of popular upstate sports personality Jack Tibaldi. Trevor Nelson is the son of Alistair Nelson of Nelcorp International, a major import-export firm with offices in Zurich and New York.

Both probationary detectives were involved in last week's failed attempt to prevent the suicide of an as yet unidentified homicide suspect.

Continued page 36

"That's great," says Tree. "Cumberstadt really backs us to the hilt. I wonder how many people turned to page thirty-six."

"I'd figure you were guilty of sordid sex with jet set midgets and turn to the sports."

"Really." Tree finishes the article, which goes on to say there were errors in radio procedure, violations of departmental rules and regulations, and just plain carelessness involved. Heads, the article concludes, are sure to roll.

"So what are they talking about?" Brophy asks. "Or rather, what aren't they talking about?"

"I have no idea."

"They're blowing smoke up someone's ass."

"Uh-huh. Looks like . . . So how was our funeral?"

Brophy looks at him quickly, then back to the road. "The usual," he says. "Bagpipes, bullshit, and phony brogues. They gave the flag to his mother and the rest of the day she held it to her chest like someone was gonna swipe it. The boys from the precinct had the old man three sheets to the wind, which was just as well, I suppose. The company sent a wreath and a check from your dad for ten grand to his kid.''

"Thanks, Broph. A lot."

"It was your father."

"That was nice."

"You should have gone today," Brophy says. "I think it would have meant a lot to his father and mother."

"I was ordered not to."

"Ordered? . . ."

"I still should have gone. But to sign myself out would have taken eight hours of forms and signatures."

Brophy nods and says, "You don't have to go home alone. Me and Martha would be glad to have you hang around for a while."

"Annie's there," Tree says. "She probably doesn't know whether to shit or wind her watch. She just told me the other day she wants me to marry her . . . I'll bet she thinks I arranged all this to get out of it."

Brophy looks mildly surprised. "Annie's still at Leo's, I believe. Some of your pals are seeing to her needs."

"I'm sure they are."

"That's funny. She never said a word about marriage. Just about how lost you were gonna be without Jimmy."

Tree shifts to a more comfortable position, happy to hear of her single-minded concern for his welfare. "I'll be okay, I guess. In time."

"You and Jimmy were what I'd call inseparable," Brophy says. "Don't think the pain is gonna go away, 'cause it ain't. I buried a partner way back when, and I'll bet a day doesn't go by that I don't think of him, catch myself wondering what he'd look like now if he'd lived, remembering what he really looks like now. It's a curse to live sometimes, I swear it is."

Tree watches their reflection flutter across the mirrored walls of the European-American Building. He is grateful to Brophy for explaining to him why he feels so dead, but he can't find the words to thank him. The hole in his chest grows bigger and bigger; he wonders when this pain, that won't ever go away, stops getting worse.

Ten minutes later Brophy double parks in front of the condo. He leaves the motor running. "Call me tomorrow," he says. "If there's something going wrong, I'd like to minimize the damage."

Tree thanks him for the ride and walks into the garage, past his 1978 Volvo, which he suspects won't start for him now, after its more than normal inactivity. It will grumble and fart, like he's got some nerve sticking it with a key.

"Good to have you home, Mr. Nelson," says the guard in the lobby.

Tree carries an armload of junk mail to the elevator and fumbles for his key as he ascends to the penthouse. But he sees he doesn't need his key; the door is ajar. "Annie?"

He can hear someone moving about inside, someone who doesn't answer to the name Annie.

He doesn't panic.

Right now the thought of being robbed is of so little concern it amounts to a minor inconvenience, like breaking a shoelace or sand in his swimsuit. He shoves the door open and calls out wearily, "Police."

"That's using the term loosely."

He sees the broad back of a white man in a hunter-green leisure suit, circa 1979, kneeling by the stereo, flipping through record albums. The man turns and grins malevolently.

"Sergeant Bolder. What a wonderful surprise."

"The pleasure's all mine, Detective Nelson."

"Why don't I think you're here on behalf of the department to welcome me home?"

"But I am, Nelson. Welcome the fuck home."

"Extending your cultural horizons, Sergeant? I've even got some books."

"You call this horseshit culture? Iron butterflies? Grateful stiffs?" He peeks inside a record jacket, then spins it across the room like a Frisbee. It comes to rest against the white teak bar, a leansie, and Tree gets the feeling that Bolder doesn't plan on cleaning up.

"How'd you get in?"

Lt. Anthony Lee steps from the kitchen, wearing a brown suit and his factory-buffed black oxfords. "With Jim's key. How'd you get home so fast?"

Brophy was right, something is very wrong. Tree checks his bedroom. The bed is turned over, the pictures off the walls, and drawers hang dejectedly from his dresser. His golf bag has been emptied on the carpet: tees, balls, old scorecards, and his clubs in a pile like Pickup Stix. He turns to Lee, who is standing right behind him.

"What the fuck is this?"

"This?"

"The mess you made."

"And we just got done saying what a slob you were."

114

"What are you clowns looking for? If you want something, why don't you just ask for it?"

"Like Bolder says, we're here to welcome you home, same as we would for any shot cop." Lee is grinning like he's got the goods. The thick cocoa carpet, the piano, the fully stocked bar, the panoramic view of the bay—Tree's luxuries have earned him the lieutenant's disdain. "I checked your phone messages for you. Some broad named Mona called. You're supposed to call her back. Two guys from *Newsday* and one from the *Times*, but if you call them back I'm gonna eat you for lunch. Also the PBA president, but I've already taken the liberty of telling him you don't need any help."

"Thanks for everything, Lieutenant. Now get the fuck out of my house before I call some real cops."

Lee walks to the door, turns, and bows. "Let's do it again soon. Say in front of a grand jury."

"See you in church," Bolder says before slamming the door in Tree's face.

Tree walks into the living room and opens the balcony doors; the curtains billow into the apartment like spinnakers. Then he opens the front door, and the sea breezes race through the rooms unchecked. In the kitchen he throws away milk that has soured and a bag of stale potato chips. Without warning, his eyes fill up with tears. He stands frozen, with his hands in his pockets, assessing damages too great to calculate in his present state of mind.

The bleat of a foghorn out on the bay brings him back to the present moment. He picks up the phone and calls the guard. "Did you let those two cops come up here unescorted?" he asks.

"Yes, sir . . . uh, yes. Were you surprised?"

"No." He hangs up.

Booze, he decides defiantly, almost as if he owes it to someone. If not Demerol for the demoralized, Moosehead for the morose. Stretching out on the couch with his bottle, he thinks of the bills he should pay and the calls he should return. But three healthy slugs of ale dismiss these mundane concerns. Fuck the bills—his creditors can wait. And the calls? He's got nothing to say to nobody, now or in the foreseeable future.

Fuck you, Lieutenant Lee. And fuck you, too, Mr. Gladstone Lanier.

More Moosehead. A shot of scotch. Feeling better. Warmer. He was told to force fluids.

She is working in the kitchen, very much the little wife. Tree is on the line between drunk and hungover, slumping in her beanbag chair, looking at the picture of her dead husband, John. John is leaning on a weeping willow tree at an angle made popular by British rock stars, wearing a lab coat and a shiny new stethoscope.

Annie was young when she took this picture, just before John went away. Young, but old. Ahead of her class and wise beyond her years. By her eighteenth summer she had finished high school, married a young doctor, and was attending Smith College while John did his military service.

In those days it seemed to her that she had been blessed with extraordinary talent and good fortune; and she remembered to give thanks when she prayed. She was one of those lucky people to whom nothing bad ever happened. Life was wonderful for eighty years and then you passed away in your sleep, surrounded by loved ones. Right? Her husband might have been away at a seminar for all the worry Annie showed the world. Until a week after New Year's, 1969, when Annie was informed by the army captain who came to her parents' house in Westhampton Beach on that cold gray day that her husband had died in a car accident. She buried him in Calverton National Cemetery, collected his death benefit, and took her act out on the road.

Talk about shitass luck and quicksilver changes of fate, Tree thinks. Talk about downward mobility. From doctor's wife to pumping gas. Tree figures she's fallen down the ladder further than he has, though lately it seems he's gaining on her.

And he knows he caught her on the rebound. He knows he was her second choice, without the normal consolation of absence when first she married. He can't even kid himself that things might have been different if he'd been there first.

A year in Aspen, two in New Paltz, Annie was a tumbleweed flower child, Tree remembers, with artsy-craftsy, shithead boyfriends. Each time she came home for a visit she broke his heart anew. She and William were doing this, she and Patrick doing that. Until finally, perhaps from sheer exhaustion, she used the last of the insurance money to buy this place and settled down.

"You got any aspirin?" he calls to her. "My head's gonna feel worse than my butt."

She carries into the dining room a platter of pancakes and bacon and Bayer. She pours hefty shots of Kahlúa into their coffee cups and he thanks her for thinking of everything.

"I can't believe they searched your house," she says.

"In-house investigations are notoriously unfair. Even if they find something they can't use in court, they *know* . . . or they *think* they know. The way the job looks at it, they're protecting the public from a possible menace."

"You?" she scoffs. "Get real."

"This ain't IBM, you know. I can't change ties and go to work for Wang. In fact if this goes down bad, the only folks who would hire me anymore are lawyers or mobsters."

"Or dear old Dad."

Tree gives her a nasty look. She changes the subject.

"The whole thing is totally unconstitutional. I'd sue their balls off."

"You would."

"You bet your ass."

Maybe so, he thinks, pouring Aunt Jemima syrup on his pancakes. Some people really don't take any shit. He's not one of them, though, never has been. He's always been the type to withhold retaliatory measures until all other options were exhausted.

"I mean," he says, "guilty or not—of what I don't know—this could be awfully embarrassing. And my father's gonna love the publicity."

"He can take it. That's what 'fuck you' money is for."

"Easy for you to say."

"Maybe so," she says, shrugging. "My worry is you. Let's concentrate on getting you healthy and forget all the other bullshit."

"If that's what it will take to cheer you up."

He doesn't remind her that a very bad man still has his picture.

"I have to go out later," she says. "You'll be okay?"

He nods, shoving food in his mouth. "I'll be fine. What is it? Starve a cold, gorge a gunshot wound? That hospital food was for shit."

"Please. Eat." She smiles at him, warm enough to stop his heart. "I need you to stick around."

8

The Trial Separation

"I can't come out tonight," Annie says. She is slouching in a phone booth in the Roosevelt Field mall.

"I'm so lonely I could scream. I was really hoping you could make it tonight."

"Not for a while, Maria. I'm gonna be real busy for the next couple of days."

"What's the matter?"

"Promises to keep."

"Am I your friend or not?" Maria says.

Good question, Annie thinks. She can't remember the last time Maria was anything but a pain. Years ago, when she was just a pretty little hippie with some color to her cheeks and a smile on her face, and not a badass junkie and dealer. "Look, Maria: Two of my friends—you're gonna hate this—two of my friends got shot. And—"

"My God, you must think I'm a stone. I feel sorry for you, baby, that's all, just compassion . . . I mean. I read the paper, I care about the world. The only thing I saw was those two asshole cops getting ambushed last week in Seaport."

"Those *were* my friends. I'd appreciate you keeping that in mind the next time you want to call them names."

"Jesus Christ, Annie! That's your boyfriend? A cop? And you doin' shit all the time, or buyin' it for someone."

"Don't give me problems."

"Whoa, Annie, get a grip. This guy's father is *rich*."

"So what if he is."

"And he's a cop."

"He's the kind of cop you'd like to have bust you if push came to shove . . . I've seen him walk up to bums and hand them money, saying he saw them drop it . . . he delivers babies and referees family fights. What do you do for people beside scare the shit out of them? I see who I want to see, girl. I'm not the doper on the run, you are."

"Just don't freeze me out. That's what Geoffrey's doing. Makin' me kick this alone. Fuck."

"Geoffrey freezes everyone out."

"That boy has no heart. But you thought he was cute . . . and sensitive."

"Just give me my list of chores."

"Annie . . . my life is in your hands."

"The hell it is!" Annie slams down the receiver and walks quickly into the mob of shoppers.

Tree's leg feels a little better when he wakes up at noon the next day. He checks Annie's captain's clock on the table by the door and figures he slept for fourteen hours, drifting off well before she came home. He tried to wait up, but the couch was so comfortable, his fatigue so complete. And now she's gone again, when he's suddenly more lonely than tired.

With a garbage bag tied over his wound, Tree showers upstairs and gets dressed. A pair of old blue jeans fit him loosely, a plain black T-shirt, low black Chuck Taylor All-Stars. It's been a week since he's shaved and he likes what he sees. He thinks he'll let it grow . . . for the boys down at headquarters, which is where he's headed if the Volvo will kick over. It always does when he really doesn't want to go somewhere.

Fifteen minutes later he is hiding the car in the corner of the parking lot, head-in to the shrubs along the fence to conceal his expired registration and inspection stickers.

The hallways are filled with the tranquil sunshine and silence of a school the day after graduation. His sneakers squeak on the fresh-waxed floors. Sergeant Baumgarten is alone in the Homicide office, sitting at his desk, his feet resting on his wastepaper basket. "Sit down, Nelson. We've got the place to ourselves," he says.

Which is why Tree wanted to meet on a Saturday afternoon. He doesn't relish the idea of being interrogated by half the job, and he doesn't want to hear about tough breaks.

"Coffee?" Baumgarten asks.

"Please. Regular."

Baumgarten plays host, then sits watching Tree through the steam rising from his cup (which says THE BOMB on it; Tree's loaner mug says GOD BLESS THE DUKE). "You've left us between a rock and a hard place," he says at last. "Internal Affairs think you're dirty as hell."

"Me? Why?"

"They think you and Jimmy were heavy into drugs."

Tree taps himself in the chest. "Me?"

"Jimmy they know for sure. You? They're betting that way."

"Tell me," Tree says. "Any word on who shot us?"

"You tell me, Nelson. Were you and Tibaldi running down a case for the department, or working a scam of your own?"

"I'm just somebody who happened to get ambushed."

"That won't do, Tree. This case stinks and you know it. You wouldn't believe the theories the guys are coming up with. You're all anybody around here has been talking about."

"That's fucking great. Criminals get treated better than—"

"Hear me out," Baumgarten says. "Please. I just might be your last friend on this job."

Tree stands up abruptly. "No deals," he says. "Don't even think about it. Not when I haven't done a fucking thing wrong."

"Sit down, stupid. Did you ever think that maybe you failed to do something right? That looking the other way was a bullshit move? Because it was. You know that now, don't you?"

"I don't know anything, Sarge, except my partner is dead, and that don't seem to *bother* anybody around here."

"Go fuck yourself."

Tree is taken aback, his feelings hurt. He likes Al Baumgarten; he doesn't want to be sitting here arguing with him.

"You make your deals upstairs," says Baumgarten. "Down here I need you clear-headed and out of jail."

"What are you talking about, jail? I don't believe this."

Baumgarten holds up his hand. "Let's not jerk each other off. A lot of serious shit has happened to you in a very short time."

"You people suck. You're in on this for them, aren't you?"

"They asked me to soften you up," he admits. "But what I'm telling you I'd tell my own brother."

"Things are that bad?" Tree says.

"I'd say so, Nelson, unless you can learn to lay low and sing on key."

"Those used to be my stronger suits," Tree says, trying to regain his composure, pretending this is some terrible mistake that his father will correct with a phone call, and not the dubious end to his chosen career. He has often thought of quitting, but being shown the door is a whole new bag of tricks. How will he fill up his days? There's a limit to how much golf one can play, how far one can run. That much free time can kill a man. "What do they want me to do?"

"Mostly I figure they want you to go without a fight."

"Go? Why? I'm clean, for God's sake. I haven't even smoked a joint in the last ten years."

"For one, it makes them look good on the kid going off the hotel roof. They can say they cleaned their own house, taking action where there was even a hint of impropriety."

"But you said yourself you think we're innocent."

"It doesn't matter."

"Are they going after Sergeant Allison, then?"

"No."

"Well what the fuck is that? He was the goddamn supervisor."

"He came, he saw, he conquered. But people aren't whispering shit about him in the hallways. And nobody's tried to rub him out."

Tree feels confused and helpless, like he's got to vomit and he can't find a toilet. He would give anything to know what they know. Or think they know.

"If you fight them things can get ugly," Baumgarten says. "I know it's not fair, but—"

"Do you see anything on the plus side?"

Baumgarten drums his fingers on the desk. "They know the press is interested in you right now. And your old man is not without influence."

"I don't talk to reporters," Tree says, "and the old man will be nothing but ashamed. I just want it all to go away, Sergeant. I want it to be a week ago, when it's not too late to do something."

"If Trimble offers you a disability pension, grab it and run like a thief. That's all I'm gonna say. In fact I've already said too much."

"What happens when I get sued?"

Baumgarten hesitates, looking Tree over just one more time, sizing him up based on limited data. "That ain't gonna happen, Tree. We know goddamn well you guys didn't kill that kid. I checked the case jacket this morning. Three different witnesses now back up your story."

"Do we even know his name yet?"

Baumgarten shakes his head. "We're calling him Roll One, which is what he had tattooed on his right bicep. Immigration is working on who he might be."

"What about picking up Gladstone Lanier?"

"For what? Living around the corner from the scene? I've got more than that on Jensen Macomber."

"Lanier had motive, means, opportunity. The man we were going to see was gonna sign a complaint against him."

"Prove it," Baumgarten says, lighting his cigar. "In fact, forget proving it. I'll settle for reasonable cause to believe."

"We get to the projects," Tree says, "no Macomber. His place is trashed; he hasn't been heard from since. Then we get fucking waxed. I'm pretty sure a decent assistant district attorney could get an indictment with that . . . Then we pick the scumbag up, set bail at a trillion bucks, and sweat him down to soap."

Baumgarten's face softens, a face well-practiced at giving bad news. He leans forward, his elbows resting on the desk. "Where's Macomber's body, then? If it's really Lanier that's behind all this, Macomber should be hanging from the streetlight at Sunrise and Main."

Tree runs his hand over the stubble on his chin, thinking about Jensen Macomber, remembering one good quality after the other, the many unsolicited favors and kind words. "Over the course of fifteen years on this job, you learn to tell the good guys from the bad guys, Sarge. Jensen Macomber was solid as a rock."

"Until maybe he was crushed by a bigger rock." There is a rueful grin on Baumgarten's face as he slugs down the rest of his coffee.

Tree says nothing. He folds and unfolds his hands, looking for some edge or fault, some mannerism or bias of Baumgarten's upon which to hang a tag of distrust. But The Bomb knows what he's about. He knows people, good and bad, nobody one thing all the time.

"It wouldn't be the first time," suggests Baumgarten.

"I just don't see it."

"I'm not telling you I do either. I'm just telling what I think it looks like . . . unless you or Jimmy was doing a married chick and the old man got wind of it, something screwy like that."

Tree thinks this possibility over for a moment, then decides against it. All of his women of late have been unattached. And Jimmy hadn't really been doing much of anything; he liked to keep his options open in the summer. "Nope," he says. "Sounds like everybody but me and Jimmy walks. Is that what you're telling me?"

"Who said that?" Baumgarten says. "You and me—we work until we get the son of a bitch who did this. And I didn't say that I thought you were dirty. I don't think you are. Your problems upstairs have nothing to do with me, Nelson."

"Whatever," Tree says. "I appreciate your support. But let's be quick about this. I was always a little paranoid, and now the feeling's getting worse."

Baumgarten opens the case jacket and flips through some papers. "You know we picked up over twenty empty shells at the scene, and thirty-six windows face that empty lot, and twenty-one people admit to being home at the time of the shooting, and we don't have a single eyewitness. They all say they thought it was kids with fireworks, or trucks."

"It sure didn't sound like no lousy carburetor to me."

"Uzi machine guns rarely do."

"What about the shootout at the Blake Hotel? Man, I don't care which crime you hang on the prick. I just want Lanier put away."

"Give me some probable cause."

"Victor told us Angel and Willy were following this white dude around for a couple of weeks, looking to rip off a drug buy. But they obviously forgot that Lanier has better security than George Bush."

"That's a good point." The telephone rings. "Homicide, Sergeant Baumgarten." He listens, then tells his caller he's just about through with Tree, that he'll send him right up.

Tree wonders how anybody knew he was here. He cocks an eye at Baumgarten, who says, "Don't look at *me*, kid. This place is crawling with rats."

He knows Baumgarten didn't tell anyone he was coming, that he was either followed from home or seen entering the building by someone. He's hot copy these days.

"The big guys want you upstairs. I can catch you up on the rest when you come back down."

Tree takes a deep breath and stands up slowly, favoring his wound.

Baumgarten also stands, and he extends his hand to Tree. "I hope it goes okay for you."

"I appreciate that."

"I find it hard to blame guys who pick up the garbage for getting some on themselves."

American flags dominate the décor and demeanor of the inner chamber of Internal Affairs. One hangs limply from a pole in the corner, one is a work of needlepoint on the wall behind Lee's desk, and finally the tack on his tie. There is a comfortable couch, a

small refrigerator, a television set, a NYSPIN terminal, and a word processor, all within easy reach of the
lieutenant's nimble fingers. Tree assumes video cas-
settes and tape recorders are rolling, and he deter-
mines to give a good performance, knowing full well
how many before him have failed. He folds his hands
behind his back, and rocks slowly from heel to toe.

"Patience," Lee says, without looking up from the
file he is reading. "I'll get to you in a minute." He
finishes the coffee in his Ronald Reagan mug, smiling
over the rim at Tree.

"What seems to be the holdup?" Tree says.

"None of your goddamned business."

Tree watches and waits. Lee sits perfectly still,
perfectly erect. It dawns on Tree that the room is
sound-proof, a vacuum beyond the reach of his constitutional rights. Hermetically sealed. Tree realizes that
Lieutenant Lee likes it this way.

The door behind him opens with a sucking sound,
and into the room walks the police commissioner.

"Interesting reading, sir," Lee says, standing and
handing him the file.

The commissioner sits down on the couch, one leg
draped over the arm in that easy manner the powerful
adopt around their subordinates. "Later," he says.
"Let's get Nelson out of the way first."

"I hope you're here to referee," Tree says.

"Hardly." He looks at Lee. "Lieutenant?"

Lee serves up an ace: "You are as of this moment
suspended from active duty, with pay. And, as you
are still in your probationary period as a detective,
you are hereby reduced in rank to police officer. If we
didn't already have your gun, we would take it from
you now. You are to shave that crap from your face

and get a haircut. You will be here Monday morning at o-eight-hundred hours for a formal reading of the charges and specifications against you. You report at o-nine-hundred to headquarters, room two-o-four, for disciplinary duty.''

"That's it?" Tree says, looking from Lee to Trimble, and then back. "When do you break my sword and throw it in the dirt?"

"That's it," says Lee. "If you and Tibaldi were as close as everyone says, you had to know about his addictions. I was *ashamed* when I walked into his apartment. His parents were ashamed. This department will not tolerate drug taking, on or off the job, nor will it tolerate looking the other way."

"You forgot the part about the right to remain silent, the right to an attorney, the—"

"I forgot nothing, Nelson. Everything else, rest assured, I'll get to. Unless, of course, you choose to resign."

Tree turns again to the commissioner. "Anything to add, sir? Or subtract?"

"I'm afraid that about covers it."

"Sir, what have I done that wipes fifteen good years off the slate? All that time in, now I'm out? What the fuck is that?"

"You're dismissed, Nelson," Lee says, standing up, his hands on his hips. "I found felony weight in your buddy's apartment. And paraphernalia. And the autopsy report showed high concentrations of marijuana and cocaine in his blood. You knew, Nelson, and you didn't report it . . . Perhaps we could have helped him."

"Yeah, into the unemployment line."

"Which is where he belonged."

"Who the fuck do you think you are?"

Lieutenant Lee smiles and says to Trimble, "He's ranting, sir. It's the drugs."

"You want a urine sample, douche bag? Fuck the contract. Fuck reasonable cause to believe. I'm gonna give you all the piss you can use."

Tree pulls the zipper on his jeans down and grabs his johnson with one hand and the lieutenant's empty coffee mug from the desk with his other, and then his anger dissipates and he is suddenly standing there, with a tremendous smile spreading across his face, filling the cup.

Lee's eyes are the size of billiard balls.

Commissioner Trimble leaps to his feet. "Jesus, Nelson. No!"

"Relax," Tree tells them, careful not to spill a drop. "And that's not the first time one of the boys pissed in your coffee," he informs Lee as he sets the mug back on the desk.

"You bring a lawyer Monday, punk. I'm gonna fucking bury you."

"Yeah, right," says Tree. Then he turns and walks from the airless room, thinking that he may have pushed a bit too hard, shoving his balls down their throats when he had only meant to prove he had them. But Jimmy would have absolutely loved it. So fuck it.

He stops at Blotto's waterfront bar on Woodcleft Canal, to regroup over cocktails with umbrellas and pieces of fruit, and spends an hour there, assuring himself that it won't be long before they have a handle on Gladstone Lanier, that no one can get away with shit like this forever.

9

HOME FIRES

They roll east on Sunrise Highway in her orange VW Beetle, through the red lights of Merrick, Bellmore, Wantagh, Seaford, past the Sunrise Mall, into western Suffolk County, where the road is open and fast and the bars boast exotic West Coast dancers. Traffic builds up at the Oakdale merge, so Annie suggests a pit stop at McDonald's, a chance for Tree to stretch his aching legs. Then, from Patchogue to Westhampton Beach, it's all downhill; they catch a Huey Lewis rock-block on WRCN and they're home.

Beep! Beep! goes Annie's horn as they roar past the gatehouse, then along the gravel drive to the rear of the Nelson home in Westhampton Beach. Annie parks in the turnaround, and she and Tree carry his overnight bags into the house—a large fieldstone colonial overlooking the bay.

Mrs. Celeste Fan, the elderly Chinese cook, is busy in the kitchen, tossing a salad on the butcher block beneath the wrought-iron halo from which pots and pans of all sizes dangle. She stops what she's doing, smooths the front of her white apron, and kisses them both on the cheek. "I'm very pleased that you are well," she says to Tree. "Your father is very upset."

He thanks her and promises to regain his strength on her generous meals. "Where is he?" he asks.

"Your father will be home for supper."

"Veronica?"

"Shopping." Celeste rolls her eyes dramatically. Tree laughs. She has stayed with the family twenty-six years by keeping her own counsel as the parade of new wives trooped into and out of the house. "Would you care for some brunch?" she says.

Annie says, "No, thanks. Big spender here went for Egg McMuffins on the way out."

"Very good," Celeste says. "Annie . . . you stay here or your house next door? It's no trouble to make up room."

"I think next door, Celeste. Thank you. I want to air out the old barn before the folks get home."

"Your mother sent me a postcard from Ireland. She deserves nice girl like you."

Celeste resumes her labors, and Annie follows Tree through the house, and then out the front door to the lawn. There is very little sun today, but the breeze off the water is pleasant, and the predicted rain seems a distant danger.

He stands with his back to the water and the hazy sunlight, and he stares at Annie, who looks like someone else's million bucks. Her hair is in a long French braid; she is wearing a T-shirt and a short denim skirt.

"Shopping," he says. "The newest, the fastest . . . God, I could never keep up with Veronica."

"She works at it. Seven days a week. Your old man's easy pickings."

Is he ever, Tree thinks, looking over Annie's head to the house. After his mother died of uterine cancer in 1956, it was one second-stringer in there after the other, each with her own set of plans to redecorate, each with her unrealized vision of siblings for young Trevor.

"I don't blame anyone for anything," he says. "The fucking deck is stacked. You want a drink? A Muddy Mary?" Jimmy's invention; vodka and Yoo Hoo on the rocks. "Wonderful for mornings after."

"Nothing," she says. "I'm gonna drive around and open up the house like the sweet young thing I am. I'll call you later."

"Okay," he says. "Don't go anywhere without me."

The afternoon winds rise, the sun disappears. Whitecaps feather the bay while small waves smash into the bulkhead. A northeaster rolling in, his father would say. Better close the shutters. But the change in the weather doesn't bother Tree nearly as much as walking in aimless circles around the house. He puts on his running togs.

A little exercise is what he needs, a chance to blow out some of the sludge. He leans on the cool brick wall and carefully stretches his legs. The pain is much reduced today, more the feeling of a rod inside his thigh than the burning and itching of the previous days. Finally, he thinks, progress at something.

He starts slowly, jogging up the street past the stately homes of family friends, headed for the country-club golf course and then Main Street, where he plans to turn around. He is glad the weather is threatening. He doesn't have to stop at every driveway and call up to every deck and porch, explaining what he's been up to; he doesn't have to hear how childhood competitors Chip and Dierdre and Todd are doing in L.A. or Houston or Provincetown. He can do without updates on the fortunes of his peers. He would rather not tabulate and compare.

Main Street looks pastel and pretty when he gets there, all busy and rich, much more cosmopolitan than when he was a boy. In Magic's Pub, his favorite hangout, he knows the year-round crowd is bitching about the summer people, all the while ogling the New York City husband hunters in Spandex body suits who pass by, shopping the crowded sidewalks for the answers to their prayers.

A downpour begins, stinging his flesh. He stops and looks around, and he see the trees behind the country club shocked into brilliant relief by lightning, as if advancing troops have cut off his escape.

Customers dash from the shops to their foreign cars. They make odd U-turns, forcing Tree to the sidewalk for safety. These assholes could gridlock the mountains of the moon, he thinks.

He leans against a mailbox for a moment, dizzy from stopping abruptly. He has a sudden sense of disconnection, of being lost in a familiar place. Goose bumps rise abruptly on his arms and legs.

A festive young woman with an umbrella, whose face he cannot pull into focus, shelters him and asks him his name. Tree thinks she is offering medical assistance. Then she asks him where he works, and he remembers where he is, on The Dating Game . . . Love American Style . . . The Hamptons.

"Nowhere," he says.

"Sorry. I have to go now," she says, backing away from him, taking her umbrella with her.

The raindrops are brutally cold, pitting the sidewalk with constant explosions. He pushes off the mailbox and hobbles for home, each step meant to catch a fall. Ten minutes later, at the northeast corner of his father's property, he slumps against the ivy-covered wall, dodging the horizontal blasts of spray. He moves hand over hand along the wall to the gatehouse, where his knees buckle.

He knows the door to the gatehouse will be terribly heavy. The copper knob is a court jester's face. He gathers his strength and with both hands turns it and stumbles inside. A dungeon, he thinks. Or a fort— what he pretended when he was a kid. He leans his forehead and elbows against the wall and tries not to vomit.

Until he smells the incongruous odor of wet wool. And then black hands cover his and night descends upon his troubled mind.

He regains consciousness on his back on the concrete floor, lost again in time and place. He can smell the damp coat laid over his chest, but the coal-black face hovering above him doesn't mean a thing until he hears a familiar voice.

"I didn't mean to frighten or hurt you, but I couldn't be sure who was up at the house."

Tree blinks.

"You see, I've been on a bit of a run myself."

And then Tree understands that it is Jensen Macomber's coat keeping him warm, Jensen's hand unobstrusively taking his pulse.

Tree, sitting up slowly, pulling Jensen's coat to his chin, says, "Every cop in New York is after your ass. They think you set us up."

"Yes."

"How'd you get here?"

"Walked, mostly."

It looks it, Tree thinks, with all his clothes soaked through to the skin. He could easily be a migrant worker, wandered off drunk from a Riverhead farm. "So what happened that day? Where the hell have you been?"

"Can we go get warm somewhere? I've a lot more than that to explain to you."

Tree nods. "There's no one at the house except the cook . . . who's seen me bring home stranger people than you."

Jensen pulls him to his feet.

"I'm very sorry about Detective Tibaldi."

"Yeah," says Tree. "Me too."

Celeste meets them at the door, shaking her head and clucking her tongue. She insists upon baths and dry clothes before they sit on her furniture.

"Okay, okay," says Tree, shivering violently. "I know when I'm licked."

After a quick shower and change of clothes, Tree finds Jensen Macomber in the den, wearing an Alistair Nelson golf ensemble, sitting on the couch eating biscuits and sipping tea. Tree sits opposite him, in a bentwood rocker, wearing blue jeans and a New York Rangers sweatshirt, looking sick.

"I've much to explain," Jensen says, "and then you'll not be seeing me again."

"I don't understand. If you're innocent, which I assume you are—"

"You don't understand," Jensen says, shaking his head. "You don't."

"They'll probably tell the next academy class all Rastas carry pictures of Jimmy and me."

"They'd be close to the truth."

"Say what?"

"Rastafarians of a criminal twist—rude boys, we call them—often carry pictures of officials who pose a threat."

"Well they can sure as shit throw mine away. I'm out of it now. The rubber-gun squad for me."

"I'm sorry to hear that. Gladstone Lanier is no one to face with a rubber gun."

"Tell him I've retired from the field."

"I can't do that. He knows I know more about his business than I should. Lanier thinks I'm an old coward who has run away to hide. With relatives in Jamaica I cannot protect, it serves no purpose to change his mind."

"Actually," Tree says, rolling the idea around on his tongue as he gives it voice, "what I should do is hold you for interrogation. You're at least a material witness, if not a suspect."

"That would likely cost me my life." Jensen sets down his teacup and brushes crumbs from his hands.

"I was kidding, man. I don't call the cops on nobody no more."

"Except Lanier. You'll need all the help you can get with him."

"What do you mean?"

"That boy who went off the roof was his baby brother. So there is no resigning from this. He will have you dead—destroyed. Nothing less."

"Jesus," says Tree.

"Lanier has only to make a phone call—to Philadelphia, Miami—and a squad of Rasta hitmen arrive. He

138

gives them your pictures and tells them where you work. Poof. Two hours later they are back in the friendly skies. The man has done people in Boston and Washington. It's all so simple. No one ever gets caught."

Celeste interrupts them to bring more tea and biscuits. When she has gone back to the kitchen, Jensen says, "Most Rastafarians are peaceful, pious people, who fully believe that the white man's world is evil and corrupt, to be strictly avoided if not overthrown. England, America, and the Holy Roman Church have conspired to deceive and oppress the Rastaman, to keep from him his royal African lineage."

"I always thought *we* were the good guys."

"Depends on how you look at it. Who's telling the story."

"I'm telling this story. It was my best friend that got killed."

Macomber takes a deep breath. It is obvious to Tree that coming here was very difficult for him, that his heart is somehow divided. He has the look of a man making a terrible mistake.

"The Rastaman don't worship death like the white man do. For the true believer, death does not exist. He skips over his grave and goes home to Jah Rastafari."

"What a great religion," Tree says. "Hang out, get wasted, and hop on the heavenly shuttle."

"All men are born Rasta, some just not come to it yet."

"You?" says Tree.

"My father believes, my brothers believe, but they are not murderers, and neither am I."

"Where are your dreads?"

"Where is your cross?" Macomber shakes his head. "Understand. Gladstone Lanier and those who do his bidding are more cruel than wild animals. They hide behind the brethren for purposes of their own."

Tree stands up and walks stiffly to the glass doors giving onto the bay. He looks out. "They say San Francisco's lovely this time of year, and straight guys make out like bandits."

"Death to a Rastafarian is like changing his clothes. Nature returning to life what is holy and good. One more door in a line of doors, returning the believer to Jah."

"Kinda like a Bible club," Tree says.

"I thought you should know what you're up against. You have illusions you'd be better off without."

"What ever happened to good old run-of-the-mill crooks?" Tree laments.

"Times have changed," Jensen says, getting up to leave. "Good luck and farewell, Trevor Nelson. It's high time I disappear."

"Any suggestions?"

"Kill him."

Tree is sitting in the kitchen, thinking about Jimmy Tibaldi and Jensen Macomber and Crazy Victor Guardina, and most of all Gladstone Lanier. He stares at the lime-colored lawn through the window, wondering what Jensen meant about illusions he should be rid of.

His reverie is broken by the sound of tires on the drive outside. He hopes it's Veronica—who has never expected much from him anyway—though he has to face his father sooner or later, certainly before Monday and the press conference, after which the many will be spreading vicious truths about the few.

The pantry door swings open. His father enters wearing a pale blue tennis shirt and khaki pants. Alistair Nelson strides across the room, with his right hand out too far, too early. "Thank God, you're alive," he says hoarsely. They shake hands; then Alistair hugs him.

"I'm okay."

Tree backs away and leans against the edge of the deep steel sink; hugs from his father still embarrass the hell out of him.

"You were shot."

"Jimmy was killed."

"Brophy told me everything. I'm very sorry about Jimmy, but my main concern now is you."

"It's not so bad," Tree says. "Really. I went running before."

Alistair's well-lined face shows instant anger. He runs his hand through his thick white hair, and says, "Are you crazy?"

"The doctor said movement was good for it."

"I hardly think he meant wind sprints."

Tree's answer is a smile and a halfhearted shrug.

Celeste serves them snifters of brandy and leads them into the den, where they sit facing each other in silence until Alistair, who seems rather uncomfortable, says, "So, how's it going?"

Tree laughs. "I got the world by the balls."

"They get the assailants?"

"Not yet."

"How were Jimmy's parents?"

"Crippled," says Tree. "Thanks for thinking of his kid."

"Glad to do it. I took it off your inheritance."

Silence again as they spin their drinks. Jimmy's

absence is so terribly obvious, so terribly forever. He's not slouching at Tree's side. He's gone and left Tree stark naked.

"I'm thinking of getting married when this all blows over," Tree says.

"To whom, might I ask?"

"Annie, of course."

"Where'd that bullet hit you?"

"Come on."

"You come on."

"Why not?" says Tree.

"If it flies, floats, or fucks, son, it's cheaper to lease."

"Says the man who's been married four times."

"Who would know better? There's no such thing as love."

"You sorry-assed old son of a bitch. That's it? That's your advice in matters of the heart?"

"In a nutshell."

"No exceptions?"

"Only your mother."

Family history has his father as the doting husband, very much in love with Tree's mother until the tragic, bitter end.

"Unfair."

"You're just lazy, Tree. You've got the hots for Annie because she lives in your building. I could put a horny young Zulu across the hall and you'd never see Annie again."

"Why are you making fun of me at a time like this?"

"To prove a point. Look: Annie's always been your next-door neighbor. She'll probably always be your next-door neighbor. Great. Wonderful. I admire loyalty. Continuity. Just leave it the way it is."

Tree shakes his head. "You're a pisser."

"I'm a pisser? You little twerp. You used to send back crisp toast because you couldn't chew and hear the television at the same time. You think the real world is the Rangers, the Giants, and the Knicks."

Tree looks down at the New York Rangers logo on his chest. "Not anymore, I don't."

Alistair pinches his lips together, nods his head as if to concede the point. "I'm sorry."

"It's more than missing Jimmy, Dad. This is a lifelong thing with me. What looks like a lackadaisical attitude is often total confusion."

"Of course it is. That's exactly what I'm trying to tell you. You're wondering if you'll be able to get up off the deck again. It's natural. All I'm saying is, don't do something permanent when you're low."

"I know that with my head."

"Too bad that's not what you use to make decisions."

"Yeah," says Tree. "Too bad."

They are still sipping brandy, debating the pros and cons of marriage to Annie Sutherland when the telephone by Alistair's hand rings twice. A moment later Celeste comes in. The call is for Tree. "It's Mr. Brophy," she says, walking him to the phone in the hall. "Very hush-hush."

"Thank you." He puts the phone to his ear. "Hey, Broph. What's up?"

"We got trouble. Did you tell the old man yet that you were shelved?"

"How do you know that?" asks Tree.

"Somebody at headquarters took a leak."

"That's the least of it," says Tree. "You should see the charges."

"A guy from *Newsday* called the company for a comment."

"Fuck," Tree says.

"What did your father say?"

"I didn't get around to it yet. The right moment just hasn't presented itself. We've been bullshitting and sucking down sauce, waiting dinner on Veronica."

"You'd better find a way to tell him tonight, before he reads it in the *Wall Street Journal*. I think he'd especially appreciate the chance to make tracks before the mini-cams roll up to the gatehouse."

"Really."

"Call me tomorrow, Tree. And keep your dick in your pants." Brophy hangs up.

"Trouble?" Alistair wants to know when Tree returns to the den.

"A guy at work needed something. About the case."

Tree wonders if this is the right time to spin yarns of urban guerrillas—remembering in particular the newspaper article he will digest with his morning meal, and the attendant damage to his own credibility.

"They closing in on the perpetrators?"

"Not hardly. Not without witnesses, of which there are none."

"There must be something that can be done about these Jamaicans."

"We could call in an air strike on their little banana republic if the tactic had worked better in Philly."

"Very well, Trevor," Alistair says, rising from his chair, empty glass in hand. "Make fun of me if it makes you feel better. . . . Veronica should be home any minute. Why don't we get refills and take this into the dining room."

"Dad?" Tree says, hanging back.

Alistair remains on his feet, clinking the base of his snifter against his wedding ring.

"I'm not making fun of you . . . I'm beating around the bush."

"What is it, son?"

"I got busted yesterday. Suspended from active duty. I wouldn't be dumping this on you now, but it's gonna be in all the morning papers . . . and probably on television tomorrow night."

"What are you talking about, 'busted'? Charged with what? God knows you don't need money."

"You're gonna wish it was money."

"Let's have it."

"Conduct unbecoming. Something to do with drugs."

His father looks at the ceiling and smiles. "Drugs. Of course. Why should I be any different." He sets his empty glass on the table and rubs his face with both hands. He looks enormously tired. "How did you manage that?"

"I didn't. The boy fucked up."

"Isn't that always the way."

"I'm serious."

"Of course you are. Not that that will do any good."

"Look, Dad—"

"I suggest you sign yourself into one of those fashionable New Jersey rehabilitation clinics right away . . . coke-enders, or whatever they call it. And I'll get Murray Olnick started on the criminal case tomorrow morning."

"I don't need rehabilitation, Dad. I don't do drugs."

"Anymore," his father says.

"Anymore," Tree says.

10

Administrative Details

Monday morning at o-eight-hundred hours Tree is standing at half-assed attention in the middle of the trial room. He has not shaved his beard, and his sweatpants have a hole in one knee. The president of the PBA, a big tough Italian cop from the Third Precinct, is sitting on a folding chair behind him, still mumbling to himself about Tree fucking up and not looking his best, deliberately sabotaging his own case.

Gathered around the conference table at the other end of the room are Commissioner David Trimble, Lieutenant Lee, Lieutenant Cumberstadt, and a young assistant district attorney Tree has seen around the courthouse—Joseph Murdoch, a recent Georgetown grad intent on building a political career. The brass band is in uniform, all spit-shined stars and bars, ready to drum his butt into the street.

"Ready, Mr. Murdoch?" Trimble asks.

"I'm ready to go home and hang myself," the lawyer says.

"We've already discussed your aversion to this 'politically sensitive' case, and—"

"However, that doesn't seem to be one of my options," Murdoch continues, running his fingers up and down his tie.

Tree notes that the commissioner has not yet taken the trouble to look at the accused. Lieutenant Lee, on the other hand, has not yet taken his eyes off him. Lieutenant Cumberstadt winks, and Tree shudders to think that the Spaghetti Boss is his only vote going into this—because that means goose eggs coming out.

"So, *Officer* Nelson," Murdoch says, making a point of addressing Tree by the rank to which he has so recently been reduced, "against my better judgment, I'm presenting evidence Thursday morning at a Departmental Trial Board against you for your failure to report the possession of a controlled substance by a member of the force. And a second charge of insubordination, to wit, your mistaking the lieutenant's coffee mug for a test tube. I suggest you get yourself a lawyer at once, if you haven't already done so. Please have him call me, Officer Nelson . . . I want you to know I'm sorry about this. I have at least managed to cancel the press-conference-slash-celebrity-roast your colleagues were so eager to stage on your behalf. A small consolation, I know, but better than nothing."

"Are they incredible, or what?" Tree says. "How'd you like to be down in the trenches with these guys?"

The PBA president says, "Hey, Nelson! I thought I told you to keep your mouth shut."

Murdoch smiles, then quickly gathers up his papers and snaps them inside his briefcase. "Gentlemen," he says, "I'm history."

Al Baumgarten is sitting at his desk with his collar open, his tie down, and his hair mussed like he's been flunking a chemistry final for hours. "What's up?" he says to Tree. "They do ya?"

"Without the Vaseline."

"Maybe pissing in Lee's cup wasn't such a bright idea. But I gotta tell you, it sure did brighten up a lot of faces around here. And Rumor Control has it that the drug tests turned up negative, so maybe things are looking up."

Tree nods. "How's the case?"

"The most promising scenario says Lanier had you guys hit."

"So let's take the prick. I'll share my cell with him."

"Anyone can dream up scenarios. None of it's worth a flying fuck in court."

"Yeah," says Tree. "I gotta go. The Bow and Arrow Squad."

"Sergeant Baumgarten! You're not discussing departmental intelligence with a civilian, are you?"

You'd think he caught us jerking off, Tree thinks, so pleased and superior is Lieutenant Lee's tone of voice.

Baumgarten replies evenly, "I was interviewing a witness, Lieutenant, in the matter of the death of a member of this department."

"See that it's all you discuss," Lee says. He folds his hands behind his back, his head held high.

"That's it for me," Tree says to Baumgarten. "I'll catch you around."

Lieutenant Lee follows Tree to the door. The cops milling around all grin and say hi to him—a small vote of confidence, but not something he can take to the bank. Maybe that's what this is all about, he thinks suddenly, why Lee hates him so much: his nonchalance, the apparent effortlessness of his life, and for having a friend close enough to share a crime.

At o-nine-hundred hours Tree reports to the headquarters classroom used by Internal Affairs to hold those officers who are suspended but not severed from the Department. He has chosen not to shave his beard, not to wear a uniform, high crimes of omission, he is sure.

Detective Woodward Mellon, a red-faced yuppie-type, snatched from an academy recruit class before street work could temper his idealism, meets him at the door. Mellon passes a hand-held metal detector the length of Tree's body, makes note of his slovenly appearance, and tells him to sit anywhere he wants.

Tree looks around the classroom, then selects a desk by the window. From here he can at least see parking-lot action, the comings and goings both voluntary and under duress.

There is one other leper in the colony, a heavyset gray-haired cop in uniform. His nameplate says P. O. CLARKE. The black leather strap above his shield is home to six multicolored medals, and the designation *Pistol Expert*. His combat boots are standing on a desk nearby. "What it is," he says to Tree.

"How's it going."

Detective Mellon taps a ruler on the blackboard, where he has written in ten-inch chalk letters the rules of their incarceration: NO TALKING, NO SMOKING, NO EATING. BREAKS AT 1000, 1200 AND 1400 HRS. HAVE A NICE DAY. DETECTIVE WOODWARD MELLON, IAD.

Mellon sits down at his desk. Holding the phone between his shoulder and his ear, he opens a container of piping hot coffee. He dunks a chocolate doughnut in it from time to time, then lights up a cigarette. Tree hears him whisper, "babysitting the scrotes," and he glares at Mellon until the baby face turns red.

At ten o'clock Mellon sends them on their break. Tree and Police Officer Clarke shuffle stocking-footed into the hallway like mental patients. They stand near an ashtray. Clarke lights a cigarette. Tree asks him what he's in for.

Clarke smiles. "A Cutty coma . . . a one-man firefight."

"How'd that happen?"

"You're not wearing a wire, are ya?"

"Are you shitting me? I'm public enemy number one."

"Yeah? Are you? That's cool. Anyways, what I did was blast the fuck outta this storefront mirror on my last set of midnights. They tell me I was shooting at my own reflection."

"Nice caper," says Tree. "The shrinks will have a ball."

"What was worse was the guys found me sitting at the curb, weeping like a baby, begging them to call my wife and tell her I was all right. Which is weird because I've been divorced for the last nine years, and I don't give a damn for the bitch, wherever she may be. I'm just here waiting for a bed to open up in rehab."

"Trevor Nelson," Tree says, shaking Clarke's hand. "Maybe you've heard of me."

"I've heard of you." Clarke leans closer. "I heard you were a scumbag."

"I've been called worse."

"Me too."

"What else did you hear about me?"

"Isn't that enough?"

"Really."

Clarke grinds his cigarette out on the wall and throws the butt on the floor next to the ashtray. "I heard you and your partner got dirty and somebody made you pay for it."

"That's bullshit, for what it's worth."

"Don't make no nevermind to me."

Detective Mellon sticks his head out of the classroom. "Let's go, fellows. Time to go back to work."

"He calls this shit work?" says Tree.

"We're supposed to be contemplating our sins."

They return to their seats. Tree opens a *Newsday* while Clarke puts his head on the desk and goes to sleep. Mellon boils water in the microwave oven and makes a Cup-A-Soup for himself. The hands of the clock barely move. The telephone rings. Mellon lunges to pick it up before it can ring a second time.

"Yes, sir," he says. "Both of them . . . five minutes."

Clarke lifts his head off the desk and groans. "Not another fucking lineup."

"Huh?" says Tree, holding his place in the day's Billy Martin story with his index finger.

"These morons feel perfectly free to drag us down to Rogues any damn time they want."

"Gentlemen, gentlemen," says Mellon. "We've been called upon to assist the Sex Crimes Unit with an I.D. What say we slip on our shoes and get down there. What could it hurt?"

Tree and Officer Clarke lace up their shoes and follow Detective Mellon from the second-floor classroom to the Identification Theater.

"I'm sick of this shit," Clarke says to Tree, as

they're trudging down the stairs. "This here's my last fucking lineup. You just wait and see."

Clarke changes into an ill-fitting brown maintenance uniform and then they join a pack of rowdy-looking thugs onstage. The lights go on. Someone with a microphone in another room says, "Okay, men, you're facing front now . . . now a quarter turn to the left. Now half a turn to the right. All the way to the right, number four."

Clarke is number four. He is facing front, peering into a blank two-way mirror, as though something is wrong, as though he can see something.

"Number four!"

"Hey," Clarke shouts. "That's her. I'd know her anywhere."

The real bad guys, the pair of long-haired Iron Maiden fans at the end who dragged the victim from her car at the Sunrise Mall, are staring wide-eyed at P. O. Clarke. Tree can hear a woman scream, then the sound of chairs banged about.

"Sergeant," says the amplified voice, "get number four the hell out of there this minute."

Five burly cops rush onstage and surround Clarke. He backs up, raises his hand, and smiles at them. "Please," he says, "brothers. Don't take it personal." And then he goes away with them without a struggle.

When order is restored, Tree and the others repeat the lineup procedure three times without incident: Walk on, show the victim three faces of Tree, walk off. Then Mellon leads Tree back to the classroom, pissing and moaning about P. O. Clarke, hoping to God Lieutenant Lee doesn't lay this mess in his lap.

"I don't see why he wouldn't," says Tree. "You were in charge."

P. O. Clarke is waiting for them in the classroom, back at his desk with his boots off, leafing through a *Penthouse* magazine.

"Way to go," says Tree. "I'm surprised you weren't taken out back and shot."

"Why?" says Clarke. "I'm nuts. They gotta expect that kind of behavior from a rubber gun like me."

"Shut the fuck up!" Detective Mellon screams at them.

Then Tree sees why: Lieutenant Lee is standing quietly in the doorway, staring at them. Tree feels his knees wobble and he looks away. When he gathers himself to look back, Lee has turned up the juice, narrowed his deep dark eyes.

"Officer Clarke," he says. "I want you to know that it took me half an hour to convince that poor woman that you couldn't see her—and that was before you pulled your little stunt. Then she got so damn upset she picked Nelson three straight times—which goes to show you what a guilty conscience can do for you."

"You're right, of course," says Clarke. "I'll admit I fucked up." Then P. O. Clarke lets loose with a two-second beer fart. Of everyone there, Tree feels sorriest for Detective Woodward Mellon, sitting at the front desk.

Lieutenant Lee says, "You just made the Christmas list, Clarke. Until then you'll be sitting here in your own goddamn mess. And Nelson . . . I don't have anything to say to you." Lee gives Mellon a discouraged wave of his hand and walks away, presumably to make a full report.

Mellon looks like he wants to cry. He dismisses them for lunch, then walks to the window, where he stands for quite a long time, perhaps trying to imagine what it is out there in the streets that turns clean-shaven recruits into madmen like Nelson and Clarke.

Lieutenant Lee is waiting for them at the classroom when they return from their forty-five-minute meal period, which they have spent sitting at the Saratoga Bay, eating Stewart sandwiches and drinking Miller Lites. Lee forms them into a work group and marches them downstairs to the dark and dusty basement.

"You men will carry these files upstairs and load them on the truck out back. These," he says, kicking the bottom box of yet another stack, "you will bring to Data Processing. There is to be no talking and no malingering. Mellon, don't you dare lift a finger to help them. Also, smart guys, your breaks have gone the way of the dodo bird."

Clarke covers his mouth and sneezes, at the same time shouting, "Blow job."

"You just bought yourself another postponement, clown. Make it Easter before you see that bed upstate."

"Make it the fucking Fourth of July."

"Detective Mellon," says Lee, "these men are drunk. I want them tested right away. Blood, urine, tissue samples if you can get them. I'll let Central Testing know you're on the way."

"Can we do that?" Mellon wants to know. "They don't look drunk."

"Smell them."

"Excuse me?"

"Smell their breath, you idiot. It's called gathering evidence."

Mellon steps apologetically up to P. O. Clarke and shrugs.

P. O. Clarke fills his chest with air and exhales forcefully, whipping his lips with his index finger, painting Mellon's face with spittle.

"Well?" says Lee. He has opened his blouse and is resting his hand on the butt of his service revolver.

Mellon wipes his face with his sleeve. "It smells like bologna, sir."

"I want my lawyer," says Tree. "This whole affair reeks of arbitrary and capricious and lots of other words that wind up on lawsuits."

"Nobody moves," says Lee. "I'm gonna find out about that, Officer Nelson. Because where you're concerned, my crooked little friend, I'm dotting the i's and crossing the t's."

Mellon and the prisoners remain in the basement, while Lee retreats to Legal. Tree daydreams about killing Lieutenant Lee: crushing his head with a carton of accident reports, reducing the body to microfilm and hiding it among the Missing Persons. Mellon stands off by himself, deeply wounded, staring out through the bars on the window.

Apparently there is someone on the ball at the Legal Bureau, for moments later a uniformed cop comes downstairs and tells Detective Mellon to get them started on the detail.

"Fine," says Mellon. "Gentlemen, you may begin."

On their very first trek upstairs, while lugging cartons from the main floor to the second floor. P. O. Clarke slips and pitches backward, bouncing down the stairs. The carton Clarke was holding flies open; black-and-white photos of dismembered bodies spin across the floor of the Visitor's Reception Center. Monsignor Martin O'Rourke and Rabbi Alev Stemkowsky, the department chaplains, are rolling in from the Rotary luncheon when Clarke arrives at ground zero.

The holy men are drunk. P. O. Clarke tells them that he can't move his neck.

The holy men overreact, sending up such a hue and cry that by the time Lieutenant Lee arrives it is far too late to stem the wave of nondenominational compassion floating Clarke, prone on a stretcher, out of the building to freedom.

Lieutenant Lee is beside himself, running around the lobby yelling about proper lines of authority and staying in one's own bailiwick. He stops ranting just long enough to assure Tree and Detective Mellon that Clarke is not going to get away with anything, then orders them back to the classroom.

Tree doesn't move from his seat on the stairs. "Tell him," he says, staring at Mellon, then Lee, then Mellon.

"He really fell," says Mellon. "I saw him."

Lee scowls. "It's cold out there, Mellon. Cold and lonely."

"I know that, sir. But it's cold and lonely in here, too."

There is a message on his answering machine when he returns to the condo: "Hoofing it," Annie says. "Be back before five."

And an envelope in his mail, addressed to him in pencil, postmarked Western Nassau, without a return address. No letter inside, just a photograph of Jimmy. A copy of the one Moffitt had in his wallet. There is an *X* across Jimmy's face.

He wanders around the place like a sentry for a while, playing old records on the stereo, stunned. Bob

Dylan, Bruce Springsteen, the Airplane, the Dead: they are a homing device on his anxiety, his only anthems. But the rooms are too vast, more space than he can fill, more sides than he can secure. He is frightened by a feeling of living in the clouds.

The telephone rings.

"How'd it go today?" Brophy wants to know.

Tree takes a moment to catch his breath. "The basic failure-to-report bullshit. Little to no publicity. I have a five o'clock appointment with Murray Olnick tomorrow."

"He's a ruthless son of a bitch. You'll be okay . . . Say, why don't you and Annie come over for dinner tonight. I'll throw a couple of steaks on the grill and try to poke holes in your story."

"That's a good idea, not that my story is clever enough to have holes . . . We'll see you later."

Tree is grateful for the invitation back to the real world of sizzling steaks and summer lawns and crickets. Annie won't mind. What has she got to do on a Monday night? Watch the Yankees on the tube? Fuck around with a crossword puzzle?

She was different before John died, less docile, much more vigorous and hopeful, always wanting to do right, always extending herself beyond reason for the smallest of causes: the snail darter, a more liberal dress code at Westhampton High, nude beaches. He loved her better way back when, but maybe not as much.

What made them change? he wonders, staring at the *X* on Jimmy's face. How does a spoiled-rotten kid from the Hamptons wind up the obsession of a madman? Make that two madmen, counting Lee. And what exactly did I prove by joining the cops in the first place? Or hope to prove? That I was braver than my father, since I would never be more successful? That I cared much less for life? Or more? I wonder if he's impressed now. Or the laughingstock of the men's grill.

Me and Jimmy, he thinks, we forgot why we were cops. That was the goddamned problem. We went from honest, working-class heroes to civil-service zombies with nary a bad intention. And the world stayed hard and fast and deadly. And the world ran us over when it roared on by. Yep, he has to admit, I've really botched this one. Things are sure to be worse than they appear. The enemy is strong, yet concealed. Obvious, yet unapproachable. And my side? Well . . . He has precious little confidence in the Department. Hell, he thinks, we can't even stamp out hookers . . . ticket scalpers . . . borough presidents. What the hell can we do with witch doctors?

They are a long way from collaring Gladstone Lanier, who, he realizes, has managed to insulate himself from the sordid doings on the street with the skill of a Mafia don. The guys who whacked them might be from Denver. They might not even have known who they were working for.

Are fight and flight really the only options? he wonders, staring out across the bay. Are there no advantages to sorrow? And what about hate, he wonders, that sickening sensation in the pit of his stomach when something reminds him of Gladstone Lanier.

He should have told Baumgarten about Jensen Macomber. He has no right to withhold information. But would Baumgarten understand why he trusted Macomber, and how would he feel about Tree not holding Jensen.

He goes into the kitchen, looking for a snack. The cupboard is bare. He checks his wallet and finds a lonely ten. By the wall clock it is four twenty, so he has time to run to the Citibank cash machine and the liquor store and the 7-Eleven before Annie gets back. He always brings Brophy a jug.

Nope, he thinks. I'll fuck it up. Comparison shopping in the Nelson family means finding a parking spot close to the store. I'll spend my money on junk, Mad Dog 20-20, and Cheese Whiz, stuff Annie will sneer at.

Better to wait. Here, where it's safe.

He wonders what route she's running, if he could find her with the Volvo; and then, while wandering out on the balcony, he sees her tie up her dinghy in the slip far below. Ozone, the little bugger, is racing down the dock. Tree doesn't call down, just watches her disappear into the building. He times her on his Casio watch. Four minutes and eighteen seconds elapse. His telephone rings.

"I'm back," she says.

"I saw you. What happened to running?"

"I felt like rowing. Are you hungry?"

"The Brophys invited us to a cookout. I figured if you aren't doing anything we could go." He waits nervously for her answer, something valuable hanging in the balance.

"That sounds lovely," she says.

So easy, he thinks. You want something, ask. Maybe you're the only one who still wants it.

The Grateful Dead are on the stereo.

. . . When I awoke, the dire wolf,
six hundred pounds of sin,
was grinning at my window.
All I said was, "Come on in."
Don't murder me,
I beg of you don't murder me . . .

11

LAWYER, GUNS, AND MONEY

Three members of the Seaport Volunteer Fire Department Emergency Company are explaining to uniformed police officers Larry Fisher and Davy Watson that Raul Santana is extremely dead, and has been now for several hours, probably from an overdose of narcotics. The emergency-room staff at South Nassau Hospital will go wild if they bring the ice-cold body there.

Watson says, "I don't *care* if they go wild. I'd rather piss a couple of nurses off than sit in this dump until the dicks get here."

"Sorry, guy. No can do."

"How soon till he stinks?" Watson asks.

"I really couldn't say."

The rescue squad packs up their first-aid gear and leaves. Watson and Fisher look forlorn and abandoned as they begin the procedures required by sudden deaths.

While Watson finds a phone in another apartment to call the detectives, Fisher checks Santana's one-room apartment for evidence or contraband. There are needles and rubber tubing next to the body on the couch. Two unopened decks of smack are on the cocktail table near a crumpled pack of Marlboros and a pile of burnt matches. He does not disturb the scene, but makes a note of the drugs on his case report. No big deal, he thinks. Ashes ashes, all fall down. Fisher checks his wristwatch for the correct time, then switches on the small black-and-white television set, flipping to the Mets game on channel 9. The picture is fuzzy, so he turns the set around to check the antenna wires. One of them has been pulled from the set, probably when someone dropped the heavy canvas sack he sees behind the television stand. Officer Fisher bends over to pick it up and suddenly doesn't care that Keith Hernandez is coming to the plate with the tying run in scoring position. He unties the leather thongs and gingerly shakes onto the floor from the sack an Uzi machine gun and two spare magazines. "Davy," he yells loudly, knowing his voice will carry through the paper-thin walls of the tenement. "Davy, get your ass back here."

Ten minutes later Homicide detectives arrive with the Crime Scene Search Team. The scene is photographed and dusted, documented for the annals of crime. Samples of carpet fibers, dust, and hair are taken for analysis along with Santana's clothing. The naked body is bagged and shipped to the morgue for an immediate autopsy. Neighbors are questioned; depositions are taken. The machine gun is tagged and delivered to the Scientific Investigations Bureau, to be dusted for prints and fired for comparisons the first thing Wednesday morning.

The Mets win in extra innings.

* * *

Murray Olnick stands up behind his desk when Tree walks into the luxurious book-lined office overlooking the intersection of Seventh and Hilton in Garden City. He is hairless, in his early sixties, tall, gaunt, and professorial. "I spoke with your dad earlier," he says, shaking Tree's hand. "I've assured him of the effort this firm will make on your behalf."

"Thank you." Tree sits and folds his hands in his lap.

Murray smiles, showing Tree all of his teeth, the essence of user-friendly. "I want you to take a polygraph tonight. I'm sure that in combination with your spotless record and standing in the community, a positive polygraph experience will be more than enough to dispose of this unpleasantness."

"Let me get this straight. You want me to plead stupidity, to say I knew nothing about the drugs?"

"It couldn't hurt."

"Sorry."

"Tree, we have an expression in this business. Actually we have several expressions in this business. One of the big ones is: Dump it on the dead. The Bill Casey Shuffle, as it were."

Tree remembers the joke about the difference between a dead skunk in the street and a dead lawyer in the street: the skid marks in front of the skunk.

"What's wrong?" Murray asks.

"I can't do that."

"Why not?"

"You don't know Jimmy's parents. I fake amnesia and it's war. His autopsy's front-page news . . . Besides, I knew about the drugs. And I don't exactly have what you'd call a poker heart."

Murray Olnick rolls his eyes and raises the skin

where there would be eyebrows if he had them. "What about a negative declaration by you concerning any narcotic abuse."

Tree laughs. "I'm not sure what you said, but I'm sure it isn't true."

Murray cracks his knuckles and stares at the ceiling. He whistles the opening bars of "If Ever I Would Leave You."

"I'm not helping you much, am I?" says Tree.

"Some of my clients are guilty, and some of them are innocent, but every damn one of them wants to beat the rap. . . . So what aren't you telling me, Trevor? I feel like my playbook is missing a page."

"I don't know . . . I guess I really resent all this. I resent even having to deal with it."

"You'd better deal with it, and the sooner the better. They're gonna play hardball on Thursday morning, going right back to service ratings for every year on the job, sick time, productivity or the lack thereof."

"It is all bullshit, Mr. Olnick. The evidence is all circumstantial, except for the pissing in Lee's cup. That's all it could be . . . They want a scapegoat, and I'm just not gonna fucking do it."

Murray flips his gold pen into the air, lets it land on the yellow legal pad. "Forget the polygraph, then. Forget putting you on the stand in your own behalf. We toss out the planned preemptive strike. You've got money and time, the two most important commodities in litigation."

"Meaning?"

"Meaning I'll request about a thousand postponements, every goddamned piece of paper they've ever heard of, and a new board every six months. One way or the other, son, we're gonna beat these worms back into the can."

"You know," Tree says, "I used to hate these tactics when I was on the other side. All the sleazeball crooks with their lawyers pulling scams."

Murray grins at him, not at all offended. Then he settles into his chair and begins the search for the words required to sanitize Tree's life.

Two security guards are sitting at the reception desk in the lobby when Tree gets back to the condo. "Everything's nice and quiet, Mr. Nelson," the senior guard reports.

He rides upstairs, lets himself into the apartment, and collapses on the couch, staring at passing clouds, contemplating prison, exile, and disgrace. The abyss . . . is staring back. There is nowhere to go, there is nothing to do.

Then the telephone rings, and his spirits soar. He leaps for the receiver, right now willing to hear even the pros and cons of aluminum siding, with perhaps a large job ordered COD for the residence of one Lt. Anthony Lee.

But the line is dead.

Someone has reached out to touch him.

His doorbell plays Annie's personal ring. Through the spyhole he sees her, looking short and fat. He opens the door and she is tall and thin and pretty, her hair pulled back in a pony tail, no bra under her pink tube top, maybe no panties under her calico skirt. Her arms are laden with groceries.

"Here," he says. "Let me take those."

"What, are you crazy?" she says, breezing past him, smelling of Giorgio perfume. She knows that if she doesn't put them away, Tree will leave the bags on the counter, eating from the top until the perishables spoil. "How'd it go at work?"

"Shitty. They're talking trial board."

"What are your chances?"

"A moron could make me look like a Mafia hitman, those things are so rigged."

She pulls her head out of the refrigerator and gives him a fatherly look. "Those jerks have you on hold and they're playing you Muzak. Pull the goddamned plug."

"Later for that kind of talk. I'd never be able to live with myself if I walked away now."

When her chores are completed, she sits Buddha-style on the living room couch, her skirt covering her knees. "You know, if I hadn't scored that blow for Jimmy, this wouldn't be—"

"I figured he got it from you," Tree says, giving her a wistful smile. "He was talking about needing toot for the Labor Day Weekend, saying Robert fucking Redford couldn't score in the Hamptons without blow."

"I know. I know. That's why I got it for him. But since they started in on you, I've been feeling incredibly guilty."

He sits down beside her, stretching his legs. "He would have got it somewhere else. You know that."

"Maybe," she says. "Maybe not."

"They had him for marijuana anyway. Lieutenant Lee made his apartment sound like an opium den."

"Still," she says.

"*You* know Jimmy always did whatever the hell he wanted, which is why I suppose I liked him so much.

He made me feel like rules were for everyone but us."

"Until now," she says.

"Yeah, right," he says. "I guess all our bills come due at once." Annie rubs his shoulders and the back of his neck, and it makes him feel like a prizefighter getting prepped for more punishment. "I'm not as worried as I look," he says. "It's only my career."

She says nothing for a moment, just frowns and shakes her head. "You're such a stoic . . . nobody can help you, nobody can apologize to you."

"That's an act."

"Well, it sucks."

"I really don't blame you for this. You've been getting him shit for years with my knowledge. I think it's a little late for me to say that I mind."

"You coulda fooled me." She hops off the couch, suddenly in a very great hurry, as if she has no more time to waste on hopeless cases.

"Annie." He has half a mind to ask the question he'd avoided asking for years, the question he should have asked earlier. Where was *she* scoring?

"I have to go to work," she says. "We're doing a party up in Muttontown, so I'll be late getting home."

"Say hi to that faggot Geoffrey," he says. "Maybe he's your way out of 'this rut.' "

"Low blow," she says. "That's not your style."

He does his best to give her a blank expression. "Maybe *that's* the problem."

He'd ask her later. Or maybe never.

Al Baumgarten is halfway home to his wife and kids in Huntington when he turns the unmarked company car around on Jericho Turnpike and heads back to Mineola. "Damn it," he says, slapping the steering wheel. The sun is setting in his face. "Goddamn Trevor Nelson."

Now both his wife and his dinner will be cold.

He lights a cigar and weaves quickly through traffic, flipping his grille lights on and off, goosing Sunday drivers with his horn. Because his sense of fair play is offended, because all his life he's been a union man, and because the reason he was a cop in the first place was to give the little guy a break.

He'll call Connie from his office, maybe tell her to let the kids chow down while she throws on something nice, and then he'll take her out to dinner at Bobby Rubino's. And goddamn Trevor Nelson can owe him one.

Tree has difficulty sleeping that night. He twists and turns and wrestles his pillow to a draw, until, at 1:10 A.M., his bedside telephone rings. He hears a little mood breathing. Then *click, buzz.*

Maybe Mona checking up on him. Or Gladstone Lanier. A snitch with information on a case he no longer cares about. A plain old wrong number, as if that's possible in these days of programmed phones. There's no telling how many spaceshot broads Jimmy gave the number to, and, if the truth be told, Jimmy was not the only one to be indiscreet. So damn near anybody could have it, a notion that does not settle his nerves.

And he knows Annie won't come up to comfort him after his parting shot about her boss. She'll make him wonder. She'll make him pay.

In the darkness faces of the dead spring to mind. He sees the mutilated corpse of Georges Crosse . . . two young black boys with Colombian Neckties . . . the

heart attacks and strokes he's covered . . . the suicides
. . . the little girl collapsing . . . Roland Lanier walking
the plank backward . . . Jimmy Tibaldi, cold and alone
in his upstate grave. A memory of his mother at Jones
Beach, circa 1954.

All those people ahead of him, waiting.

In the dark.

He rises early and runs just far enough to break a
sweat before turning around; but it's not fun for him
now, looking over his shoulder every couple of steps,
feeling like he's being chased by hounds and horses.
The uneatable pursued by the unspeakable.

Back upstairs, he showers slowly, letting needles of
hot water sting his back until the bathroom is filled
with steam. Then he wipes a section of the mirror
clean and considers shaving off his beard. He wonders
if shaving now might not be letting Jimmy down, that
he ought to let his freak flag fly in their faces; then he
shakes his head and laughs at himself and lathers up.
The damn thing was starting to itch anyway.

He takes the elevator down to the garage, where he
is happy to find Annie's car parked where it should
be.

As he drives away from the building he sees in his
rearview mirror that her curtains are drawn. He turns
on the radio. There is still no publicity. No negative
waves on the FM stereo. All clear at 1010 WINS.
Elliot Kash, Geraldo Nowhereo, Jerk-his Johnson, and
Roseanna Roseannadanna have been otherwise occupied lately. Apparently conduct unbecoming an officer
is fairly commonplace. No bogus quotes from the high
command interrupt his ride up the Meadowbrook to

Headquarters. Where he used to work, is what he must suppose, though the idea makes him feel old.

He signs in at the front desk and limps upstairs to the Homicide office, where the phones are ringing with the persistence one associates with disaster. At every desk shocked families cluster around detectives. Some of the little children are crying, which makes some of the other children cry. Threading his way through the grief-stricken mob, Tree can only think it was a terrorist's bomb, perhaps in a shopping mall or school.

Through the beveled glass Tree sees Baumgarten typing hunt-and-peck. He pokes his head into the office. "Got a minute?"

"Come in, Nelson," he says without looking up. "Close the door." Baumgarten's fingers fly from tab to space to carriage return, as if by efficiency and diligence he might ease the sorrows of the bereaved. "Hey, you look good. Rested."

"Big deal. I shaved."

"It couldn't hurt."

"What happened?" Tree says.

"A senior citizens' bus whacked a fire truck . . . on its way to a false alarm. I've got two dead volunteers and broken hips from here to Massapequa. So far."

"I could come back," Tree says. "Hell, I'd chip in with the paperwork if I thought it was kosher."

"Thanks, but no thanks. Stick around, though. I want to talk to you." Baumgarten continues typing. The smoke from the stub of his cigar curls into his nostrils and eyes. He lays it in the ashtray and stops to rub his face.

Tree's palms are sweating and he's tapping his foot. "Someone is doing a very good job of scaring the shit out of me, Sarge. I get weird phone calls at home, and pictures of Jimmy with an *X* across his face. I gotta tell you, they're driving me fucking crazy. I want my goddamned gun and shield back, at least until Lanier is put away. After that, they can stick 'em both where the sun don't shine.''

Tree draws hope from the fact that Baumgarten doesn't say anything right away. He flips open the manila case folder on Detective James C. Tibaldi, which is made up largely of I-don't-knows, dead-end leads, and overtime slips.

Baumgarten looks at Tree and wonders what it is like not to need a job. Hell, he thinks, his twenty are up in two more years, and he can't even begin to contemplate packing it in. He's still got one in elementary school, and two in junior high. And he'll probably have to take a second mortage on his split-level house when they want to go to college, away from their father who comes home cranky from work.

"Well?"

Baumgarten rubs his eyes again. "I don't blame you. This witch hunt's getting old. The only thing they found in your piss was Sweet 'n' Low."

"It must have been Lee's. I don't use it."

"I went through your file last night after everybody else went home."

Tree squirms uncomfortably in his chair.

"Lee's been saying it proves a long-standing conspiracy to thwart the department's objectives, that only guys that were dirty could do so little work."

"Would you believe we gave a lot of warnings?" Tree says sheepishly.

"Actually, I would. Not that I think you ever knocked yourself out."

"You're right. We were dogging it. But we weren't taking money and I wasn't doing drugs."

"I'm gonna go to bat for you, call in a couple of markers. But if they let you back, you're gonna come back with a different attitude this time," Baumgarten tells him. "You're gonna act like you give a shit. No more of this life-is-hard, then-you-die bullshit. No more of this I-don't-need-the-money, so-why-should-I-give-a-good-goddamn. I want you obsessed with this until we either lock up the bad guy or blow him away. Do we understand each other?"

"If I'm lying, I'm dying," Tree says. "And that's no joke."

"Okay, then . . . here's the good news. We got the gun."

"The gun?"

"The gun that wounded you . . . the gun that killed Jimmy."

Tree's legs go weak and his stomach flutters. He puts his arms on Baumgarten's desk and buries his head in them. "God, I hate guns," he says. "Where'd you get it?"

"From the apartment of Raul Santana, a Puerto Rican DOA who overdosed on high-test heroin. We found money, too. Sixty-five hundred and change."

Tree picks his head up. "Sounds like that makes the going rate for killing a cop about ten thousand dollars."

"Or five each, in advance."

"One of Crazy Victor's boys?" Tree asks.

"Oh, yeah," says Baumgarten. "One of the inner circle, according to Aviles."

"You think he pulled the trigger?"

"That would be awfully obvious, don't ya think, just a little too pat."

"It's typical," says Tree. "Every time someone dies around here, he looks guilty of the shit we're working on."

"So now I don't know what to think. I've been leaning kind of heavy toward Lanier. Yesterday one of the narcs told me Jensen Macomber's shop was probably a wholesale outlet for crack, with real bad dudes in and out of there up until the shooting."

"He's wrong. Way the fuck off base."

"Maybe Macomber had the Rastas do it for him. You and Jimmy were getting too close. What makes more sense? It was business."

Tree doesn't say anything. He can't believe how overmatched cops are when it comes to professional crooks.

Baumgarten says, "We both know he's been to Cuba."

Tree's face grows pale, his knees weak. He is in Jensen's apartment with Jimmy, holding the passport and wondering. Someone with an Uzi is waiting outside.

"Who found who?" Baumgarten asks. "How did you first come in contact with him?"

"His store was robbed a couple of years ago, when me and Jimmy were in uniform. We got to talking about this and that, and I suggested he form a merchants group to interface with the department. The Arabs and West Indians thought they were getting the shitty end of the stick. He kept telling me his problem; I would do what I could. I'm telling you you're wrong, just like your narc buddy is wrong. I've seen Jensen

Macomber since the ambush. If he wanted me dead, he had his chance."

"When did you see him?"

"Last week, out at my father's house."

"And you let him *go?*"

"*He* let *me* go."

"Do you know how to reach him?"

"No. And if he's got brain cell one, he's astala-bye-bye."

Baumgarten runs his fingers through his curly hair. If he loves his work, it doesn't show. "Make me think you're helping me, Tree. I can't walk out on a limb if I see you got a chain saw in your hand."

"Sorry, Sarge. Attempts on my life tend to throw me for a loop. I get all . . . I don't know . . . flustered."

Baumgarten laughs long and hard, perhaps for the first time all day. "Okay," he says. "I'll back off if you'll come forward."

"Deal."

"So talk to me."

"Macomber told me that the kid at the Blake who went off the roof was Lanier's baby brother, Roland."

Baumgarten shakes his head. "How does a florist know shit like this?"

"He had a friend who liked to flap his gums, someone who didn't like Lanier all that much. I don't know. Maybe Lanier stole his woman."

"Maybe. Supposedly. Could be. Can't say for sure. I'm getting a little sick of this."

"You and me both," says Tree.

"Nobody knows as much about these scrotes as you do."

"God, we're in trouble."

Baumgarten takes one more gulp of his coffee, then

holds the cup in front of him with both hands. "Nobody has better reason for wanting them stopped."

Tree wonders if Baumgarten is suggesting revenge, the killing of Gladstone Lanier—what Tree feels he probably should be thinking about as well. A back-alley hit, an accidental drowning, something. Because no one can get away with murder better than a cop. But he does not find in himself the overpowering urge to retribution—the guts to do something wrong. He would much prefer the criminal justice system grind Gladstone Lanier to dust for five or six consecutive twenty-fives-to-life.

Baumgarten says, "It's like this son of a bitch Lanier is made of air."

"What about I talk to Victor," Tree suggests. "Man to man. Dick to dick."

"You want Aviles to bring him in?"

"Hell, no. Get me my gun and my badge and I'll do it myself."

"I'll do what I can," Baumgarten says. "Also, I've got a team setting up court-ordered wiretaps on Lanier's three telephone lines tomorrow night. Maybe we'll get lucky and he'll say something dumb. Or dial your number direct, so we can start him off with a little aggravated harassment."

"My gun, Sarge. Quick."

"I'm on it," says Baumgarten. "In the meantime, you stay the hell out of sight. I gotta go pull somebody's string."

Police Commissioner David Trimble has a decision to make.

Sergeant Baumgarten has always been a man worth listening to, and here he is, with all the nay-sayers aligned against him, putting his reputation on the line for Police Officer Trevor Nelson.

"He's a hairbag, crooked cop," says Lee. "And maybe a murderer."

"Lieutenant," says Baumgarten, "if the district attorney saw no reason to bring charges against Nelson and the others, don't you think it's a bit unfair of you to keep bringing it up?"

"The district attorney doesn't know what we know about Jimmy Tibaldi. Maybe they were high when they caught the kid; maybe Tibaldi freaked out and the other two are covering for him. Come on yourself, Sergeant. How many perps have you seen kill themselves rather than be caught?"

"It's not that much different than killing yourself in jail, which happens all the time."

"Commissioner Trimble," says Lee, "I don't care if the evidence against Nelson smells like dogshit in court. I don't care if he pisses Perrier. He knew about Tibaldi, and he didn't report it. The guy's *apartment* had hash pipes and rolling papers scattered all over the place."

When asked for his opinion, Lieutenant Cumberstadt says that both Nelson and Tibaldi were chronic complainers and frequently called in sick together. He doesn't know, didn't know, about the drugs. He would have taken action. "They were very secretive," he says. "They mostly talked about golf."

Lieutenant Lee snorts. "You're damn right they were secretive. Tibaldi, Nelson, and Jensen Macomber were probably involved in a conspiracy to distribute drugs, and they wouldn't share the vig with Lanier. You said yourself Lanier controls the turf. Why wouldn't he have them hit? What else could he do about a couple of crooked cops?"

"Damn it, what do you say, Sergeant?" Commission Trimble asks. Like the others at this late afternoon meeting, he is not happy about another Trevor Nelson imposition on his time.

"I think we've got our heads up our asses, sir . . . with all due respect. Try this out for a moment: Nelson and Tibaldi, by the record, good cops, not great. Book-smart, street-smart, but not what you'd call overachievers. Reasonably capable types who could make some money doing other things. But like most of the people around here, they were coasting."

"I'm not so sure about Jimmy Tibaldi," Cumberstadt says. "I wouldn't have hired him to rake leaves."

"Maybe they did give a shit about the job. Maybe they were more honorable than we give them credit for. What's a bad attitude? A little grumbling about rules and regulations, or a string of brutality complaints? It's the ones who don't complain that are brain-dead or crooked. You gotta remember, these young guys are from the generation that kidnapped their deans. Most of them have taken one drug or another, I suppose. It doesn't mean they're rotten to the core. Hell, everyone our age drinks and drives and fucks around."

"Not everyone," says Lee.

"Everyone who can pull it off," Baumgarten says. "Anyway," Baumgarten continues, "Tibaldi gets whacked. His blood shows dope. Not Nelson's."

"We don't know that for sure," says Lee. "The hospital refused to give me a sample without his permission and by the time we secured his urine it was too late to tell if he was high at the time of the shooting.''

"You, sir," Baumgarten says to Lee, "are a wonderful human being."

"I do my job. Thoroughly. I was the one who found the marijuana and cocaine in Tibaldi's pad."

"Right. In Jimmy Tibaldi's pad. Commissoner, Nelson's a marathon runner. Those people are fanatics about their bodies. A week after a bullet up his ass, he's out running laps. I think the point we're missing, is that he didn't come forward, crying about his partner. He held the thin blue line. If anyone besmirched the good name of the department, it was the morons who put out those half-assed press releases before they knew what was going on. I don't think we ever had a reason *not* to believe Trevor Nelson."

"Let's not overdo it, Sergeant. Don't make him out to be supercop," says Commissioner Trimble. "Even my credulity has its limits."

"Okay," says Baumgarten.

Lee and Cumberstadt study their gold cuff links.

"They really were pretty good guys," Cumberstadt says wistfully.

"I think we owe the man immediate reinstatement," says Baumgarten. "He needs us and we need him. They're gunning for him, too. He cares now, if he didn't before."

"You understand that this won't be good for discipline?" says Trimble.

"No sir. I'm just a Homicide sergeant."

"A very fine one," says Commissioner Trimble. "Remind me I said that if Nelson goes belly up."

* * *

Tree knows he's being followed. He picked up the dark brown Duster with tinted windows and without a front plate just south of Merrick Road. Since then he has been making circles around Seaport's central shopping district, speeding up and slowing down, running red lights and stop signs, and still the Duster hovers in his rearview mirror.

What he wouldn't give for Jimmy's Vette right now. And as long as he's wishing, what he wouldn't give for his gun and shield and a bulletproof vest.

He shoves the Volvo through three tight turns, and then roars down Lombardo Avenue toward the water. Four blocks from the condo, next to the baseball field at Lombardo and Cedar, he pulls to the side of the road and kills the engine.

He would like to think he's lost them, whoever they might be. And, for a moment, nothing on the road behind him moves.

Peace and quiet dominate on the sunny suburban street. A sea breeze ruffles the tops of the tall shady trees that ring the field. Four young mothers have circled the strollers in front of a dugout. Five elementary school kids are playing running bases between second and first, laughing and sliding in the dust.

It would be simple to make it home on foot from here, he thinks, sticking to backyards, hopping fences. Simple and stupid. He remembers that they know where he lives. He also remembers that he is not playing running bases. Getting tagged means getting dead. Forever. None of this three-lives bullshit.

He looks forward again, and there it is, turning onto Lombardo at Front Street, awesome and deadly, like a Soviet tank in Red Square.

The Volvo won't start, and it's too late to take it on

the arches. Blue smoke piles up in the air; the fenders rattle and shake. "You Swedish piece of shit," he yells, pumping the accelerator.

Ninety feet away the Duster downshifts to ramming speed and hurtles toward him. Tires screech, sand flies, and the nose of the auto rises. But that's all he sees before diving across the passenger seat and knocking the wind from his chest on the gearshift.

He hears whoops of laughter, then what sounds like a rock bouncing off the hood of his car, then a deafening explosion, and he knows that they've missed him with a hand grenade and blown third base to kingdom come.

Short of breath and draped across the seats, he struggles to sit up, trying to catch a look at the rear license plate through the curtain of dust and smoke that pours from the fuming hole. Nothing. Nada. They've disappeared again. Returned to the bowels of the skyline city.

To get more bombs.

The innocents in the park slowly rise to their feet, and then run to each other screaming.

"I'll go get help," he calls out to them. "Please stay right where you are."

The wailing continues, but Tree can see that no one has been physically hurt. He rubs his ribs and turns the key. The Volvo, in spite of all the new dents and holes on the passenger side, kicks over smartly, but Tree cannot hear this over the ringing in his ears, so he grinds the starter twice before pulling away.

He double-parks in front of The Barge Inn and runs inside to use the phone. His hands are shaking so badly he has to dial the number 911 three times before getting it right. Then he orders a beer and chugs it down, to calm himself. Then he steps back into the phone booth and calls Baumgarten.

"Get me my tools back," Tree tells the sergeant, "and I'll drop that boy too short to shit."

12

FUTURE PERFECT

A woman in her early forties steps off the bus in front of the Blake Hotel. She has waist-length brown hair and is wearing a sweatshirt and faded blue jeans. Before closing the door behind her, the old Negro driver warns her to get where she's going quick, that getting off here ain't exactly a common practice of white girls. " 'Less they looking hard for some crack and don't care what it cost."

"Go fuck yourself," she says. She lifts the waistband of her sweatshirt and shows the Tom her piece. The door slams shut in her face and the bus roars away. It makes her laugh out loud, to see herself as the odd white woman who has less to fear in the ghetto than she does at the mall.

She walks into the seedy hotel and briskly climbs the steps to his door. She knocks hard on it three times, then once.

"Yes?"

"Maria from Geoffrey. I have something to give you."

"You were saying?"

"Good news, my friend."

"You wish to come inside my rooms?"

"For a moment."

"Will you let me take your clothes off, little white girl? To see that you aren't wired for sound?"

"Yes . . . of course."

"You may come in."

The door opens and she walks inside. Lanier is alone in the barren room, smoking a big fat joint. He is wearing black gym shorts, a red Lacoste tennis shirt, and orange rubber sandals, and he is casually holding an automatic pistol in his hand.

Maria Delgado smiles at him, then pulls her sweatshirt over her head. He stares at her little breasts with his beady bloodshot eyes and takes another hit on the spliff. Then another one as she sets her gun on the shelf and wiggles out of her blue jeans and panties.

She turns around slowly twice for his benefit; she has the body of a much younger woman, and she is not ashamed to show it off.

"You brought me a gift?" he says. "A sign of respect?"

"Yes. May I get dressed?"

"The gift I was hoping for would require you to leave your clothes where they are. You are so much more attractive than your predecessor. I must remember to compliment Geoffrey on his choice of replacements."

"Men don't attract me. I'm sorry. But my gift is more valuable," she says, bending over, sliding quickly back into her jeans, pulling on her sweatshirt.

"What are you talking about?"

"The cops you're after. . . . I have a plan."

His face does not change expression. His dreadlocks look like snakes to her. "And why would I be after cops?" says Lanier. "Wouldn't you think I'd be giving them wide berth?"

"Not at all," she says. "Not when vengeance is demanded."

"You know a lot, it seems," he says. "You have never met me and yet I am to understand that you have already assembled a plan for my revenge?"

"I have been watching you for Geoffrey for quite some time now, and it has always been with the utmost admiration. Your name is spoken of with pride."

"But you like girls?"

"Exclusively."

"What a pity. I do some of my very best work on white meat."

"You're not taking me seriously."

"That's true."

"You won't be sorry that we've met. I mean that."

"We'll see, eh?" he says, smiling lewdly.

Gladstone Lanier puts the joint down and lights a cigarette. "Very well, then. Tell me stories, woman. Show me your cunning. Your plan is brilliant?"

"No," she says. "It's simple."

Lanier flips his lit spliff out the open apartment window and takes a step closer to Maria. "I want you to know that I'm mulling over your proposal." He puts his hands around her neck and kisses her forehead. "I'm thinking about doing what you want." Then, with steadily increasing pressure on her shoulders he forces her down to her knees. "Show me, Maria. Convince me."

Tree wakes from a three-bucket night on the balcony, hooking, slicing, and shanking balls into the bay. Sound sleep was impossible. Sirens, bells, and fire whistles from north Seaport throughout the night saw to that. He looks forward to hours of safe and silent skin diving, shagging the range balls from the sandy bottom of the bay while Annie floats above him in the dinghy with the police babysitter assigned to him.

The phone rings. He answers it without opening his eyes.

"Hey, there," Annie says. "Can I come up? I want to apologize for how I've been these last few weeks."

"You've been fine," he says, "considering. Stay where you are. I'll be right down."

"No," she says. "I'll bring you breakfast in bed."

"So come up."

He hangs up and rolls out of bed, noticing that his laundry pile has grown beyond the confines of his hamper, and he thinks of asking Annie if she'd mind . . . he's got so much to do today. He's supposed to play golf with his father and Brophy this afternoon, and there are still September's bills to pay. What else? he wonders.

The guard on the door lets Annie in. She is balancing a tray and is dressed for work: overalls, hiking boots, work shirt. She says she can't stay long; she's needed at the gas station. "I couldn't find anyone to take my hours."

"If by chance you have some time later, do you think you could run my clothes through the washing machine with yours? I'm kinda behind on the domestic shit."

"I'll even iron."

"You're a hell of a woman," he says. "I'm glad we talked."

There's no reason to tell her about the hand grenade, no reason to worry her pretty little head. If she notices the new damage to the Volvo amidst all the old damage, he'll be very surprised.

"How about a hug?" he says. "It's been a long time."

She stares at her feet, frozen, unable to provide.

"What's the matter?"

"This isn't working out."

"What isn't working out?"

"Us. Our lives."

Tree doesn't say anything. He hates these conversations. He will not encourage her probing.

"Tree, I'm pregnant. About two and a half months."

Pregnant. He slowly nods, many things coming clear to him at once. Her questions, her threats to disappear, no more drugs. "So much for living for the moment," he says. "Am I the father?"

She lowers her head, her shoulders slump. "You have every right to ask that," she says. "I wish to God that we'd lived in such a way that the question would be ridiculous. I guess we . . . I guess I didn't." She looks up. "I want to now."

He is still waiting for an answer; the truth or at least a pretty lie. He's not fool enough to raise some other guy's kid. He hopes that she knows this.

"Yes. You're the father. My last little fling was in April, just before the marathon."

He knew about Geoffrey, and the lifeguard from Point Lookout last summer. She knew about Mona and Casey and some of the others he used to retaliate.

"Cutting this kinda close, aren't we?" he says.

"I'm sure."

"I suppose we should count our blessings," he says.

Annie gives a bitter laugh, then collapses in a chair. All the starch is gone from her. "God, I'm sorry."

"We're both of us sorry."

Her despair stands between them, cool and faultless.

"I gotta go," she says.

Like a dog he follows her to the living room. She picks up his socks, a pizza box, his golf glove, and properly sees each to its appointed place. He loves this: that she knows his home by heart. He loves her, whether it makes him feel good or not.

"How long have you known?" he asks her. "Since you stopped getting wasted?"

"I could tell you the night it happened."

June, he thinks. The night she chose not to use the diaphragm, to see if fate had anything in store for her.

"You *will* marry me?" he says.

She looks surprised. Did she expect him to offer another ride to the abortionist?

"Just the basics, Annie. Don't panic."

"The basics?"

"I thought girls grew up dreaming about marriage."

Annie has just been reminded of a ghost. Her eyes brim over with tears.

"Hey," says Tree. "We can cherish John's memory but we can't include him in all our decisions."

"I know that, you asshole," she says as tenderly as that can be said.

"So?"

"Let's hear your idea of the basics."

"I play all the golf I want, and never screw around. You hold the frowning to a minimum and never screw around. Simple. We'll get along famously."

"No."

"To which items?"

"The frowning and the golf."

"Wanna use my last name?"

"Yes," she says immediately, so he knows that she has thought about this. "Anne Adams Sutherland Nelson—it does sound a bit WASPy, though, don't you think?"

"Like you came over on the *Mayflower*, my dear. Will you kiss me when I'm drunk and you're not?"

"You sound like you're negotiating a treaty," she says.

"I am." Tree smiles, thinking that most golf bets are won on the first tee, haggling the handicaps. "Well? Will you?" This could be a valuable concession.

"I'll do anything you say. Don't you know that yet?" She puts her arms around his waist and kisses his nose, his mustache, his lips, his chin, then buries her face in his chest.

"Oh, yeah, sure. I've known it all along. Never a doubt." He looks over the top of her head, out the balcony doors, at the sky and the ocean and the future, and squeezes her. "I think this is fucking wonderful," he says. "I know you don't believe that, but it's true."

"One more beer and we get the hell out of here," says Sgt. Robert Allison. He is wearing a white T-shirt and his dark blue uniform pants. He is off duty and drinking hard at Puddles Pub, as he has been since 4 P.M., when he heard the notification that the John Doe from the Blake Hotel the other week was Gladstone Lanier's younger brother. He is supposed to see the precinct commander tomorrow about it, but he is currently regaling two baby-faced rookies with the highlights of his career in law enforcement.

"No more beer," says one of the rookies, waving a hand. "I got to get home before my wife cuts my balls off."

"She'll get over it," Allison says. "Doing without you. It comes with the fucking job. I could stay out a week and my old lady wouldn't notice. . . . You gotta break 'em in right, is the key."

"Look, Sarge—"

"Hey!" Allison insists on telling just one more war story. For the edification of the troops. "Dig it," he says. "They send me to this uppity colored guy's house one night. Which was mistake number one. He's got his white-man tweeds on and he's waiting for me in a taxicab with the meter running. Seems he's lost his keys somewhere during his *very busy* day. He needs immediate access to his house and automobile. Chop chop, you dig? So I tell him there could be a bit of damage getting him into his house and have him sign my memo book, authorizing entry, you know. So he's happy as a clam, this fucking gleep, 'cause whitey's gonna handle some of his light work. Now, I don't have to tell you, I'm fucking fuming. I'm ready to shit hand grenades. But the wheels are turning," he says, tapping the side of his head. "I see these two concrete lions he's got guarding the front of the hut, just as uppity and arrogant as if he had a statue of a white guy holding a lantern at the end of his driveway."

"Oh, no," says the shorter rookie. "What did you do?"

"I picked one of those hundred-pound babies up

over my head and launched it through the front door before Buckwheat could say boo."

"No."

"Fucking A."

"What'd he do?"

"What could he do?" says Allison. "He stood there looking at this huge fucking hole. I give him a friendly pat on the back and say, 'There you go, bro. . . . You're all set.' "

Shots of Jack Daniel's are ordered, beers again topped off. The story is gleefully celebrated, until the rookies finally leave, and Allison is alone with the bartender, an elderly man who could recite the whole of the sergeant's career. He stays by the TV, polishing glasses, until Allison orders another shooter to go with his beer.

The sarge swallows the whiskey whole. The bartender pours him one more and raps his knuckles on the bar. "With me."

" 'Bout time. Hey, where the hell is everyone?" Allison asks.

"Home . . . with their families . . . eating dinner."

"Home whacking their beef, is more like it."

"To each his own."

"Fucking A."

A single woman enters the bar—slender, brunette, in her forties. She is pale and her nose is running. Allison immediately makes her for a cocaine whore, that subspecies of female who will do anything with anybody for the chance to wrap their nose around some blow. She sits one stool away from him and orders a margarita. Allison stares at her nipples beneath her halter; he taps his wad of bills when the bartender delivers her drink.

"Thank you," says Maria, licking the salt from the rim of the glass. "God, I need this bad."

"Times are tough all over," he says.

She wrinkles her nose and sniffles at this piece of information. There is sleep in one of her eyes, or maybe it's dirt. Whatever, she's got that just-fucked look he can't resist.

He prays to God she don't have AIDS. Damn near anything else he brings home he can blame on the scrotes he wrestles during the normal course of business; it's way too late to tell the old lady he's Haitian.

She removes a Marlboro 100 from her purse. Robert Allison lights it for her, and then lights up a Camel for himself.

"Thanks again," she says.

"Bobby Allison, at your service."

"Donna. Nice to meet you."

"The pleasure's all mine."

"Look," she says. "You seem very kind, I wonder if you might help me with something else."

Like the rent, he's thinking, or that goddamn itch between your legs. "And what's that, doll?"

She smiles and tosses back her long hair. "I hate to trouble you. Your day has probably been as rotten as mine."

"What's the matter?" he singsongs, the way he used to talk to his daughters when they were scared to death of some silly little thing.

"My car's outside with a tire that's flatter than shit. . . . I'm afraid I don't know how to change it. Never did it before, in all my life. Isn't that amazing?"

"Nothing's amazing to me," he says.

"Will you help me? I'm already late getting home as it is."

He takes a long slug of beer and sucks the foam out of his mustache. "Don't sound like that leaves much time for you to show your appreciation."

She gives him a naughty, dime-store smile. "Old-timer, you won't last five minutes with me."

" 'Old-timer'? Fill these up again," Allison calls to the bartender. "We'll be right back." Then to himself: "I'll bring you back the pelt."

She leads him out of the bar and around the corner to where her old brown Duster is parked. A Connecticut license plate is wired to the bumper with a clothes hanger. He sees that the right rear tire is indeed lacking air, as well as tread. This chick's old man must be a winner.

She opens the trunk for him, and Allison reaches inside for the jack and spare. He has the start of an erection growing in his police pants, thinking of cold tools and honest effort, the hard and the soft. Snap-On. Hard-on. Lugs and screw.

Then his brain explodes with blinding pain and darkness wraps around him.

He wakes to find himself bound hand and foot, and gagged, riding in the closed trunk of an automobile, a Duster from the fucking Nutmeg State, he supposes, remembering with chagrin the events leading up to his major-league headache and surprisingly upset stomach. His wallet is gone and his off-duty revolver is missing from his waistband.

Jesus, Mary, and Joseph, he thinks. Rolled, by a freaking bimbo. The guys'll shit. But why, he wonders. She's got his money, his gun, his badge. He entertains for a moment the idea that she might want him to be her sex slave, that this minor adventure is nothing more than the caveman scene reversed.

Don't bullshit a bullshitter, he thinks. He knows she didn't do this by herself. He draws the sign of the cross in the darkness with his nose. "Our Father, Who art in Heaven. . . ."

The car doesn't stop until he's halfway through the Rosary, using his fingers and toes to count. The car swerves and stops, the trunk opens, allowing him to see again in the dying evening light.

Three dreadlocked Rastas yank him out of the trunk and stand him up in front of another black man. They are parked on the side of the Seaford-Oyster Bay Expressway, on the overpass of the Southern State Parkway, out in the goddamn country, where nothing ever happens.

The snow witch is sitting in the back seat of the Duster, smoking a cigarette, her hair brown without the wig. She does not turn around to look at him. There will be no long good-bye.

He grunts at the brothers. What more can they want? To kick his lily-white ass? Motherfuckers. These faces he's gonna remember.

"Say hello to Roland," the shaky one says to him.

Then the three hairy Rastas hoist him up like so much rolled-up carpet remnant and dump him over the side of the bridge.

During the free-fall moment, Bobby Allison hears the tires screech and Dopplered horns and understands what is going down. He lands on his knees in the middle of the center lane, facing traffic, and struggles on broken femurs for the briefest instant to maintain a position of prayer, a supplicant swaying to the altar, asking mercy of a grinning grille doing sixty.

13

Mr. Blue

Tree peeks through the spyhole, something he would not do without hearing a familiar voice. He's seen stiffs with bullets through the eyeballs before, victims of misplaced trust and cheap doors. Baumgarten is alone, dressed in blue jeans and a St. John's University sweatshirt.

"You got a warrant?" Tree says through the door.

"You want a punch in the nose?"

Tree opens the door and Baumgarten walks right in. He nods at the balcony, impressed, and purses his lips at the stark modern furniture, the illusion of endless space reaching out through the balcony's glass doors to the horizon.

"I was just gonna call you," Tree says.

Baumgarten raps his knuckles on the Steinway keyboard. "Great touch. You play?"

"Jimmy did, now and then. I use it as a planter."

Baumgarten grunts and sits on the couch. "You were gonna call me at home? What, did someone take another run at you?"

"Not exactly."

"What the hell are you doing home?" Baumgarten says.

Tree sits on the edge of the sofa, toweling his hair. "I'm supposed to be getting out of town."

"Wrong. You're supposed to be downtown working with me. I need you on this, right."

"I need protection."

"Tree. You're the only one who knows all these bums."

"You want a beer?" Tree says.

"In spite of the clothes, I'm working. Been down at the shop since four this morning."

"What happened?"

"All kinds of shit, all night long. You wouldn't have believed it. Uniforms stopped a William Outerbridge driving on Nassau Road in Roosevelt. Everything he owned was stuffed into an unregistered Subaru, including about a pound of marijuana, a nine-millimeter Beretta and a sawed-off Remington shotgun. Said he was moving out of state. There was another guy with him, but he took it on the arches and our guys couldn't catch him. Outerbridge is a Rastafarian and he's a heroin addict. He knew he couldn't make station-house bail on a weapons charge so he started asking for you, to make a deal."

"By name?"

"Right."

"Don't know him."

"He says his street name is Mongo Blue."

"About thirty years old?"

"Right."

"He's not one of Lanier's board of directors, but he knows his way around," Tree says. "He used to pick up scrap metal and bottles and cans to get the bread to feed his head. Then I guess Lanier showed him the better way.''

"Correct. Anyway, the cop tries to get hold of you through the main office, but you're suspended, right, so they get in touch with Lieutenant Lee, who tells them you're the last person on earth authorized to make deals with prisoners and hangs up. About this time old Mongo starts getting sick, so he ups the ante. He tells the guys that he knows about a plot to kill you. The guys call Lee back. He tells them to stop breaking his balls and gives them my home phone.''

"Is Lee a prince or what?''

"I get up, I go in, I talk to Mr. Mongo Blue. He's sweating his ass off now, puking every ten minutes. He tells me Lanier's gone wild. Says Lanier's been having terrible headaches lately, and visions. Smoking crack from dawn to dusk. His crew is terrified.''

Tree nods. "So what about we pick Lanier up. Let's have a little chat with him now that he's so strung out.''

"My sentiments exactly. Unfortunately, Lanier's ahead of the game. By the time I got to the Blake Hotel around dawn it was empty. Gladstone is gone— checked out.''

"Holy shit.''

"Yeah. Nobody home. The other tenants and hangers-on said the Rastas split about midnight and suggested it was a marvelous time for everyone to take a nice long walk.''

"What did the suddenly homeless Rastas have to say about that?''

"Ya got me. They were all out of there. Every damn one of them. The hotel is empty. We're sifting the debris, but I'd be willing to bet Lanier didn't leave much behind to trace him with. I found out from the manager that Lanier never paid dime one in rent. The landlord was afraid to throw him out. Oh, yeah, another thing, Lanier put out an open contract on you for ten big ones. Same on Allison and, get this, Victor Guardina.''

''Anyone looking to make a buck would be after me then.'' Tree folds his arms across his chest.

Baumgarten slumps onto the couch, a look of disappointment in his eyes. ''You know,'' he says, ''I'm beginning to think what they say about you is true.''

''And what's that?''

''Nice guy but a few bricks short of a load.'' Baumgarten shakes his head. ''Damn right—open season. It's not gonna go away like a bad cold either. So we got errands to run.''

''Small problem. Jensen Macomber wants to meet me.''

''Beautiful. Where?''

''Behind his shop. Tonight.''

Al Baumgarten raises his eyebrows suspiciously. ''For what?''

''Whatever.''

''Knowing what you know,'' Baumgarten says, ''you still want to go?''

''As long as we bring along the fleet.''

''No fleet. No fanfare. No local cops. Not everyone has the faith in you that I do.''

''But—''

''I will call my buddy at the Bureau for a little backup. That way, if it turns out to be nothing, I won't have Lieutenant Lee breaking my balls, second-guessing me to the boss.''

''Whatever.''

"That don't mean this won't be dangerous and probably stupid. Your friend Macomber might have had a gun to his head when he made that call."

"I know that."

Baumgarten reaches into the pocket of his sweat-shirt. "Here's your gun and shield," he says. "You're back on the payroll. Now come on, get dressed. We've got a lot of things to do."

Tree and Baumgarten drive north to headquarters. Mongo Blue is still handcuffed to Baumgarten's desk when they arrive. He's wearing blue jeans that are wet at the crotch and an orange T-shirt that says A RACE WITHOUT POWER IS A RACE WITHOUT DIGNITY. The smell of sweat and urine and vomit fill the office.

Tree pretends not to notice. "How's it going, Mongo my man," he says to him. "Cool runnings, babe?"

"I'm dying here, Nelson. Right before your eyes."

"Would you like me to cut you loose?" Baumgarten asks.

Mongo turns to Tree. "Tell him, mon. Tell him what happen to me if Gladstone finds me now. I'm caught with guns and then I'm free? He'd hear the thirty pieces of silver clankin' in me pocket."

"He's meat," Tree says.

"Seems like you've got a problem," Baumgarten says.

"Yeah, I've got a problem, but so do you, Mr. Policemon."

"But my problem isn't like yours, is it, Mongo? I can go home at five o'clock and not have to think about it."

Mongo Blue looks at Tree and says, "That ain't necessarily so, now is it?"

"What do you want from us?" Tree says.

"You've got to give me money and a car, and at least one of my guns," says Mongo. "Withdraw the charges against me, too, because I won't be comin' back."

"So far you've told me shit," Baumgarten says. "You don't know where Lanier is, you don't know much about the place you just moved out of, you got no fucking idea about any of the murders your friends have been committing. You've got to open up a little more, William, shine the light in a couple of dark corners for me. If I like what I hear, I'll give you some money. If I love it, you'll walk on the weapons charge. Make my dick hard and I'll get you a running start."

"I told you before. Gladstone Lanier is planning to kill Nelson."

Baumgarten looks at Tree and rolls his eyes, then slams his fist down on the desk, half an inch from Mongo's pinky. "What about Gladstone Lanier already killing a cop, William? When are you gonna tell us something solid?"

Tree walks behind Mongo. "My partner, Mongo." Tree squeezes Mongo's deltoids hard enough to cause pain in most men, but the Rasta's shoulders feel like they are made out of wood. "The best friend I had in the whole fucking world."

"I don't know nothing 'bout that, mon. I already tol' the sergeant. But Gladstone is settling scores."

Tree is thinking of tearing his dreadlocks out one by one, and stuffing them down his junkie throat. Baumgarten is sitting placidly, scratching an ear, a man with time on his hands, playing the sales game of he-who-talks-first-loses.

"You're absolutely right," says Tree, softly. "You already told everything."

Mongo exhales. "Now how would a poor black foreigner, who picks up junk, know the big man's plans?"

"You read the *Daily News*," says Tree.

"Go on," says Baumgarten. "Tell me what wasn't in the paper."

Mucus drips from Mongo's nose but he does not seem to notice. "I don't know all the particulars," he says, accepting from Tree a tissue that he does not use. "Gladstone keep an awful lot to himself. We have good guns, though. Many men I never seen. This white bitch he fucking and white dudes been around."

"Why has Lanier gone?"

"He buggin' out."

"Why?"

"I don't know." Mongo shrugs.

"Were you with Gladstone in the murder business?" Tree says.

"Oh, God," Mongo says. "I never said that. You never heard that from me." Mongo places his index finger between his teeth and bites it hard, a sign that he's not speaking.

"Somebody told me Lanier put out an open contract on me."

"That's not precisely so. Gladstone wants to do the job himself."

"Is that so? Himself?"

"That's the truth of it."

Tree sits down on the edge of Baumgarten's desk, trying to regain some control over his suddenly twitching knee. Mongo looks up.

"I know you, Trevor Nelson," says Mongo. "I

didn't think that was right, what happened to you and your partner.''

"Thank you, Mongo,'' says Tree, thinking all the while that Mongo might have fired the rounds that killed Jimmy. The round that nicked his butt. "You don't know how much that means to me.''

"Yeah I do, but I say it anyway.''

"Is your dick hard, Sarge?'' Tree asks.

"Where did Lanier go, Mongo? The Blake Hotel is history, so where's the new headquarters? Where are you supposed to meet up with them tomorrow?''

"I don't know.''

"Fine. Well, you have a nice time in the exercise yard at the county jail tomorrow afternoon.''

"That's not fair.''

Baumgarten smiles at Mongo, then lights his cigar and flicks the lit match into Mongo's dreads. While Mongo is patting down the smoking mat of hair with his free hand, Baumgarten says to Tree, "You know, I haven't tuned a motherfucker up in a coon's age. Close the door.''

"Okay, okay, forget it, mon. . . . I heard they got a smuggling boat the other day. And Gladstone was saying something crazy about pirates. I don't know. I told you, he's cracking it up. I swear that's all I heard.'' Mongo starts to cough, begging them to believe him, choking on his phlegm.

"Sarge?'' says Tree.

"Okay, so I got a semi. We'll stash him in jail until after. Then, if what he says is true, we'll sneak him out of the county with a couple of bucks in his pocket.''

"Please,'' Mongo says to Tree. "You can't do that. If I don't kill myself in there, Lanier will have someone do it for me. I've got to go now. Straightaway. I swear I told you the truth."

Tree looks at Baumgarten and shrugs.

"Please . . . God . . . You don't know how bad I'm hurting." Mongo even smells sick.

"Okay. Fuck it," says Baumgarten. "I've got my neck stretched already. What's one more reason to get dumped back into uniform?"

"You're a good man," says Mongo.

"Yeah, yeah, yeah," says Baumgarten. "I'm a fucking prince."

"How?" says Tree.

"We'll take him downstairs and sneak him out of here in the van."

"Where do you want to go?" Tree asks Mongo.

"What do you mean? Now?"

"There is no later, Mongo," says Tree.

"Could we make a couple of stops?"

"No," says Baumgarten. "We're not gonna help you score. We're easy, not sleazy, William. Don't believe everything you read in the paper."

"Kennedy Airport, then."

"Fine."

Baumgarten rapidly types a supporting deposition for Mongo, aiding and assisting his memory where it is lacking detail, color, and clarity. Mongo Blue signs the statement implicating Gladstone Lanier in drug dealing at the Blake Hotel, then stands up next to the desk and shuffles his feet impatiently while Baumgarten uncuffs him.

"Watch yourself, Nelson," says Mongo. "He talk about *you* all the time."

* * *

They take Baumgarten's unmarked car south to the Spanish section of Seaport and begin a drive-by check of the local crack parlors, the Stadium Bar, the beauty parlor, looking for Victor Guardina's shiny white BMW 325.

"You know," says Tree, "this is the first time anyone on this job ever asked me to use my head for something other than a hat rack."

Baumgarten chuckles.

"Slow down!" says Tree. "There's Victor's joy-ride, in front of the diner. And guess who's sitting behind the wheel."

"Got him," says Baumgarten, one-handing a U-turn across Merrick Road and pulling up behind the BMW. "You were right."

Victor remains in the driver's seat, watching Tree and Baumgarten approach in his rearview mirrors.

"I am perfectly calm," Victor calls out the window. "My hands are visible on the dashboard. I will make no sudden movements. I wish only to cooperate with the police."

Baumgarten crouches by Victor's window. "Knock it off, willya, Victor. Save your speeches for the courtroom."

"I will do anything you want me to do, Officer."

"That's Sergeant Baumgarten to you, Victor. I understand that you already know Detective Nelson."

Victor ducks his head and leans across the passenger seat to look at Tree, who has taken up a position by the opposite window. "Hello, Detective Nelson. Allow me to say that I am sorry for what happened to your partner."

Tree bends over and stares into Victor's dark eyes.

Victor says, "Truly. All this violence—"

Tree draws a blank; there is nothing in Victor's demeanor to suggest guilt or fear of revenge. He hardly seems annoyed at being rousted.

"Some people down at headquarters think you're a part of the problem, Victor," Baumgarten says. "We'd like to talk to you about a couple of things."

"Will I be needing my lawyer?"

"Have you done anything wrong?"

"I mean, am I a suspect?"

"Aren't you always?"

"When and where would you like to have this chat, keeping in mind I have an image to maintain?"

"Meet us at the Ranger Restaurant, down on the canal. We'll buy you lunch if you promise to behave."

Victor grabs Baumgarten's hand to stop him from walking away. "As you may know, Sergeant Baumgarten, I don't have a valid driver's license, courtesy of Detective Wilfredo Aviles. I suggest you clear my travel plans with him."

"You're a really funny guy, Victor. We'll see you in fifteen minutes."

The outdoor deck at the waterfront restaurant is filled with customers unable to get into Blotto's or the Riptide. Most of them are wearing boating clothes or T-shirts and jeans. Only Victor Guardina is wearing gang colors, the crossed fists of the Spanish Brothers on the back of his sleeveless dungaree jacket. People are smiling at him condescendingly, the way they do at mental patients on holiday furloughs. Tree wonders if he feels stupid in ghetto garb, so far away from his turf, or if he thinks all these white folks dress like clowns.

"Best chili in New York," Baumgarten tells Victor as they take their seats.

"I came to talk, not to eat."

"That's too bad, Victor, because I came to do both." Baumgarten waves a waitress to their table and orders three chili cheeseburger specials and a pitcher of beer for them. Then he sits back in his chair and admires the busy canal, with its pleasure craft slipping back and forth, and its large charters loaded with anglers heading out to sea. The air is pungent with the smell of brine and fish and gasoline exhaust.

Victor mentions the extraordinary amount of contraband smuggled in through the south shore canals of Long Island. "You wouldn't believe all the people involved."

"Tell me something I don't know, Victor. Tell me what your boy was doing with the gun that killed Detective Tibaldi hidden behind his Magnavox and thousands of dollars in his sock drawer?"

Victor thinks this is funny. "Why are you fucking with me, Sergeant? We come down to the water, we gotta go on a fishing trip?"

"Watch your language, Victor. And please don't get the idea that just because we're breaking bread, we're buddies. You're here because only a sleazeball like you would be involved in shit like this."

"You know I didn't have nothing to do with hitting cops. I'm a businessman, with roots in the community. And I know Lanier was looking to spend big bucks to make me look bad. . . . So how much was it, Sergeant? Three thousand? Five thousand? What is my absence worth to Lanier? Maybe he could just pay it to me and I'd go away until he self-destructs."

Baumgarten smiles. "Name your price, Vic. I'll see if Aviles and Gonzales want to chip in."

"We think Lanier may be leaving town," says Tree.

"Don't believe that," says Victor. "My luck has never been that good. Yours either. You know he's not leaving without a fight. There's too much here. Too many dudes who like to get down. I'd bet my ass he's out house-hunting right now."

"Yeah? Then where are all his Rastas? I haven't seen a dreadlock all day."

"Maybe they have gone to the mattresses, Detective Nelson. Maybe his big-money friends in New York have put them up. I don't fucking know."

"But you could know, couldn't you?" says Baumgarten. "If you really wanted to."

Victor taps a cigarette up from his vest pocket and lights it with his Bic. "What makes you say that?"

"You're still alive, after three months of feuding with him. You don't have even one bodyguard. That means, to me, that someone he knows talks to someone you know."

"Everybody talks too much," says Victor. "That don't mean that I listen."

"You think he planted the gun and the money and then fried your amigo?" says Baumgarten.

"That's obvious," says Victor. "But I am only a businessman. What do you professionals think?"

"*Someone* set it up," Baumgarten says. "The gun was totally clean of any prints except the alleged shooter's, which bothered me right from the get-go. Plus we found several strands of very dirty hair in the trigger mechanism that came from the head of a male Negro in his twenties or thirties."

The waitress returns with their baskets of goodies.

Victor sips his beer but again refuses to eat. Tree knows Victor is high on coke, that underneath his calm exterior his heart is pumping ice. Food? What are you, nuts? he is probably thinking. Booze and blow and cigarettes are all he needs. Even women are for later.

"You're a fucking wreck, Victor. You know that?" Baumgarten says. "I can smell your fear from here."

"I've spent a lot of time and money on this town. I've got a lot of friends . . . a lot to lose."

"Their numbers are dwindling," says Tree. "Aviles says you're almost broke. And the IRS is up your ass with a microscope. The money's stopped rolling in, hasn't it, Vic. Your people are afraid to go to work."

Victor curls his lip and sneers. He crushes the butt of his cigarette in the ashtray. "What is broke to me is different than what is broke to Detective Aviles."

"Still," says Tree. "When the money gets short . . ."

This must be a sensitive subject; Victor's face is getting red. "You know Lanier gave my man a hotshot and then dumped the gun in his lap. You're so worried about my finances, carve out a hunk of the mother-fucker's dreads and match them up and then throw his ass in jail."

"You're thinking Lanier did the job himself?" says Baumgarten. "Isn't it more likely that one of his soldiers, maybe one of the women, got next to your boy to do some partying. How many guys that work for you would trust Gladstone Lanier with a needle in his hand?"

Victor taps another cigarette up from the pocket of his vest and lights it. His hands are delicate, trembling.

"Raul?" he considers. "Depends on how bad he needed to get high."

"The bigger question is: How would you like to help get the son of a bitch?" says Baumgarten.

Victor furrows his brow and cocks his head to one side: his Scarface look borrowed from Al Pacino, though Victor would say he invented it.

"Would you really strip away the last of my self-respect?"

"You bet your ass, Victor. We're done playing fuck-around."

Victor looks from face to face, unsure of himself, wondering if he is the butt of a joke.

"What do you say, Vic?" says Tree.

"Goddamn it, stop calling me Vic! My own mother doesn't have the nerve to call me Vic."

"Sorry."

"Victor," says Al Baumgarten. "I didn't know you were so touchy."

"I'll need time to think about your proposal," he says, getting up from the table suddenly. "I'll have to see if my friend can talk to his friend. But thanks a lot for the beer and the sunshine. I must come back here some evening with a woman."

Baumgarten points his finger in Victor's face. "Think hard about it, Victor. All those friends you were talking about need your help. And if you can't help them, for shit-sure someone else will."

Victor shoves his chair in and stands before them. Baumgarten cuffs Victor's shoulder, hard enough to force him to replant his feet to keep his balance.

"You open the door, Victor, and we'll clean house."

14

Talking Heads

At twenty past eight, Al Baumgarten and Special Agent Walsh of the FBI pick up Tree Nelson in an unmarked gray sedan. He hops in the back seat, behind Baumgarten, and they drive away in the gathering dusk.

For the first time since the ambush, Tree feels a purpose to his life, a sense of camaraderie, the thrill of the hunt. Hemingway was right, he thinks: Once you've hunted men, animals just don't make it. He is wearing his bulletproof vest and packing both his Smith & Wesson and Jimmy's off-duty 9, a Sig Sauer.

Five minutes later they're rolling up North Main Street, past the deserted Blake Hotel. They circle for a while and then park behind the gas station at Sunrise and Long Beach. Walsh turns on the interior light and reads aloud to them from the folder he has on Lanier and something called the Jungleites, information, he tells them, that was developed by law-enforcement agencies and the customs service.

"... They have, over the last decade, seized control of the marijuana trade in Washington and New York and are fighting their way into cocaine. We believe some members have been trained in Cuba. However, there is still no concrete evidence to support this assertion. The Jungleites. This group is rumored to have been successful in raising funds by robbing banks and getting state-of-the-art small arms by intimidating Jamaicans who work at U.S. arms factories . . . etcetera, etcetera. Lanier is a charter member.''

Walsh looks at Tree. ''Let's keep this in perspective, Nelson. We have shit like this on fifty groups, a hundred groups. Just off the top of my head, right now you've got your United Freedom Front, the Republic of New Africa Group, who want five southern states to make their own country. The May 19 Communist Organization, the Revolutionary Armed Task Force. All the wacko groups that were in on the Brinks job in Nyack and knocked off those two cops and the guard. And that's not even considering the FALN, Omega 7, The Order, the Jewish Defense League, and the Red Guerrilla Resistance.''

''Jesus,'' Tree says.

Walsh nods. ''You see what we're up against. Plus these guys do something crooked every day. Most of their time is spent moving from one hole to another. Worse yet, they pool their lethal talent and lease out shooters.''

''What do you think Jensen Macomber wants?'' Baumgarten says.

Walsh shrugs. ''I really don't know. Let's see what he has to say.''

At ten to nine, after five slow trips through the area, they park in the alley behind the shop and kill the headlights.

"You don't happen to have a spare Uzi lying around?" Tree says.

"Under the seat."

Tree engages the ammunition clip and flings the safety off, then holds the stubby barrel out the window, a kid with a fishing rod, unsure if he really wants the shark to bite.

Baumgarten's final instructions are short: "If Lanier, or anyone else who ain't kosher, is spotted, shoot first, then yell, 'Freeze. Police.' And then watch your goddamned back."

They get out of the car and spread out, each taking a position of cover that affords them a view of the back door of the shop. They look at, and listen to, everything, as if their lives depend on it.

Tree is stationed at the western end of the side street, near Leonard Avenue. He smiles grimly to himself, thinking that he already knows about the art of ambush—from the target's point of view. His head swivels continuously, trying to make sure it doesn't happen again. The crowd on Main Street is typical. He searches face after face; but for what, he isn't sure. Who among these nattering nabobs looks guilty or overly innocent? Who has a stiff leg? An unnecessary coat on this hot night? Long hair, short hair, Rasta dreads? Who is looking the wrong way?

The minutes drag by, the muscles gradually coil tight, and still no break in the rhythm of the street. Tree watches himself prepare to die, as if it is somebody else, somebody conducting himself with honor. "He should have been here by now," he says softly into his walkie-talkie. It is twenty minutes after nine. He has his back protected by the brick wall of Macomber's shop, and the cast-iron dumpster in front of him will roll, if necessary.

"I should be home with my wife and kids," says Walsh.

"Ssh." Baumgarten thinks he hears something. "Voice."

Tree listens hard. He hears it, too. "Yeah . . . No." Something is dripping.

"Nope," says Walsh. "Nothing here."

Tree moves one step closer to Baumgarten's position on the cellar stairs. Then another and another, his back against the bricks. He can hear something but he doesn't know what. He takes the last step he can without giving up his cover, and feels a drop of rain land on the top of his head.

But the stars are out. So that doesn't make sense. It's too dark in the alley to see. The wall behind him is wet, but the liquid in his hair is definitely not water. His spine tingles in horror. He digs in his pocket for his flashlight and turns it on. A stream of blood is dribbling down the brick wall of Jensen Macomber's shop. He follows its course up to the roof, where he can just about make out . . . a gargoyle.

"Mother of God," says Baumgarten.

"You'd better get some help down here quick," says Walsh. "That head's definitely facing Ethiopia."

The search for Gladstone Lanier is concentrated in the northern half of Seaport, and conducted by every available officer from the Twelfth, First, and Seventh Precincts. Suspicious cars are pulled to the side of the road at gunpoint. Every black in dreads is stopped and frisked. The officers exercise extreme caution during these sidewalk encounters, erring on the violent side of vigilance; the usual constitutional amenities are temporarily not observed. Crowds of the resentful are gathering on street corners throughout the area, bitching.

Standing on the roof of Jensen's shop, outside the glare of the neon and the store lights, Tree hears the whine of overtaxed machines and the occasional sound of breaking glass. Like a sci-fi movie, he thinks, or a hard rock video. When a fire breaks out in the unemployment office, there are cries of pain and the clang of heavy glass windows cascading out from their frames.

At twenty-three-fifteen there is a radio call for shots fired on Broadway. Sirens howl and a moment later the tree-lined street looks like the parking lot behind headquarters. The call is unfounded: no victim, no crime. Tree watches from the roof as sergeants descend upon the scene, imploring the disappointed cops to resume the hunt.

Baumgarten walks up behind Tree and puts his hand on his shoulder. "We found the rest of him," he says. "The guys found it sitting behind the wheel of some poor schmuck's parked car. Funny boy made it a substitute head from one of Macomber's balloons."

"Where?" asks Tree. "Where in this leper colony did Lanier dump the body?" Tree can't resist looking again at the canvas bag that Baumgarten carefully placed over Jensen's head when the photographers were through.

"The train station. I've got a team from the Railroad P.D. calling in all the crews that stopped here from eight o'clock on. We've got a lady lives down the block who saw Macomber earlier, she thinks around seven o'clock. He was going into his store with a couple. A clean-cut black guy and a skirt.''

"The motherfucker is having his own way.''

Baumgarten nods and shrugs. "I'll call you in the morning. How about that?''

"Whatever.''

Tree climbs down the ladder and finds the cop with the time log to sign himself out of the scene. He gets into the unmarked car with Agent Walsh, who has been good enough to hang around. "Please, take me home,'' he says. "I've had a bellyful.''

"You?'' says Walsh. "I wasn't even here, remember? I got to go home and explain to an angry wife why I was out half the night and didn't make any money.''

"What did you mean about the head facing Ethiopia?'' says Tree.

Walsh starts the engine and pulls out. "A couple of these fucking witch doctors in the Bronx cut the heads off some Jamaicans who wouldn't knuckle under. They lined the heads up on the roof of their apartment building, facing east, so the souls would know to follow the sunrise home.''

Tree draws himself a bath when he gets home, and he spends the next two hours soaking in it, so that he does not have to contemplate reality; Mongo Blue on a plane to Jamaica, Macomber on a slab at the morgue, Gladstone Lanier on a rampage.

The phone rings twice; but he lets his machine do the talking for him. No sense slopping suds all over the rug.

"Meet George Jetson,'' he sings. "His boy Elroy.''

Reinforcing his belief that environment holds sway

over heredity, he finds in himself the energy of a sponge, with not even the strength to abuse the erection that pokes unbidden through the bubbles. He's too scared to have sex, even with himself.

It's just after one o'clock when he hauls his sodden body from the tub and dresses in winter pajamas. He turns on the television for companionship and checks his phone messages. The first is from his father, expressing the fervent hope his only son is well, and goddamn it, keep in touch.

The other is from Annie. He plays it back a second time:

"Hey, Tree. Mom and Dad called. They're blowing through New York on their way to a conference. I have to meet them for dinner at La Guardia. I'm gonna tell them what we're doing, if that's okay. Mom is gonna go berserk. I love you. God, I hate talking to machines."

He throws a Stouffer's French Bread Pizza in the oven, then does some chipping and putting on the living room carpet, trying different stances, different grips. His TV plays the theme for David Letterman.

"Have we got an animal trick for you, David," he mutters.

He wonders what his child will look like, if it really is his child, and if they'll have anything in common besides a need for Annie and a trust fund. He wonders what Annie will tell her folks: "Tree knocked me up and now he's gonna do the right thing," or "Tree and I have decided to marry and raise a child."

He wonders if she is celebrating life's good fortune with her parents. No, he thinks. That's improbable. She has always been an embarrassment to her parents: not sufficiently lofty for a Smithy. Getting knocked up by a cop won't get her off the hook. Not by a long shot.

Wow, he thinks. There's a baby on the way. Their lives are coming true.

He looks at the letter he felt compelled to write Jimmy's daughter when he first got home from the hospital, but never got beyond the salutation.

Jesus, Jimmy, I'm making a mess of things. What the hell do I say to your kid? Tree exhales. He remembers the time last July when they stopped by Northeast Park at the end of a boring day, and sat in the car watching some fairly good ballplayers slam-dunking some hackers.

"Enter the cavalry," Jimmy said. "Enough's enough."

They locked their guns in the trunk of the unmarked car and joined forces with the underdogs. Jimmy was the playmaker, the tough guy dishing out elbows and assists, fouling his opponents unmercifully on defense. Tree always could play the game, and he was leaping and slam-dunking over the crooked rim with the best that were there. Back door, pick and roll, throw it up and crash the boards. The two of them hung tough with the kids for over an hour, then they bought a case of Coors for twenty-four dollars at the corner bodega and split it up among the playground hustlers.

They had a grand old time that day, the ghetto blasters, the sweat, the competition complete with racial slurs, then the cool evening beers as the sky turned red.

Jimmy was feeling good too, momentarily worthwhile. Susan was down for her semiannual visit, probably stretched out next to Annie on the sand at Lido Beach; she was proud of her father for making detective; and Lt. Dwayne Cumberstadt had not yet caught on to their shtick. Life was good. Very good. Driving in to the station house, Jimmy said out of nowhere, "I do love kids, you know. Most of all Susan. I'm not the cold motherfucker everybody thinks I am."

Tree couldn't tell that day if Jimmy was smiling or fighting back tears under his aviator Ray-Bans. Not that it matters anymore. He holds his head in his hands for a moment, his stomach empty but not hungry.

Tree takes out a fresh sheet of writing paper and proceeds.

Dear Susan,

I think I know how you must be feeling right now, missing your dad and everything. I miss him, too. I also think you might be feeling cheated, that you never really got a chance to know him well enough. I know I felt that way about my mother for the longest time.

You might have some questions about your father from time to time. Things might occur to you years from now that you'll want to know. Please remember, Susan, you can always call me or write to me, and I'll tell you what I know to the best of my recollection.

For now, just remember that he loved you more than anything. His very last thoughts were of you.

Love,
Tree

P.S. Use the money my father sent to start a college fund. And when you get there, go to class.

"Can you take me closer?" says Lanier, looking up into the well of the night sky. "I want to see him. I want him to feel me watching him."

"Sure," she says. "But the less time we spend on the water the better. At least until we get the boat painted and change the registration number."

Gladstone Lanier is sitting low behind the windshield, wearing a yellow rain slicker with the hood pulled over his head, smoking a spliff of ganja.

Maria is exhausted by their hours of oddly gentle sex, yet invigorated by the adrenaline of action, inspired by his decisiveness. He had no sooner withdrawn himself from her body for the last time than he was planning for all-out war.

"It's dark, Maria. When the black man holds the edge, you have nothing to fear from the night."

"Very well," she says.

Maria runs the boat at one-third power past the uninhabited marshlands that dot the bay between the south shore of Seaport and Lido Beach. At the 5 MILE PER HOUR sign she trims power even more. They don't want to be throwing a wake down the canal that might get the attention of the waterfront homeowners. Not a white girl with a black man in dreads.

"What happened to his light?" Gladstone says. "I don't see it."

Maria kills the motor, setting them adrift in the middle of the bay, two hundred yards from Tree's building.

"His balcony is dark now," she says softly. "The tan light to the right is his living room."

"Quiet," he says. "I need to feel him." He bows his head, as if in prayer. "I want my spirit to brush up against his."

The bay side of the large condominium reminds Lanier of the Kingston hotel where he held his first and last regular job.

"Okay?" says Maria. "Seen enough?" She is resting her chin on the steering wheel of the Whaler, doing her best to look bored.

"I still can't see him."

"That means he can't see us, which is very good for our side, because you, my friend, are badly in need of a haircut."

"Silence, woman."

Shave the holy dreads, the white woman tells me. Give away my strength for coins, the way she gives away herself for power. My dreads will grow back, when I am ready. Her hole will never close.

Nelson will not grow back. For Nelson, I am ready. I who am homeless, brotherless, a sufferah adrift. Live well, Rastaman, they say. Die trying. A sufferah.

He whistles in the wind, imaging the face of the men and women he has killed, despising their souls, their duppies. Mourn a birth, celebrate a death. Perfect readiness. There is no other perfect readiness but mine. No one else can be ready. Not this time around the wheel.

An outlaw, he thinks. What I was and what I'll always be. Can you feel it, Nelson? Can you hear me coming after you? I've got a picture of you in my head that's not very pretty, Nelson.

"Nellllll-son," he sings very quietly across the stillness.

He wants to kill me, this little po-lice man. But he is dreaming. Because Black is hard. Black is flight. I am darkest night. He sees only my ghost, this Babylonian impostor.

Something whistles past Gladstone Lanier's right ear and lands in the water with a startling splash. "What was that?"

"Probably a fish jumping out of the water."

"Damn it, woman. That didn't sound like no fish to me."

"Let's go back, then," says Maria. "You've got the general idea. I can cut off your beautiful locks tonight."

"Wait." A terrible picture assembles itself in his brain: Trevor Nelson with a nightscope on a high-powered rifle. He stares again through the binoculars at Nelson's balcony, and this time he sees a flash, not of flame, but of steel . . . and a second later . . . another splash!

"What the fuck was that?" he yells at her.

"I didn't see anything," says Maria. "Cut it out, willya. You're scaring me."

They stare at each other in the dark. Another splash to their left. Lanier sees something strike the water.

"Golf balls."

"Jesus," says Maria. She quickly starts the Evinrude outboard and turns the Whaler around. They far exceed the legal limit during this maneuver, kicking up a roostertail, throwing heavy wake into the bulkheads. Still, no one comes outside to yell at them to slow down. Soon they are well south of the mouth of the canal, slicing across the open water in the moonlight.

15

THE NEAREST FARAWAY PLACE

Annie ships the oars as her dinghy glides to a stop.
Ozone hops onto the dock as she fastens the bowline
to a cleat and steps out herself. The shack is quiet in
the hot summer light, the curtains drawn.

She carries two bags of groceries into the house and
sets them on the counter. Maria is sulking on the
couch, looking desperate.

"Two days, Annie. Two fucking days you missed
my calls. The phone just rings and rings. I've been
beside myself with worry."

"Worry?" she says. "Worry for who?"

"You know you're the only one I can talk to, the
only one I trust."

"If I'm your best friend, you're in serious trouble.
. . . This is it, Maria. It's done, you know? You could
come up for air now."

"Thanks a lot, Annie . . . Really."

"You're just like a man," Annie says. "God forbid
you're taken lightly. Here you go," Annie says. "Final installments. You've taken the cure—kicked it.
I've come to say good-bye."

"Just like that? Geoffrey said you had a customer who might be interested in our wares."

"I'm sure there are plenty of other people to involve in your deals."

"Please don't leave me out here all alone."

"You left you out here all alone. No one else." Annie fingers the top of the brown paper bag and shakes her head. "The best of luck to you. I really mean that. But I don't want any part of what you and Geoffrey might be into." Annie smiles. "There's macadamia Häagen-Dazs in one of the bags. Eat it before it melts."

Ozone is curled up on the couch waiting for her to head home.

"Annie," says Maria, "there's a surprise for you in the bedroom."

Annie pauses, taken aback by anything like generosity from Maria. She goes to the door and turns the knob, still looking at Maria. The door flies open, a fist explodes in her face.

She staggers backward. Someone shoves her again and she lands against the table, knocking ashtrays and magazines to the floor. A black man with a shaved head is standing over her, a gun in his hand. Maria stands at his side, her arms across her chest. Ozone arches his back and spits.

"What are you people doing?" Annie cries out.

Maria closes the door and locks it from the inside. "Shut your mouth, Annie Sutherland."

Gladstone Lanier squats by her side and squeezes her hand. "You're staying with us, Mrs. Sutherland. We need you . . . now. While your man is chasing his tail."

"You got one hell of a nerve," she says, throwing

off his hand and propping herself up on her elbows. "They get you on kidnapping and you two won't ever see the light of day again."

"Nor will you," says the black man. He shows her his gun, its silenced barrel. Then makes his point by shooting Ozone in the face.

"See," he says. "Sounds like champagne."

Geoffrey sits on the dirty chair with visible disdain for the threat it presents to his immaculate linen suit.

"You jumped the gun on me," says Geoffrey. "Both of you. I don't like my hand forced."

"But it's a perfect opportunity," says Lanier. "One too good to be missed. The groundwork is already done."

"By you," he says. "For you. For personal revenge."

"Yes," says Lanier. "That too."

The kitchen shades are down. The men are drinking cans of Budweiser beer at the table. Maria is sitting on the counter, near the sink, looking out at the late morning light.

Geoffrey frowns like a schoolmaster. "I was not prepared for this. I was not consulted. It does not align with our collective goals."

"Our pleasures," says Lanier.

"Do I detect in you a sudden softening of will?"

Lanier's face does not move, nor does the skin on his slick skull.

"I told you to stay hidden, to avoid the police," says Geoffrey. "And what do you bring me? A stupid gang war and a vendetta against cops. And a kidnapping, which means the FBI. Then a half-assed plan for another import. So what is it—in or out?"

"Every man has his price," says Lanier. "Thank Maria for helping you find mine."

"The work does not benefit by the death of policemen."

"I don't care anymore about your business. I care about the last man living who killed my brother."

Maria says to Geoffrey: "The logistics are right this time. I've walked it through."

Geoffrey lights his cigar. "I agree. The plan is not without its attractions. Especially the size of the jackpot."

"Only men and women who are willing to risk can do it," says Maria.

Geoffrey corrects her: "Calculated risk. But can we do it? Can we get away with it?"

"Give me sole authority and responsibility," says Lanier. "It will go as you wish. And as I wish. No one will ever know about you. I promise you that."

"Any problem with that?" Geoffrey asks Maria. "Are you ready to try it, too?"

Maria turns the cold water faucet on and off, on and off. "Have I ever let you down?"

"I would not have cut my dreads if I didn't think it was worth it."

"And you agree to the terms we discussed?"

"Aye. The very same ones. We get two million," Lanier says. "You pay me half before we go. Then another million after the stuff is sold. Any extra shit I get is mine to keep."

"Those are the figures we agreed upon," says Geoffrey. "The money is in New York. I just wish we had more time, Gladstone, that it wasn't all such a last-minute rush. Mistakes may have been made."

"Be assured," says Lanier, "nothing has been left to chance."

"Very well. You know I'll be watching you."

"I would expect no less."

They rise from the table and shake hands, then Gladstone walks Geoffrey down to the dock.

"Until tomorrow," Geoffrey calls out as the boat pulls away, then swings out into the channel.

The sky is filled with the cries of hungry sea gulls and the fair morning light.

Lanier's men and their women, outside the derelict bay shack on North Cinder Island, are making preparations. Maria is keeping her eye on Annie on the porch, and shaving the dreadlocks off the skulls of the Rastafarian men. Gladstone Lanier struts around the small front yard, supervising from a distance the repainting of the speedboat tied up at the dock.

"Dot's coming out beautiful," he says, as the Fiberglas above the waterline of the stolen boat is changed from white to royal blue by three of Lanier's accomplices using cans of spray paint. "Don't ya think so, girls? Being that the weaker sex has the greater appreciating of lines and colors?"

"As long as it don't come out looking like graffiti," says Maria. "Or you might as well hang a sign on it— Attention police officers. Us niggers stole this boat."

Annie, unshackled but nevertheless a captive, says nothing to Lanier; her eyes studiously examine the rotten floorboards under her feet.

Maria puts down her electric razor and sweeps the pile of shorn dreads onto the sandy lawn. "I wish you'd change your mind," she says to Annie. "You can trust Geoffrey to do right by you."

"You're crazy," Annie whispers.

The men assemble in a clearing behind the shack, nine of them, speaking in thick Jamaican patois, laughing bravely, cleaning and loading weapons.

Maria stares hard at her, a look Annie is sure she has learned from Lanier. Then her face softens and she nods slowly, sadly. "We're all of us victims. I know what you're going through."

"Please." She has her baby to protect. Perhaps if she's somehow less of a witness. . . .

"You can go inside, Annie, but if you try anything smart—"

"I just want to live," Annie says, and she goes in.

Annie curls up on a cot in the living room. A moment later rude hands shake her, then pull her to her feet. "Hello, again, lovey," Lanier says to her. "I want you to see something, so that you will not make errors when I need your utmost cooperation."

"What?" she says. Can he think her insufficiently terrorized?

"Come. I want you to see something."

"I don't want to."

Lanier's eyes grow wide with anger. "Does Nelson let you talk back to him like this? Eh? Answer me." He grabs her by her hair and snaps her head back; with his other hand he twists her arm behind her back, well past the point of pain. He drags her to the back of the shack and kicks open the door. His smell is in her nostrils, of marijuana, cigarettes, and booze. In spite of all her workouts, he so easily overpowers her.

"Lloyd French," he says to one of his men. "Call him to the boat. Toby, as well."

"Right away," says the bald Rasta.

Lanier leads Annie to the dock and lets her go. She rubs her arm and looks out across the water for help—a charter fishing boat, a clammer—but there is no one in sight, and in truth she would not risk a cry.

Three of Lanier's men appear, roughly shoving a fourth in front of them.

"Something wrong with the boat?" French asks. "I can fix it right away."

"Something wrong with you." Lanier points a pistol in his face, then taps him lightly on the forehead with the barrel.

French cracks a nervous smile. "So my mother often said. What is it I've done to cause you worry? Tell me and I'll do my level best to make it up."

He is a wiry man in his thirties, with the blackened hands of a mechanic. Shirtless, he wears only blue jeans and work boots. He blinks rapidly as sweat runs down his forehead into his eyes.

"I don't trust you anymore," says Lanier. "I can't bring you with us . . . This pains me greatly, Lloyd . . . I want you to know that. I wish this day had never come. Tie him up," he tells his men.

"You're wrong, Gladstone," says French, not struggling as his comrades bind him hand and foot with rope from the boat. "We've been friends for twenty years. Back 'o Wall, Ghosttown, remember when we robbed tourists together behind the Hilton. I would give my life for you. Please."

"Your life is no longer yours to give."

Lanier instructs his men to carry French to the end of the dock.

"I told nothing," French yells. "Nothing."

"Last chance, Lloyd."

"He loaned me some money once, but he doesn't know my business. He doesn't want to know my business," French says urgently. The *he* is unnamed, as if this identification was unnecessary. Lanier hears guilt talking.

Annie wonders if Lloyd French thinks this is a test, that Lanier will stop at the very last moment. Can he think complacent acquiescence will earn him a future?

"Face first into the water," says Lanier. "Right this bloody minute! I can't stand the stink of the nigger anymore. Hold his legs. Hold them! . . . Goddamn it, *hold* them! . . . That's better. There, there—isn't that pretty? Watch him fight to keep the water from filling his lungs. Watch the natural force of the water win."

Annie stands mute throughout the screaming and then the thrashing. The man is strong. Desperate. A minute goes by. Two. Then a final silence. Lanier's men release the bound legs, letting the body slip beneath the surface.

"A nice trip home," says Lanier.

"We don't know he sold us out," one of the soldiers says.

"That's true," says Lanier, looking thoughtful. "That's true."

On the way down to the garage, Tree decides to check on Annie, to see if she made it home okay from seeing her parents. He steps out of the elevator on the second floor and slides his key into her lock.

"Annie?" he says so softly that were she home she would not hear him. "Are you in here, my little dumpling of love?" he says, half sarcastically.

He walks into the foyer. The coatrack is on its side,

as if she knocked it over, bustling out on her appointed rounds. He looks on her desk for notepaper and a pen. When he turns on the lamp to write her a note, he sees Ozone's carcass draped across the shade, and he suffers the thorough violation of the soul Gladstone Lanier has troubled himself to arrange.

16
Gladstone's Grief

Tree can barely sit still, so overcome is he by the desire to look for Annie everywhere and anywhere. But Baumgarten is calling the shots now, so at least he knows things are being done right and by someone still capable of using his head.

Her apartment is being searched for clues, her description broadcast throughout the region. The local hunt for Lanier has intensified, and with the kidnapping charge, Agents Walsh and Nikro of the FBI are officially on the case.

Baumgarten grinds his cigarette into an ashtray that is full and peers sullenly into his coffee mug.

"Terrific. So what kind of plan do you have?" says Tree, seemingly annoyed.

"I hate to say this to men who know better," says Agent Nikro, "but our only hope is constant vigilance. That and the statistical probability that elimination of the victim will not take place."

"Wonderful," says Tree. "The statistical probability . . ."

"Look," says Nikro. "Combined, we've got a hundred agents and cops out there working on this. That's a hundred chances to nip this shit in the bud. Every cop out there has a picture of Lanier in his pocket, with and without dreadlocks, courtesy of the photo lab. They've also got a picture of Mrs. Sutherland. What the hell more would you like me to do?"

"Find the cocksucker," says Tree. "Then let me rip his lungs out."

Nikro raises his eyebrows and checks his watch. "It's thirteen-thirty. Why don't you return to your command post upstairs and watch my boss briefing your boss. See if it has anything remotely to do with what I just told you, or if it's been changed beyond recognition again. In either case, don't say anything. My boss may not be telling your boss the truth." He looks at Baumgarten. "You got to love them statistical probabilities, eh, Sarge?"

"And dumb fucking luck."

"Maybe the guys will turn something up," he says.

"It's possible," says Baumgarten. "Anything's possible."

Hours have gone by and nothing has changed. Half of the day shift is working on an armed robbery, the other half on the missing Mrs. Sutherland. The shift change is approaching and nobody is going off duty. Every available clue is being followed. The condo security guards have assisted in the preparation of composite sketches of the perpetrators, the hair and fiber teams are bent over their microscopes. Nothing has panned out.

Tree's heart is pounding; sweat pours into his bullet-proof vest. Come on, Lanier, he thinks. Where the fuck are you? For he knows in his heart a terrible truth: He wants something to happen, for the good or the bad; and not because he will look the fool if it does not. He wants to see Gladstone Lanier's bullet-riddled corpse, and feel it clammy and cold, and watch the medical examiner tag the toe and zip the green rubber body bag shut. He wants this over and done with.

"Nelson!"

Tree spins quickly, panicked at the mention of his own name. It is Baumgarten, babbling about shit hitting fans and swamps filled with alligators, things Tree cannot comprehend until his heart resumes its normal beat from its normal place. He says, "Run that by me again."

Baumgarten leads him out of the crowd, to the edge of a filing cabinet where they will not be overheard. "The commissioner had to divert some manpower from your security detail, but that was no great loss, seeing as how they were only window dressing anyway. Still, he wants everyone advised, so that they can 'fully appreciate how dire are our straits.' His words. He wants everyone to 'dig way down.' If even a cop shows up on your doorstep that nobody knows, he said to shoot the son of a bitch on sight."

"All I want is Gladstone Lanier on a slab. Trimble doesn't have to tell me to dig way down."

"I know that."

"So what's happening here?"

"Nelson?"

Tree recognizes the voice. "Lieutenant Lee. Top of the morning to ya."

"Don't address me in that insolent manner, you son of a bitch."

"Go fuck yourself, *sir*."

"You are hereby ordered—"

"Hold your water, big-time. Check the scoreboard. I'm on the clock again."

"Look, kid, I'm just doing my job," says Lee, trying to sound properly sympathetic in front of the other men.

"Your job is to lick ass, Lieutenant. Not mess with guys trying to survive in the streets. You're lucky I don't slide by your house tonight and lock you up in front of the wife and kiddies."

Lee makes the sounds of one being strangled; Tree has not enjoyed himself so much in weeks.

"Let's see," says Tree. "Burglary, harassment, all kinds of civil-rights violations . . . and you made chopmeat of the fourth and sixth amendments to the Constitution. Where'd you say you lived?"

"This isn't over, Officer Nelson."

"You got that right, scumbag. Your rank don't mean jackshit to me now." If this pleasure Tree enjoys is the exercise of power, maybe his father is right. Maybe he should take up the family work. He seems to have found the knack.

"Be in my office in an hour. It will have a lot to do with where you are permanently assigned." Lee turns smartly on his heel and walks away. Behind him Nelson gives him the finger.

"You should go home," Baumgarten tells Tree. "If he's gonna make contact, he may try to get to you there."

"You think he wants money?"

Baumgarten chews his cigar. "Would you like me to piss in your pocket and tell you it's raining?"

"Yes. Yes, I would."

Baumgarten says, "Sorry, pal."

"Maybe there's something I ought to be doing here. Something we're forgetting."

"Everything is being done. I mean that, Tree. I'm looking for Annie like I'd look for one of my own kids. I even got Berezuk and Stack to stay after and help. They're riding north Seaport now, handing out posters."

"Okay," says Tree. "I'll go home."

"You want some company?" Baumgarten asks.

Tree says no, that he'd rather be alone.

"Stay in touch."

"Yeah," says Tree. "You too."

The security guards are away from the desk when he enters the lobby, the low sun a shiny yellow reflection in the glass doors. He finds them in Annie's apartment, watching a real cop do his thing. An exasperated look in their direction sends them running from the room, bowing and saluting, apologizing for leaving their posts.

"Anything?" Tree asks Sergeant Gallo, who is the lone representative of the police department at the scene.

"The description fits Lanier, except for the shaved head. Neither guard took his eyes off the woman's ass long enough to make note of her face. And naturally, neither saw anything like a cat's corpse. But he was carrying a sports bag."

Tree cannot wait to meet this chick, whom he is sure also lured Bobby Allison out of Puddles Pub, according to the statement of the bartender. "You find anything else in here?"

"Just some narcotics paraphernalia that I'm sure you would rather I forget."

"I . . . Yeah, thank you."

"No one has called on the victim's phone, or yours, and there ain't no mail. Looks like it might be a long one, Nelson. I'm sorry."

Tree nods, his eyes taking in the once familiar living room, the icons and artifacts of Annie's short life.

"I'm going back to the shop," says Gallo. "You'll lock up?"

"Sure."

But Tree can't stay in her apartment when Gallo is gone; his eyes want too much to give up and cry, his body wants so much to collapse. He locks the door and rides up to his apartment in the elevator, staring mournfully at his distorted reflection in the triangular mirror.

Once behind his own locked doors he sees the red light pulsing on his answering machine.

Maria watches the horizon through binoculars. Something is wrong, she thinks. The men have slipped away, deserted, and Gladstone has barely noticed. What will Geoffrey say when he comes back with the down payment?

Annie sits on the couch in the shack, hands and feet tied. Since Lanier sent his lone remaining accomplice to patrol outside, he has been standing by the front window, toking on a crack pipe, watching and waiting, occasionally coughing violently and spitting up phlegm. His clothes are dirty and soaked through with sweat. He has paid no attention to Annie's attempts to engage him in conversation, to humanize him, to convince him that her man is one of the kindest on earth.

Gladstone is waiting. For what?

"Look," Annie says. "It's not too late to call this off."

"Silence," he tells her. "You're better off than you know."

"I find that hard to believe."

"You know what your fellow thinks?" Lanier giggles. "He thinks I've got a soldering iron up your snatch."

Annie's stomach turns. She thinks of Tree, and what he must be thinking, of the mistakes he will make in his haste.

Lanier cocks his ear for a better listen outside. Annie cannot hear anything but wind and birds and water slapping against the dock. He pulls aside the shade.

"Lighten up," Maria says. "Please." She puts her hand on Lanier's shoulder for a moment, then pulls it away like she's touched a hot stove. "Let's get out of here before we have to spend the rest of our lives in jail."

Lanier smiles arrogantly, as if the thought of that possibility has never crossed his mind. "There are accounts to settle," he says. "I hope you're not running out of faith." Gladstone Lanier frowns. "You worry me, woman. I don't think you comprehend what's going down."

"What makes you think *you* know what's going on?"

"Worry me much more," he says, "and I might mail you a letter."

"I'd like to talk to Mrs. Sutherland," she says. "I'd like to be able to untie her hands and feet. I see no reason to treat her like this."

"I sometimes like my women tied up," he says with a leer.

Maria frowns sharply, as if a sudden pain has wracked her stomach. "Gladstone."

"You gotta be kidding," says Annie. "I'm three months pregnant. For God's sake." Her eyes plead with Maria.

"Ooo," he says, "Trevor Nelson is about to be a father."

"Please?" says Maria. "She has done nothing wrong."

"Wasn't this your idea?"

"But not that, Gladstone. We're not savages."

"I'm told quite frequently hostages come to worship their captors, given enough time and attention. How do you suppose Nelson will like it when he sees that I've stolen her heart?" He is taunting both of them.

"He'll probably kill you," Maria says, "the way he killed your little brother."

Maria is airborne, suddenly flung across the room. And Lanier is pouncing on her, ready to smack her face again.

"You!" he screams when she has slumped to the floor in a ball. "Don't talk ever to me again. Don't ever mention Roland . . . Because I will do things to you . . ." A big white crooked smile lights his face. "You're jealous, aren't you?"

Maria whimpers, curled up in a fetal position.

Annie screams for someone to help. Lanier turns to slap her. She struggles but the cord is thick, the knots too well constructed.

Lanier raises a finger, and Maria crawls breathless out of the shack.

A boat is approaching, a fancy pleasure boat with

one man steering it alone. For a moment Maria thinks it is Nelson, then recognizes Geoffrey's stance as he guides the boat to the tiny dock.

Gladstone appears from the house. The boat docks. Geoffrey, suited, disembarks and ties off the bowline as Lanier saunters over.

Geoffrey says, "I think that you will make me very happy today."

"The money, mon."

"Many people will be happy," Geoffrey says, trying to impress Lanier with intimations of the powerful who back him.

"That's too much static for my head, without dreads. Give me the money, errand boy."

Geoffrey squints at him, as if he were crazy.

"Look at me, Geoffrey. Place your bets. Make your deposits and withdrawals."

"I have done my part," says Geoffrey. "Here's your money."

Look at this, thinks Lanier. He hands me two Gucci suitcases, as if I am still working at the hotel, hauling the white man's bags while Mama scrapes their excrescences from the sheets. Geoffrey, with his cars and spic-shined shoes, thinking he is the sun.

Geoffrey says, "We'll meet a week from tomorrow night for the second half."

"Money, money, money. Trinkets. Colored paper."

"At that same place in Brooklyn."

"If Jah is willing."

"God *is* willing," says Geoffrey.

"Yes," says Lanier. "So very true."

The pick is incredibly light. It slips under the man's sternum, directly into the aorta, just the way the Cuban once said it would.

Imagine that.

Geoffrey grabs Lanier's shoulders to support himself. His eyes fill with fear and hate. But no questions. Even in death Geoffrey will not allow himself to look surprised.

"Check-out time, Geoffrey."

"You have reached the Nassau County Police Department. All of our lines are busy right now. Please hold . . . *click* . . . Nassau County Police, Operator Fifty-one."

"This is Detective Trevor Nelson, from the Twelfth Precinct, shield one-one-six-nine. I need to know where the Five boat is right away."

"Stand by . . . Marine Five is in Wantagh, Detective Nelson, assisting on an aided case."

"We got any choppers in the air?"

"Negative. We used all of them at the Coliseum today. They're being inspected and refueled. Anything else?"

"Connect me to Sergeant Al Baumgarten at Homicide, please."

"Stand by."

In less than ten seconds the sergeant picks up.

"He called," says Tree. "Listen." Tree replays Lanier's message for the sergeant, then tells him about the lack of helicopters, the status of the Five boat.

"Let me hear it again," says Baumgarten.

"I have your woman, Nelson, naked and spread-eagled in the only bay shack on North Cinder Island. She wants you to come for her, and quick about it, too. Alone. See, I stole a soldering iron from a friend of yours, the late Mr. Crosse, which I have just

239

plugged into a generator, which I will plug into her if you bring help. And then I'll start the generator and disappear, Mr. Detective, so as not to suffer the sounds of her a-gony.''

Click.

''*You* got a boat?'' asks Baumgarten.

''I have the use of one.''

''Get moving then. I'll be as close behind you as I can. We're gonna change the maintenance schedule on a couple of those birds.''

''Hurry.'' Tree grabs both his guns from the kitchen counter and sprints past the elevator and down the four flights of stairs to the dock.

Annie's boat is there, with her skin-diving equipment tucked under the bow: a snorkel, a mask, flippers, a life preserver. He steps in and unties the dinghy when he hears a man behind him call out his name. He draws and turns in one motion. Crazy Victor is standing on the dock.

''I heard about your woman,'' Victor says. ''From that friend of mine that talks to the friend of his.''

''Look, Vic . . . I'd love to chat, but Lanier's going to torture her to death.''

''That's why I'm here,'' says Victor.

Before Tree can say anything Victor steps into the boat with him and shoves off.

Tree fits the oars and pulls mightily away from the dock.

Victor slips a canvas sack off his back and sets it between his feet. ''I knew he wouldn't cut and run without doing some damage first. I figured it would be you or me that he came after in the end. When Aviles told me who his brother was, I knew it had to be you, you lucky guy.''

Tree is working far too hard to make small talk. He nods his head and grunts.

"Here," says Victor. "You're getting tired. Let me do that for a while."

"I got it," says Tree. "You pull out the map and figure out which one of these marsh bogs is North Cinder Island. The odds are good we can make it before Baumgarten arrives with the troops."

"We'll make better time if you'll rest a minute."

His burning muscles agree. Tree gives up the oars and switches seats with Victor, who is soon powering the boat down the canal. Tree tells him what Lanier said he was going to do to Annie. Victor spits in the water.

They pass a man on his dock in a swimming suit, hosing down his runabout. "Hey," yells Tree. "Is there gas in that thing?"

"What business is that of yours?"

"I'm a police officer . . . I need it for an emergency."

The man looks them over, mostly Victor, in his dungaree vest and black leather headband. "Sorry, Officer. Dry as a bone. I got the tanks out front in the car."

They pass Waterfront Park, at the end of Long Beach Avenue, and then turn west for a while, finally turning into a shallow cut through the reedy marsh, which, if Tree is reading the map correctly, will exit some thirty yards from the tip of North Cinder Island, directly opposite the bay shack. The late afternoon sun is shining in his eyes, cloaking Victor's face in shadow. "You have a gun?" he asks him.

Victor grins. He cocks his head to one side. "You know something?"

"What?"

"For a motherfucking cop, you're okay."

"You know something?"

"What?" says Victor.

"I don't believe a word you say."

Victor slows down. "Why not?" he grunts.

"Because there's a real good chance we're gonna die very soon . . . and I don't believe you're gonna put yourself in that position just to avenge a couple of friends or enhance your reputation. Certainly not to help me." Tree points his weapon at Victor. "Stop rowing," he says. "Get out."

"I can't swim."

"I'll bet you learn quick."

Victor continues to pull on the oars. "The odds ain't that bad. Gladstone's tribe has dumped him. There's maybe one or two left. Something else, too," he says.

"What's that?"

Victor lifts the oars from the water and crosses the handles in his lap. "Lanier got a million dollars in cash delivered to him this morning. And you know I have some pressing financial obligations. I was hoping that—in the confusion of his capture—some of that money might find its way . . . Either that or a reward from you. I understand you got means. Whatever."

Tree feels a tremendous sense of relief. Profit as motive is something he's grown up with. And he's sure Victor's obligations are not to banks who send collection letters, but to loan sharks who send shakers. He nods. They switch seats again.

At the mouth of the cut, Tree pulls the dinghy into the reeds. Across the channel, the turquoise shack appears deserted. He goes ankle deep into the soft brown muck and squats down low to listen.

"The tide's running out," Victor says. "I can make my way through the marsh to those trees down there, and then swim around to the far side of the island."

"I thought you couldn't swim."

Victor says, "I just learned. It makes sense to come from two directions." Tree agrees; they will split up here.

"Are you going to take the boat across?"

"I don't know," says Tree. "I was thinking of trying to swim underwater to the dock."

"The dock's probably booby-trapped," Victor says. "His guys are very good with explosives. And that would be a natural."

Tree nods, well aware of the many areas in which Gladstone Lanier excels.

Victor removes his vest and folds it like a flag. He tucks it in the bow of the dinghy. "Wait five minutes, then start across. That should give me time to get behind them."

"Hey . . . Victor. I owe you, man."

"Some day you may be sorry." He winks at Tree and then moves off through the marsh grass, crouching low, trying not to rustle the reeds.

Tree takes his shoes and pants and shirt off and stuffs them under the bow of the dinghy with Victor's colors. He puts on the mask and snorkel and flippers. His five-shot revolver and Jimmy's 9-millimeter go inside Annie's plastic bait bag, which he cords around his neck.

Five minutes go by.

Two teenage boys in a speedboat pull a female skier the length of the channel and disappear behind the island; Tree hopes Victor does not have the bad luck to be run over by them, chopped to bits by the prop.

Tree slips into the warm water behind the dinghy and is about to pull it into the cut between the reeds when he steps on something that moves, something that feels alive. He scrambles out of the water.

The water is too murky for him to see anything. He puts on the diving mask and ducks his head and shoulders below the surface.

He is eyeball to eyeball, nose to nose with a black man. A corpse who used to be Lloyd French. The body is bound with ropes and tangled in the roots of the marsh grass.

Tree lifts his head out of the water and sucks down a barrel of fresh air. His legs go weak and his arms are shaking under his weight.

God, he thinks, please. Make this roller coaster stop.

Tree drops into the water and hauls the swollen body to the surface. Hungry crabs have left marks on the face and back that look like bullet holes. Tree wrestles the shirtless Rasta into a sitting position at the back of the boat, ready to be ferried to his tomb. Then he shoves the dinghy out into the channel and slips in behind it, keeping his head below the stern, kicking hard with Annie's flippers.

The current is strong, the boat unwieldy; he has to work too hard to keep the bow pointed toward the dock, the boat advancing. Progress is painful and slow, moving in under the enemy's guns.

17
Accidentally Like
a Martyr

"Now what am I to make of that?" Gladstone Lanier says to Annie.

He is standing by the small front window of the bay shack, wearing a white tennis shirt with dried blood on it and gym shorts, smoking crack from a little glass pipe. She is sitting on the couch, waiting to die.

Big Noel Richardson, the last remaining Rasta on the island, is on patrol outside, armed with an AR-18. He has one hundred thousand dollars hidden in a knapsack, his payment in advance for helping Gladstone waste the cop.

And Maria Delgado's corpse is stretched face down on the porch by the front door. Lanier had walked up behind her in the kitchen and shot her in the head. Her hands and feet twitched for at least a minute; then she died.

Annie doesn't know what has become of Geoffrey's body. They may have buried it in the marsh grass bog, they may have dragged it to the other side of the island

and torched it . . . they may have eaten it for all she knows. Lanier had snapped open the Gucci suitcases and handed big wads of bills to each of his men, laughing loudly about passports home, letters of introduction from great American presidents. "Arise," he said to the men on the beach, scattering the colored paper while they shamelessly chased the fluttering bills across the sand. "Scatter yourselves on the wind."

After that Lanier drenched what was left of the money in gasoline and set it ablaze. He said he would not need it.

All but Noel Richardson took off in Geoffrey's speedboat, some of them gleeful at the chance to make tracks. There was no telling on whom Lanier might turn next.

"A rowboat," he says to Annie. He looks past the window shade again. "I see a rowboat that's floating on air."

Around the dark living room, thirty small candles are burning, casting an eerie glow.

"Anyone ever tell you that crack fucks up your brains?" she says.

"White men fuck up black brains, hiding from them their proud and truthful heritage."

"That may also be true," Annie says, doing her best to engage his attention, now standing and stretching her legs, trying to see outside. "I think we all of us fuck up each other."

"Sit down and shut your mouth," he tells her. "I don't really need you alive, if you think about it."

She rapidly does as she is told. He peeks past the shade once more. Then he puts down his pipe and lights up a joint. "I don't like what I'm seeing," he says to her. "Because what I'm seeing cannot be true.

The ganja settle me down, and make clear business of the truth."

"What are you seeing?"

"The dead, little girl."

"Run," she says to him. "Run like the wind. No one will ever catch you."

"Now, when the last of my enemies is near? You must be crazy, woman. I have dreamt this moment, and seen it come true. Roland was nineteen years old, woman. Do you know how young that really is? . . . I do not fear this death. I welcome it."

Annie nods, thinking of her unborn child, aware that her errors in judgment may cost the baby's life, not just her own.

"Imagine that," says Lanier. "Him, coming after me. Lloyd French adding his restless spirit to the dread."

"Gladstone!" Noel Richardson calls from his place of concealment in the marsh grass. "Do ya see it?"

"Aye."

"What do you make of it?"

"I take it as a sign of insolence. I take it as a challenge of the highest order." Gladstone Lanier picks up the Armalite and sticks three extra ammunition magazines in his belt. "I see," he says to Annie, "that I'll have to do the job myself."

Lanier takes one more hit on the joint and stares at her, considering tactics. He'd planned on walking out behind her when her hero arrived, forcing the Babylonian to do the killing of them both and the unborn manchild, if that was the way it was going to be. But he certainly doesn't need her to face down one duppie spirit what don't want to stay dead.

"Maybe I'll see you again," he says. "And maybe I won't. Don't forget me, eh?"

He drops the red-tipped joint on the cocktail table and walks outside to the porch. The excrement the black-haired witch has spilled onto the floorboards disgusts him. He steps around the corpse and drops to his knees in the sand.

"You don't worry me, Lloyd," he calls out across the water. "I'm gonna close my eyes, mon, and you'll be gone."

In a trance, Annie gets up and one by one blows out the ceremonial candles. Then she curls up on the couch and says her prayers.

The bow of the dinghy is thirty feet from the end of the dock and closing slowly. Tree can hear Lanier quite clearly.

"You don't mind if I just shoot you this time, do you, Lloyd? You're a better swimmer than I thought," Lanier calls out.

Twenty feet from shore, Tree risks a look around the side of the dinghy, and catches the briefest glimpse of a Rasta walking slowly across the lawn with a gun in his hands. A naked white body on the porch.

"There's nothing for you here, Lloyd! Get back where you belong, mon."

A burst of automatic-weapon fire slams into the hog-tied corpse, spraying dead flesh from the back of the dinghy.

Ten feet from the rickety dock Tree pulls the mask over his eyes, puts the snorkel in his mouth, and shoves hard against the stern with his feet. He fills his lungs with as much air as he can hold and dives for the shallow bottom, praying that Victor was right about the dock. It takes only a fraction of a moment for the dinghy to make contact.

The explosion pounds him into the sandy bottom and rips away his mask. His ears ring like Sunday morning in Rome. He is bruised and blinded; but he still has the guns. The mouthpiece of the snorkel is clamped between his teeth. He swims away from the wreckage as it cascades into the water above him; until he is surrounded by the peaceful, otherworldly silence of submersion. He might be in the bay, retrieving golf balls, or sleeping with his head under a pillow, hungover, hearing only the sound of his heart pumping blood. He floats down the channel for as long as he can, until his lungs harden and his limbs feel swollen and weak. Then he comes almost to the surface and blows the water from his snorkel, hoping Lanier won't recognize the spout for what it is amidst roiling water and debris.

Tree draws his first breath of fresh air in over a minute. Incredible, he thinks—sinking below the surface again—how fast you miss oxygen.

Tree doesn't hear any muffled gunfire; no silver-slashes rip the water. He pokes the top of the snorkel above the surface again. More welcome air pours into his aching lungs.

He waits, suspended at periscope depth, counting. Thirty seconds elapse. Then he risks allowing his eyes to rise above the surface. His vision is blurred, but he can make out the shirtless Rasta at the shoreline, aiming a rifle at him.

He hears a shot, like the crack of a whip. He tears off the snorkel, takes one last deep breath and submerges, breaking into a frantic anaerobic breaststroke. Face muscles clenched, cheeks bulging, he sprints for the shattered pilings of the dock. If he can make it that far. If his lungs don't collapse, or his brain or his heart.

Just ahead and above, the surface light is broken by the remnant of a log. Ten yards away, eight, two—into the murky water churned up by the blast. He finds the footing of the dock by touch. His chest is ready to explode. No time for thought. No time at all. With Jimmy Tibaldi's 9-millimeter in his right hand, the five-shot Chief in his left, his head breaks the surface. He peeks over the shattered pilings.

Lanier is looking the other way. The muscles ripple across the hard brown back, an inviting target.

Tree gives a kick with the flippers and rises at the water's edge with both guns blasting. "Rrrrrrah!" He is firing and screaming. Lanier wheels to face him, then jerks straight up and pitches backward onto the sand. The body jerks with each shot. Then Tree's weapons click empty.

He slides below the surface again in search of that submarine silence. His ears are ringing and the salt water stings his eyes. He glides forward. His lungs burn. He rises to his feet in the quiet shallows and kicks off his flippers. He feels alone, the first man to walk out of the water on two legs. He stumbles, his sopping underpants around his knees, pointing his empty guns at Lanier, at the shack, then at the tall reeds that surround it. "Yo!" he screams. "Victor?"

Nothing moves but the wind through the head-high grass. He pulls up his boxer shorts and wipes the water from his face.

He kneels next to the body and checks Lanier's carotid artery for a pulse.

Nothing.

A bullet has entered the shaved skull above the right eye, another through his upper lip. The face is damaged beyond recognition. The muscular chest is still. Good, Tree thinks, go fuck yourself.

"Victor?"

Tree wonders if Victor has made it safely around the island. Had something happened to him when he came ashore. If Lanier had hidden reinforcements, wouldn't they have made their presence known by now, while his pants were down and his weapons empty. Tree takes the Armalite next to the body and slides another magazine in place.

"Annie?" He stares in horror at the body on the porch.

"Tree . . . I'm in here. I'm alone."

"Annie?" he says. "Annie." He leaps onto the porch and flings open the door, the Armalite against his hip.

She's sitting on the couch. Fully clothed. Pale. From far off he can hear for the first time the whoop-whoop-whoop of the helicopters closing in.

"I couldn't watch," she says, crying. "I was sure he was going to kill me. I was sure they were gonna kill you . . . He was talking crazy about boats in the air and dead spirits coming after him. His partner was out front shooting. And then . . . ."

"His partner?"

"Yeah," she says breathlessly. "This guy—Noel."

He holds his finger to his lips and presses her down on her side on the couch. "Stay. Right here, Annie. I only saw one bad guy out there."

Tree crawls to the door of the bay shack, his weapon over his elbows, then onto the porch, sheltering behind

Maria's body. He lays the barrel over her back and scans the beach, prepared to fire.

"*Nelson . . . over here,*" he hears Victor calling.

He watches Victor emerge from the tangled marsh grass at the edge of the sandy clearing. His underclothes are shredded and covered with brown muck.

"Get down," Tree calls to him. "I think there's still one more."

Victor dives back into the grass for cover, and shouts, "I didn't see anyone else. But this island is bigger than it looks."

Tree can't hear what else Victor is saying because the helicopters are directly over them now, bristling with the cavalry. Baumgarten uses the public-address mike to ask if they are okay. Tree holds up one finger.

One of the choppers dips, then races forward along the shoreline. The other hovers over the beach by the devastated dock, then descends.

Tree runs from the porch to the dead body on the beach, to make certain it is Gladstone Lanier. He is bent over the body, holding the rifle like a pistol. Twenty feet away the beach opens before him and a head, streaming sandy snakes, appears. Then a torso coated like a sugar doughnut, holding an automatic rifle. The monster is blinded by sand sticking to his eyes; he holds the weapon with one hand above his head and wheels his arm, blindly spreading an arc of fire around, causing Tree to slip under his deadly rope.

"*Nelsonnnnn!*" the head screams.

The Armalite fairly dances in Tree's hands. He misses Lanier with his first ten rounds, but not the second, which spatters the sandy-white face and chest beyond all resemblance to a man, turning the pastry to jelly. It's not enough. Not even if Jimmy has Lanier now, kicking his ass from cloud to cloud. He is shaking when Baumgarten pulls the rifle from his hands.

"Easy," says the sergeant. "Are we sure now that's everybody?"

Tree exhales deeply. "I think that's the lot of 'em. But then what the fuck do I know?"

Tree wipes his hands on the back of his underpants and returns to the bay shack. Victor is on the porch with an air bureau cop, examining the hole in Maria Delgado's forehead among other things. "Whoa," he says, offering Tree his high-five. "That was some outrageous shit, Detective. You a bad motherfucker."

"Thank you, Victor. I'm sorry about your clothes." Victor doesn't seem to be carrying anything. But he looks satisfied.

Victor laughs and punches Tree in the arm. "Not to worry," he says. "You'll make it up to me, I know."

"Sure I will, Victor."

"Hey, whatever. I'm glad I was here."

"Yeah," says Tree. "I'll bet you are." He is pretty sure now what took Victor so long. But he'll never be able to prove it. Victor can come back later to locate whatever he has managed to find and to hide. Let Aviles try and stop him.

Tree shoves open the wooden screen door to check on Annie. She is standing next to the couch, clutching her throat, making shapes with her mouth but no sounds, a vain attempt to speak.

"Easy, girl," he says. "You're gonna hyperventilate."

Her lips tremble as he pulls the hair from her face and kisses her teary cheeks. "Relax," he says. "The good news is that people don't shake until they're safe."

"He's really dead?" she says.

"Oh yeah."

"He's dead," she says, as if to convince herself.

"And we're alive."

She puts her arms around his waist and hangs her chin over his shoulder, and they make each other a momentarily perfect fit.

18

THE LAST WALTZ

Mona is in. It's time, he thinks. She has to be told, now, before Annie starts answering his phone.

She sounds woozy when she answers, or half asleep, and he sees on the clock that it is almost midnight.

"Whoa . . . it's the celebrity. Finally remembered to call an old friend."

"Come on, Mona. Don't make a big thing."

"You're in the papers every other day: 'Single, wealthy, handsome, doomed.' I read what they've been saying. It's like the best personal ad I've ever seen. Send photo."

"It ain't like I've been having a good time, you know."

"No, but it ain't like you're broke, either, as I was surprised to discover. How come you never told me you had bucks?"

"It never seemed important with us."

"Yeah, right," she says. "Us. Ha! Gimme a break, Tree. You never come over unless you're drunk, and you're gone ten minutes after you come. I'm supposed to think that's love."

"No," he says. "You're not. I never thought you did. That's why I called, Mona . . . I wanted to tell you I'm getting married and having a kid—a boy—and I won't be stopping over anymore."

"You've got to be kidding, Tree."

"No, I'm not."

"Married? A daddy? You? Get a grip."

Tree is smiling, remembering Mona at some of her finest moments, thinking now that those moments are over.

"What really happened? Some bad girl give you Herpie the love bug?"

"You're my only bad girl, Mona."

"For real? Till death do you part?"

"For real."

"Whoa . . . What a bummer."

"That's one way of looking at it."

"I mean, how drastic is that?"

"I'd say it's fairly drastic."

"Is there a place for old friends in this new arrangement?"

He knew she would ask that, that she wouldn't just wish him luck and send him on his way. "I don't think so, Mona. I'm gonna give this thing my very best shot."

"Yeah, right. Of course. And what are you gonna call the little rugrat? Trevor Junior, or what'd the paper say your father's name was . . . Mortimer?"

"Jimmy," he says. "We're gonna call him Jimmy."

He hears her exhale, maybe a smoke ring. He's gonna miss those trips to Mozambique.

"Don't lose my number, Tree. I'll be here when it doesn't work out."

"Yup," he says. "So will I."